THE WRITER'S DIGEST

GUIDE TO QUERY LETTERS

THE WRITER'S DIGEST

GUIDE TO QUERY LETTERS

WRITER'S DIGEST BOOKS

www.writersdigest.com
Cincinnati, Ohio

WENDY BURT-THOMAS

For more fine books from F+W Media, visit www.fwmedia.com or www.writersdigest.com/books/. To receive a free weekly e-mail newsletter delivering tips and updates about writing and about Writer's Digest products, register directly at http://newsletters.fwpublications.com.

12 11 10 09 08   5 4 3 2 1

Distributed in Canada by Fraser Direct, 100 Armstrong Avenue, Georgetown, Ontario, Canada L7G 5S4, Tel: (905) 877-4411. Distributed in the U.K. and Europe by David & Charles Brunel House, Newton Abbot, Devon, TQ12 4PU, England, Tel: (+44) 1626-323200, Fax: (+44) 1626-323319, E-mail: postmaster@davidandcharles.co.uk. Distributed in Australia by Capricorn Link, P.O. Box 704, Windsor, NSW 2756 Australia, Tel: (02) 4577-3555

Library of Congress Cataloging-in-Publication Data

Burt-Thomas, Wendy.

  The Writer's Digest guide to query letters / by Wendy Burt-Thomas.

    p. cm.

  Includes index.

  ISBN 978-1-58297-566-5 (pbk. : alk. paper)

  1. Queries (Authorship) I. Title. II. Title: Guide to query letters.

  PN161.B87 2008

  808'.02--dc22

                              2008036208

Edited by Lauren Mosko
Designed by Claudean Wheeler
Production coordinated by Mark Griffin

DEDICATION

To my children, Ben and Gracie, who I hope will be inspired to write on paper (instead of walls) one day.

And to Aaron, who pretends not to notice.

TABLE OF CONTENTS

CHAPTER 3:
NONFICTION BOOK QUERIES

CHAPTER 4:
NOVEL QUERIES

UP FOR THE CHALLENGE?

So you wanna be a writer, huh? Are you sure? Really, *really* sure? Okay, then. As long as you're serious about it, let's get right to point because there's good news and bad news. (You kept your receipt, right?)

The bad news is, everyone wants to be a writer. That means every Tom, Dick, and Harry (or Harriet) with access to a computer (or worse—an old typewriter!) is littering the path to YOUR big break with horribly cli-chéd, poorly formatted, and downright unsellable pitches. And as much as you'd like to break in that four-hundred-dollar leaf blower, there's no way to get rid of the competition. Your only hope is to write a query that stands out in the crowd—a genuine nugget among a river of gravel, lime-stone, and fool's gold. It's hard work and it's not for the easily discouraged, but if you're still up for the challenge, here's the good news: This book will tell you how to do it.

WHAT'S A *QUERY* ANYWAY?

If you're planning to pitch article ideas to magazine editors or book ideas to agents or publishers, you're going to need a query letter about 99 per-cent of the time. This is a one-page letter used to get an editor or agent in-terested in the work you'd like to send him. Sometimes you'll be querying to send a piece you've already completed. In other cases, you'll essential-ly be asking to determine if you *should* write the piece, as in the case of a nonfiction book idea you have. (Yes, you can sell a nonfiction book to a publisher based on an idea. More on that later.)

A query letter is an opportunity to use your brilliance to not only impress an editor (or agent) with your idea, but also demonstrate your ability to follow the specific submission guidelines the publisher or agency gives. In the case of a nonfiction magazine article, for example, you'll use the query to tell the editor what angle and topic you'll cover, whom you'll interview, how long the piece will be, whether you can supply photographs, how your piece will help readers, and for which section of the magazine the piece fits. Whether you send this letter via e-mail or snail mail will be dictated by the guidelines.

In a nutshell, *your query is your sales pitch.* You're selling your writing before the editor has even read your manuscript. This is no time to be shy (or conceited); getting published is as much about marketing yourself as it is about the quality of your writing. Maybe more so.

WHY USE A QUERY LETTER?

When I teach my class "Breaking Into Freelance Writing," one of the questions I'm asked most frequently is, "Why can't I just send the article/story/proposal?" While querying for permission to send an article may seem like a waste of time, there is a bit of logic to the apparent madness.

The short answer is editors, agents, and publishers are busy. Very busy. They want the CliffsNotes version of your idea so they can skim it and see if it's a good fit. They don't have time to read 4,000-word feature articles, 90,000-word tomes, or even the first few chapters of your historical-paranormal-romantic-science-fiction-western (no matter how highly your mother recommends it). The sheer volume of material that comes across their desks (and virtual inboxes) would be enough to send a paper shredder into early retirement.

"First reads" require almost everyone in the publishing industry to make snap judgments and immediate decisions. If they didn't, nothing would ever get published because they'd be too busy reading (or sleeping atop of) the unpublishable manuscripts.

WHO WRITES QUERIES?

As a beginning or intermediate writer, expect that you'll be writing query letters a lot. More experienced writers can often circumvent the process because they're either getting regular assignments from an editor or have a strong enough relationship with the editor that they can simply shoot her an e-mail saying, "Hi Jane, I have an idea for an article. What do you think?"

Granted, there are times when less experienced writers can also skip the query letter. These include:

- When a publication's guidelines clearly state no query is necessary
- Letters to the editor (submission to the so-named section of the newspaper) or other reader-feedback sections (because contributions are generally solicited from readers, not professional writers)
- Submissions to certain local or regional publications (which are often comprised of pieces contributed by residents in the area who aren't necessarily professional writers)
- Submissions to small-readership online publications (which often don't pay and therefore don't require professional queries)
- Submissions of poems, greeting card ideas, flash fiction, or fillers (which are short enough to skim and therefore don't require a query)

If you're not sure when it's necessary to query, your best bet is to read the writer's guidelines of the publication or agency. (When querying an agent, some will require just a query, while others will ask for a complete book proposal.)

KNOWING WHEN YOU'RE READY

When I first started pitching to magazines, I thought it was about quantity. I would throw together a quick query letter, send it to every magazine I could think of, and then get right back to work on another (poorly written) query. (And this was back before e-mail queries so I just cringe at how many trees I killed, not to mention how much money I wasted on postage and envelopes.) Now that I'm more experienced, I realize that getting published isn't about throwing everything at the wall and seeing what sticks; it's about *quality*. Learn from my mistakes and focus on crafting one good query to pitch to a few quality magazines (or agents, if we're talking about a book). This will entail doing some research, reading sample queries (both good and bad), and creating a solid piece of writing.

I wouldn't be so Pollyanna as to say, "You'll know when you're ready." You might. You might not. If you're new to this, you'll be scared out of your mind the first time and probably experience one or more of the following:

- "They're going to know I'm new at this."
- "If they like my query then I actually have to WRITE something!?!"
- "They're going to post my query in the staff lounge and laugh at me while they sip their espressos and dine on their cucumber sandwiches." (This is a common misperception. As an editor, I can attest that we are neither snooty nor dainty. More likely, we are chugging our cup of coffee and eating our second—OK, *third*—Hershey's bar ... while laughing at your query.)

The truth is, you'll learn as much from your rejections as your acceptances, so sending a well-prepared query is the best you can do to get ready. You'll learn more about the details of how to prepare a great query later in this book.

THE EVER-EVOLVING QUERY LETTER

Perhaps the biggest—and best—transformation in the query-writing world is the advancement of technology. The computer, the Web, and e-mail have helped writers and editors save time, money, and heartache.

Computers

With computer functions like "copy and paste" and "save as," it's much easier to modify a query from its original form. Long gone are the days of reinventing the wheel. Received a rejection from one magazine? Simply replace the contact info and send to Editor Number Two.

Computers also make it easier to keep track of submissions. Once you start sending out multiple submissions, you'll be able to easily find and update files. Can't remember if you pitched that article on artichokes to *Woman's Day*? A simple "find" will help—if you know how to organize.

The Web

What did we do before Al Gore invented the Internet? (He didn't, really. His comment about taking the initiative to help the Defense Department create the Internet while he was in Congress was taken out of context. But it's still funny.) The World Wide Web is a writer's best friend (and sometimes worst enemy). It allows us to search for sample queries, review online writer's guidelines, skim back issues of archived publications, and find the right contact person to whom we should submit queries. It's a wonderful resource for statistics, public domain works, and interviews with editors who share what they look for in queries and articles. It can't write a query for you, but it sure beats yesteryear's researching at the library.

E-mail

Get to know your mail carrier. He will be a vital part of your query process—picking up stacks of queries and returning tons of self-addressed, stamped envelopes (SASEs) and hopefully several on magazines' letterhead. That said, you probably won't need to know your carrier as much as those of us who were writers a decade ago. Today's writers will be pleased to know that a large majority of magazine editors, agents, and publishers are now accepting e-queries—that is, queries submitted via e-mail. It's not only an incredible money-saver (stamps, paper, ink, envelopes, gas to the post office, if needed), but also a great time-saver. With some editors responding in mere seconds, you'll either be able to get right to work ... or right back to the drawing board. (And a rejection is much less painful if you can immediately submit the idea to another magazine/agent/publisher.)

E-mail also allows you to get writer's guidelines much faster (if they're not published on the publisher's Web site) and to correspond promptly with questions about word count, payment, deadlines, interviews, and other such assignment details. Three caveats regarding e-mail:

---

1. Choose an e-mail address that you'll check regularly, and keep it professional. "HotGirl24@yahoo.com" or "Studmeister48@hotmail.com" might work for the online dating scene, but editors, agents, and publishers will view it as tasteless. (Unless you're writing for *Hustler*. Then you're in like Flynn. Or Flynt.)

2. Use an e-mail address that's easy to remember—your name only, if possible. Or, if not available, try your name with a number or two after it.

3. Get an e-mail address and keep it. It's a pain for everyone to update your e-mail address every time you change it. Plus, not everyone will, which will make it impossible to track you down for clarification or future assignments. I've had editors, after six or seven years without contact, e-mail to offer me work.

One much-discussed dilemma regards how to send clips by e-mail. There are several suggestions making their way around writers' circles. Some of my personal favorites include:

- Copying and pasting published clips right into the body of the e-mail. This is particularly useful because many spam filters reject e-mails with attachments.
- Attaching Microsoft Word documents or PDFs and then following up with a separate e-mail (with no attachment) to let the editor know to check her spam folder.
- Sending a link to published articles on the Web.
- Directing an editor to your Web site, on which you have posted clips.

Increased Foreign Correspondence

As opportunities for publication and representation in a country outside your own increase, it becomes more important to study submission guidelines and requirements. Technology has made routine correspondence easier, but there may be times when you need to use the good ol' postal service. Foreign countries (including Canada) do not allow you to use American postage on SASEs. In order for an editor to reply to your query by mail, you will need to purchase several International Reply Coupons (IRCs). An IRC can be exchanged for that country's postage. Your post office can help you determine how many IRCs you will need to cover the return postage. Most standard queries will only require one IRC, currently running about two dollars in the United States.

KEEPING TRACK OF SUBMISSIONS

Rumor has it that you can buy tracking software, but many pros do it just as easily on their own. I started off keeping mine in a Microsoft Word document, just because I wasn't familiar with spreadsheets then. There are as many ways to keep track of queries and submissions as there are writers, and you'll have to find the one that's right for you. Here are a few tips to consider:

- Designate a one- or two-word title for each piece you write. A piece titled "Rage Against the Machine: How Computers Are Working Against Us" might best be designated as "RageMachine" rather than "ComputerArticle" because you may end up writing another computer article in your lifetime.

- Be sure to include the *year* of your query or submission or you're likely to get confused when you're in your third year of freelancing.

- Include *all* pertinent information in your tracking: date sent, publication, editor, query/submission, title of piece, and response. (I've sent a previously rejected query to a new editor at the same magazine and gotten an acceptance.)

- Update information immediately upon receipt. This includes editor changes, new addresses, publication closings, etc. Don't assume you'll remember, or it could cost you time, energy, and money if you resubmit.

- Write rejection comments like "no simultaneous submissions" or "no reprints" in your copy of *Writer's Market*. (If you own it. The library frowns upon writing in its books, even if you're updating it for future borrowers.) It might keep you from resubmitting to a publication that has gone defunct or that doesn't use freelancers.

Feeling a bit more informed now? Good, because we're just getting started. You've got a lot more to learn about queries, so if you need a minute to stretch your legs, feed the dogs, or just process the fact that you're on the verge of getting published, go ahead. You'll need to feel refreshed as we head into chapter one and discuss the Ten Commandments of queries. They'll offer some insider tips on major dos and don'ts, and thou shalt not feel groggy for the lesson.

CHAPTER 1

QUERY BASICS

Oh good, you're back. Talking about "hard work" in the introduction is usually a great way to weed out the "wannabes" from the "wanna writes." ("Wannabes" are typically people who want to be *known* as writers but don't want to put in the effort to actually write, rewrite, or submit. Prolific authors can usually smell them coming from a mile away; they're the fans who slip Janet Evanovich their phone numbers saying, "If you ever run out of ideas ...") The truth is, writing queries isn't so much about doing *hard* work as it is about doing *smart* work. Building a pyramid by hand is hard work. Reading the forklift operator's manual is smart work.

This chapter is your operator's manual to query letters. You'll learn what to do (push the lever); why to do it (you'll build the pyramid faster); what not to do (drive over a mound of bricks); and why not to do it (you don't have disability insurance). Best of all, you can see real examples of queries that worked (*yeah!*), a few that didn't (*hiss!*), and side-by-side comparisons of opening "hooks."

Even first-time query writers without any publishing credits under their belts can follow these "Ten Commandments" to increase their chances of impressing an editor. Some are more obvious than others, but I'll address everything so the lessons are as comprehensive as possible. This is an immersion in queries. So take a deep breath and dive in.

I. THOU SHALT LOOK PROFESSIONAL

Your first obstacle at any office (magazine, agency, or publisher) is to get by the "gatekeeper." This is the receptionist or editor's assistant or lowly intern who reviews the *slush pile*—industry jargon for the mound of unsolicited submissions—to weed out the good, the bad, and the maybes. If your query letter (or possibly even *envelope)* arrives with several spelling mistakes, on fluorescent pink paper (a dead giveaway that you're trying too hard to get their attention), emblazoned with bunny stickers or with a five-hundred-page tome (when the guidelines specifically state to send a one-page query first), you're headed for the round filing bin in the sky. (This is the garbage can. Or, at least for coastal publishers, the recycling bin.)

In the query world, "professional" largely means demonstrating you've done your homework. It's the writer's responsibility to send a self-addressed, stamped envelope (SASE) if you're querying by snail mail; address your query to the right editor or agent (and spell his name correctly) with the right title; format your query according to industry standards; spell the name of the magazine, agency, or publishing house correctly; and get its address right. (Unless the business moved very recently, using an old address will indicate that you haven't referred to a recent issue of the magazine or been to the business's Web site.)

For some of you, these guidelines are obvious, and therefore boring. Others may be thinking, *Is the publishing industry really that strict?* As someone who has worked as an editor at several publications, I can say that these guidelines are in place for a reason: so editors can maintain their sanity and not waste so much of their precious editing time.

Imagine this: You're an agent at a major literary agency. *The New York Times* just ran an article about how you landed John Writerdude a million-dollar advance for a novel about his life. While John Writerdude's life is fascinating and exciting (think James Bond meets Casanova), the lives of the other forty-thousand wannabe writers who are now submitting their life stories to your agency are not. You are now plagued with thousands of manuscripts and queries a month and you need a way to weed out the bad ones before the guy in the mailroom cuts your car's brake lines. Your first line of defense is to dump the unprofessional-looking queries and manuscripts before you even read them.

On one hand, this sounds intimidating to new writers. On the other hand, look how easy it is to beat your competition out of the gate!

Still concerned? Let's look at these guidelines in more detail one at a time.

Include an SASE (If You're Querying by Snail Mail)

Because amateurs often *don't* include an SASE, remembering this courtesy differentiates your submission from theirs. In addition, including an SASE is vital because no company is going to pay for the postage to send you a rejection. (And chances are, if they make a point to ask for an SASE in their guidelines, they're not going to accept your idea if you didn't include one.)

Yes, it gets expensive to include an SASE with every query, but you don't have a choice. (For publications that allow you to submit complete manuscripts without queries, use this trick: Place a sticker on the back of your SASE that says something like, "SASE is for response only. No need to return manuscript." This will save you money on return postage. Besides, you don't want to resubmit manuscripts that have been folded to other publications or agents.)

Address Your Query to the Right Editor or Agent, With the Right Title

Granted, staff members will often forward mail to the appropriate editor, but you can't always count on that. Even at literary agencies, there may be one agent who handles nonfiction and another who handles fiction. Take the time to find out who does what and you'll increase your chances of being considered and decrease the time it takes to be considered.

Also, don't assume that only men work at *Men's Health* or only women work at *Woman's Day*. If you run across a name like "Chris Smith," either call the publication to ask if Chris is a male or female or do a search on the Web for an interview in which they indicate "he says" or "she says." When in doubt, address the person as "Dear Chris Smith" instead of "Dear Ms. Smith" or "Dear Mr. Smith."

Format Your Query According to Industry Standards

This means printing your query from a computer, not a typewriter. (And don't even think about sending something handwritten.) Queries that aren't computer generated are an indication that you haven't written much. I had a friend who constantly submitted work that he typed on an old typewriter ... on onionskin paper. (Remember that see-through paper you used in grade school to trace pictures?) He couldn't understand why he kept getting rejections. Did I mention that one of his letter keys was also broken, causing him to handwrite the letter *W*?

In addition to clean, typed copy (white paper, black ink, Times New Roman size 12 font, please!), industry standard dictates you'll need to include the date, the editor's/agent's name and title, the magazine or agency name and address, and your name and contact information (address, phone, fax, and e-mail) on the one-page query.

Spell the Magazine, Agency, or Publishing House Correctly and Get Its Address Right

Larger magazines may have more than one mailing address so be sure you know at which location your editor works.

II. THOU SHALT PITCH A GREAT LEAD

Remember the great scene in the movie *Jerry Maguire* in which Renée Zellweger's character says to Tom Cruise's character, "You had me at hello"? The first paragraph of your query needs to make your editor or agent feel the same way. By the time she gets to your second or third paragraph, it's just icing on the cake. Your lead needs to excite her on a Monday afternoon spent skimming boring queries. Don't disappoint.

One way to accomplish this is to "cite the lead." This basically means you're opening your query with the first paragraph of your article. You can indicate you're doing so, if you like. See **Example 1.1** for a query where citing the lead worked well for me (*Home Cooking* bought the article).

Another style is to throw in something the editor can really relate to, such as a funny parenting anecdote (if you're pitching to a parenting magazine), a

EXAMPLE 1.1   GOOD (E-MAIL) ARTICLE QUERY

February 1, 2004

Shelly Vaughan James
Home Cooking
House of White Birches
306 East Parr Road
Berne, IN 46711
Home_Cooking@whitebirches.com

Dear Ms. James,

Cinderella used hers as a taxi. The headless horseman used his as a noggin. But it was Peter, Peter, Pumpkin Eater who seemed to put his pumpkin to best use.

Dating back to the Greek's *pepon*, meaning "large melon," pumpkins have a long-standing history of odd uses. From "removing" freckles and "curing" snakebites, to the Native Americans' more practical craft of weaving dried pumpkin into mats, the orange gourd has taken on many forms.

Today, the tradition continues, as the benefits of pumpkin are continually touted by dietitians, doctors, and scientists. Offering lots of taste for its considerably low-fat, low-calorie content, pumpkin is an excellent source of fiber, beta-carotene, and vitamin A, and a good source of potassium. Nutritional benefits include the promotion of bones and teeth; formation and maintenance of healthy skin, hair, and mucous membranes; increased resistance to respiratory infections; and treatment of many eye disorders. When applied externally, pumpkin can also aid in the treatment of acne, boils, and open ulcers.

Of course, no one wants to eat chunks of fresh pumpkin for breakfast, lunch, and dinner. Luckily, you don't have to. Incorporating October's most edible decoration can be as easy as pie ... or bread ... or muffins.

The above is the opening to my article, **"Jack-O-Lantern of All Trades: Putting Your Pumpkin to Good Use,"** complete with nutritional and historical information about the gourd, six pumpkin-based recipes, and a sidebar of trivia.

At 33, my credentials include more than 500 published pieces, including work in *Family Circle*, the Diabetes and Wellness Foundation's newsletter, *Complete Woman*, *Woman's Own*, BlueSuitMom.com, Vital Living, the Nemours Foundation's KidsHealth.org, Cub Foods' magazine, and Streamedia.com's Women on the Edge. I've also written two women's humor (nonfiction) books for McGraw-Hill. (And lucky me! Many of my food/nutrition articles have final review from my mother, a Registered Dietitian.)

If you have any questions, please do not hesitate to contact me at the number or e-mail listed below. Please note that I am also open to assignments.

Thank you for taking the time to review my query. I look forward to hearing from you.

Best regards,

Wendy Burt-Thomas
(address, phone, e-mail)

"near-miss" story if you're pitching to an adventure magazine (where, chances are, the editor is an avid outdoorsman), or a quirky tidbit that will make him want to read more (e.g., "Why is this lady talking about her uncontrollable need to throw cheese down the stairs?").

Example 1.2 shows a query that landed me not only publication, but also an interesting response from the editor. He wrote, "How fun! Please *do* send me the article for review. And would you also send me directions on how to play Kick the Can? It's been so long that I've forgotten and I'd love to play it with my kids."

See how this works? Your opening paragraphs have to make the editor laugh, cry, reminisce, or jump online to see if pumpkins really do cure snakebites. But most importantly, your lead has to make her want more—even if "more" is directions to the simplest game since hide-and-seek.

III. THOU SHALT TAILOR YOUR QUERY TO THE MAGAZINE

If you have an older, same-sex sibling, you're probably all too familiar with concept of hand-me-downs. (Unless you were raised with money. In which case, you should not become a writer.) Like you, editors enjoy the (rare) occasion when something is specifically tailored to them, and the more perfect a fit you can create in their minds with your query, the more likely you are to see your article in print.

There are several ways to do this. As with any publication, you'll start by reading its writer's guidelines and at least *skimming* a few recent copies of the magazine. You can:

- Tailor your query by targeting the voice/tone/style of the publication's past articles (as should be done in most cases)

- Mention a specific section where your article might be a good fit ("Home & Hearth" section, "Words of Wisdom" page, "From the Heart" column that's always written by readers)

- Give a specific word count (e.g., "I've written this personal essay to fit within 600 to 700 words, as per the writer's guidelines for your "Full Circle" section.")

EXAMPLE 1.2   GOOD (MAIL) ARTICLE QUERY

April 15, 1999

David Dunn
KidsPlay Magazine
1234 Main St.
Burlington, VT 05401

Dear Mr. Dunn,

THE ARTICLE
As a writer, I am by no means "anti-computer." As a child trapped in an adult body, however, I am sometimes disturbed that today's kids know more about "surfing the Web" than "surfing the waves."

With dreamy visions of Kick-the-Can, tire swings, and my old disco roller skates, I set out to write an article with realistic suggestions to help parents reintroduce their children to "real play" (that is, play without the computer).

I'd like to send you **"Growing Up Online: Reinventing the Lost Art of Play."** The 1,000-word how-to piece offers 10 realistic suggestions for parents who'd like to reacquaint their children with old-fashioned play.

Although the article does not aim to negate the positive attributes of computers, it does address certain parental concerns (computer games, access to pornography, and lack of interaction) in order to encourage a healthy balance between "technologic" and "real-life" play.

CREDENTIALS
My writing credentials include over 250 published pieces and a parenting column in a local newspaper. I also write for three local newspapers and teach "Break Into Freelance Writing" at Colorado Free University to freelance writers.

If you have any questions, please do not hesitate to contact me. I would be more than happy to send the article upon request.

Thank you for taking the time to review my query. I look forward to hearing from you.

Best regards,

Wendy Burt-Thomas
(address, phone, e-mail)

Encl: SASE

- Reference an article the publication has run, pointing out that you write in a similar style

See **Example 1.3** for a letter that incorporates all four of the above-mentioned ways to tailor a query to a specific publication. You'll notice in the query that I am not only paying them a compliment (by saying that I enjoyed the article *and* by letting them know they're hitting their target readership), but also showing them that (A) I've actually *read* the publication, which is more than some writers do; and (B) I'm aware of things like tone, style, and voice. Talk about tailoring your query! What editor wouldn't at least ask to review the article based on such a "measured" approach? (Do not use bad puns in your query.)

Another way to tailor your query is to cite the magazine's editorial calendar, referencing a specific upcoming theme (perhaps seasonal) under which your article would fit. Some writers have even found success by doing so in the opening sentence, saving their "hook" for the second paragraph. (This is especially true for seasoned writers or those who have already developed a relationship with the editor.)

Example 1.4 (pg. 19) shows a letter that cites the publication's editorial calendar. You'll note that there's not really a strong hook in this query, but rather I'm relying on several other factors to hold the editor's interest: my expertise as a writer specializing in cognitive development; my ability to provide fun and interesting "brain training" exercises; and my promise to interview experts, including a professional brain trainer (relevant), an author (impressive contact), and a *local* expert. The last is especially important because this is a small, regional publication, many of which like to use local resources in their articles. I also offered to fit the length to the editor's desired word count (many small regional publications don't use writer's guidelines) in order to better tailor the piece to her needs. Note: Even if your article is complete, you can offer to fit the word count to the publication. Just be prepared to cut down your piece or bulk it up, if needed.

IV. THOU SHALT OFFER A FRESH IDEA

In 2001, I heard a National Public Radio interview with the editor of a national women's fitness magazine. The program was about how specialty

EXAMPLE 1.3   GOOD ARTICLE QUERY

July 29, 1999

Allison Kyle Leopold, Editor-in-Chief
Flair c/o Hearst Custom Marketing Group
P.O. Box 755 Radio City Station
New York, NY 10101-0755

Dear Ms. Leopold,

I just received my copy of your premiere issue of *Flair*. I was quite impressed with the variety of topics covered and was thrilled to see one of my old hangouts (Sunset Beach Restaurant on Shelter Island) in the article on summer hot spots.

I was perhaps most intrigued with the article "Dough Girl" by Kelly Love Johnson. The piece was funny, interesting, and informative—three traits that always appeal to me as a single, 28-year-old freelance writer. (Note the similarities of my bio to Kelly's. It's no wonder her writing captured my attention!)

Because your premiere issue seemed to really speak to women of my age (my interests, my concerns, my income), I thought I'd submit one of my own articles, written in a similar tone, style, and voice to that of "Dough Girl."

THE ARTICLE
"A Woman's First Home" is a how-to piece that takes the first-time female homebuyer through the process step-by-step, from "Are you ready to buy?" to "Choosing a home inspector." The article is based on my own experience, and includes quotes from a realtor, a home inspector, and a mortgage broker, as well as a financial chart and sidebar glossary of terms.

I think the piece would be a nice fit for your "Milestones" section and, as per the word count indicated in your writer's guidelines, I have written the feature to 2,000 words.

CREDENTIALS
My writing credentials include over 250 published pieces, including articles in *American Fitness, Woman's Life, Columbia*, and *New Living*. I also write for three Colorado Springs newspapers and teach "Break Into Freelance Writing" at Colorado Free University.

Thank you for taking the time to review my submission. I look forward to hearing from you.

Best Regards,

Wendy Burt-Thomas
(address, phone, e-mail)

Encl: SASE

magazines have to work harder to come up with new approaches to the same topics so as not to sound stale. It's a tough job, and the more specialized your publication, the harder it gets. *Shape* magazine has to offer articles on how to flatten your abs in every issue—because that's why women are buying it. If you laid six consecutive issues next to each other, here's how the cover blurbs would read:

- "10 Tips for Flattening Your Abs"
- "5 NEW Ways to Get Flatter Abs"
- "Get Rid of Your Gut Without Exercising!"
- "Drop Your Belly Fat in 5 Minutes a Day"
- "Lose Your Stomach by Christmas"
- "Eat Chocolate to Tighten Your Abs? YES!"
  (Okay, this one's wishful thinking.)

Think you can do better? Prove it. Come up with a new spin on a must-be-covered topic and, as long as it's well written, you'll be cashing your check before you can e-mail a reminder to send a contributor's copy. (Yes, this happens sometimes. But more often you'll have to remind them to send your check. Get used to it.)

Here are some ideas to get you started. We'll use the "flatten your abs" example, since it's a tough one.

- Ab exercises for someone who is wheelchair-bound or bedridden
- Safe postpartum ab exercises
- Helping your husband lose HIS postpartum gut
- Ab exercises you can do with your kids
- The coolest outfits to show off your abs
- Ab exercises you can do at your desk
- Reviews of the latest abdominal exercise machine(s)
- The truth behind pills that claim to "fight the flab"
- Dance/bowl/roller-skate away your belly fat

Are you starting to get it? Good. And remember, you don't have to be an expert to write an article. Just come up with a new spin and then *interview* an expert.

EXAMPLE 1.4   GOOD ARTICLE QUERY

December 3, 2007

Kim Dearth, Senior Editor
brava
P.O. Box 45050
Madison, WI 53744-5050
kdearth@ericksonpublishing.com

Dear Ms. Dearth,

I see on your editorial calendar that you'll be covering "Adult Attention Deficit Disorder" in your December 2008 issue.

As a full-time freelance writer specializing in cognitive development, I'd like to propose an article to fit this edition. **"Pay Attention! Improving Attention the All-Natural Way— With Brain Training"** would include the following:

1. Brain exercises that your readers can do at home to improve the three types of attention: selective, sustained, and divided

2. The latest scientific research on brain training (why it works)

3. Quotes from a psychologist, a professional brain trainer in Madison, and an author

I could fit the article to your desired word count.

My credentials include a B.A. in Psychology and more than 1,000 published pieces, including two nonfiction books for McGraw-Hill. I've written for countless parenting, health, and women's magazines and currently work as a freelance editor for several publications.

Thank you in advance for your time. I look forward to hearing from you.

Best regards,

Wendy Burt-Thomas
(address, phone, e-mail)

Clips and books available on www.wendyburt-thomas.com

Here's another way to put a new spin on an old topic: Interview a celebrity. You don't need any innovative approach other than "How Kirstie Alley Flattened Her Abs" or "A Playboy Bunny's Tips for Looking Good Naked."

Can't get any celebrities to return your calls? Go for the next best thing: the people who work for them. Trainers, hairdressers, stylists, personal chefs—they all *love* publicity. And although they may be limited in what they can talk about, they'll probably be able to talk the celebrity into allowing them to speak to the media—with certain stipulations.

It's important to remember that "celebrity" doesn't necessarily mean "Hollywood." Land an interview with a world-renowned theorist, the chef of a five-star restaurant, or the manager of a "resort to the stars" and you'll be able to spice up your query with tidbits that inquiring minds want to know, like:

- What's Brangelina's favorite drink at the La Mancha Private Villas Spa and Resort?
- Why do scientists now believe there's life outside our galaxy?
- What food does Paris Hilton order in the shape of her dog at London's Che restaurant?

Likewise, "famous" doesn't necessarily mean world-renowned. If you're querying a small, regional publication, find out who the local celebrities are—the mayor, the has-been actress, the ghost that haunts City Hall—and run with it. Of course, you'll have to review several back issues (or better yet, search the online archives) to make sure the story hasn't been done to death. But if the story is new (or at least to that particular publication), you'll have a great leg up on your competition.

V. THOU SHALT BE CREATIVE IN YOUR PRESENTATION

This is different than Commandment IV in which I talk about presenting old ideas with a new twist. I'm talking about the actual approach you take in your query. Why not open your query with a sample of your multiple-choice quiz from your article entitled "Are You as Smart as You Think?" Or a few outlandish true-or-false questions from your article on urban legends? (Not the obvious ones. Everyone knows Bill Gates is not going to send you money for forwarding that e-mail to seven of your friends, aka soon-to-be enemies.) If you're a graphics whiz, you could even include a small perception test of some sort ("What do you see in this picture?") as a sample from your article "Are You a Serial Killer in the Making?"

Although query letters should adhere to some basic format (one page, contact info, salutation, pitch, credentials), that doesn't mean you can't play around by adding bullet points, bold, italics, underlines, etc. You might want to stay away from all caps and lots of exclamation points (things that indicate yelling) ... unless your article is about poor punctuation, which would be rather amusing.

Example 1.5 (pg. 23) shows a good query letter that used some of these creative presentation tips.

VI. THOU SHALT TIGHTEN YOUR QUERY ANGLE

You already know that queries need to fit on one page. For new writers, that might seem like an insurmountable task. "But how will I ever summarize my idea on how to travel in style in one page?" The answer? You won't. And news flash: You're not going to write an article about "how to travel in style" in less than twenty pages, either. The topic is just too broad.

Instead, you'll need to take the inverted pyramid approach, brainstorming on topics and filtering ideas out as you go to narrow your topic down to the smallest molecule of an idea.

For example: "Travel in style" can be narrowed down to ...

1. When flying
2. With your family
3. On a cruise

Each of these can be broken down even more. Let's take "When flying." It can be narrowed further to become:

A. For frequent world travelers
B. For business people
C. With young children

Each of *these* can be narrowed down even further. We'll use "For frequent world travelers":

1. How to exercise when you're always in the air/in hotels
2. Foods to avoid before a long flight/best foods to consume
3. The latest and greatest clothes for frequent world travelers

Now we're cooking with gas! An article that is more focused is not only more likely to get published, it'll actually be easier to write. Ditto the query.

Many new writers (myself included) start their careers by mistakenly pitching pieces that are just way too broad for a magazine. Do you honestly think an in-flight magazine like *Hemispheres* (the full-color glossy you find in the back of the seats on United Airlines) hasn't covered "Travel in Style" about a hundred different ways? You'll need to not only narrow your focus, but also add a bit of newsworthiness/timeliness to it (the *latest* in clothes for business travelers) in case they ran something similar three years ago. See **Example 1.6** (pg. 25) for this type of query.

VII. THOU SHALT SWEETEN THE POT

Everybody likes freebies and, despite the rumors, editors are people too.

There are lots of ways to add weight to your article with "extras." These might include one or more of the following.

Photos, Graphics, Illustrations, or Renderings

Offering to send these will not only add visual dimension to your piece but also save the editor from having to find stock photos, send a photographer, or use a graphic designer. In most cases, those won't require you to do much more than request a photo (from the person you're interviewing, the library, the architect, the clothing manufacturer, a media representative for the company, etc.). Look for ways to go above and beyond the usual "photo available upon request." How about suggesting a "then and now" photo of the hotel that was built in 1920 but recently remodeled? (Check with the hotel first to see if they have such a photo, if you could use it, and if it's available to be sent via e-mail. If it's not, you'll need to find out how to make a duplicate of the original.)

EXAMPLE 1.5   GOOD ARTICLE QUERY

December 6, 2007

John Smith, Managing Editor
The Latest: A Magazine of News
999 Strange Avenue
Los Angeles, CA 90001

Dear Mr. Smith,

The privacy of the Internet has allowed sellers to pawn off some incredibly freaky stuff. (My friend once sold photos of her husband's feet. Seriously.) eBay is no exception, offering a clearinghouse of bizarre options for those who are willing to shell out their hard-earned cash. Just see if you can figure out which of these items were actually offered. (Hint: Eight are real.)

A. A serial killer's fingernails	F. The Meaning of Life
B. A date with George Hamilton	G. A UFO detector
C. A (real) shrunken head	H. The Internet
D. The chance to be a bridesmaid	I. A ghost in a jar
E. A vampire-killing kit	J. A Falcon missile

The above quiz is just part of my 2,000-word article:

"FOR SALE: Ghost in a Jar
25 of the Strangest Things Ever Sold on eBay"

If you'd like to consider the article for publication (and have me immediately e-mail you the answer to the quiz above!), I can be reached at the e-mail below.

As a full-time freelance writer, my credentials include more than one thousand published pieces and two books for McGraw-Hill. In addition, I have worked as an editor, writer, columnist, and copy editor for a variety of regional and national magazines and newspapers.

Thank you for your time. I look forward to hearing from you.

Best regards,

Wendy Burt-Thomas
(address, phone, e-mail)

Encl: SASE

Sidebars and Sidelights

From Top 10 lists and "Did you know?" trivia to resource boxes (Web sites, addresses, and phone numbers to pursue for more information), smaller companions to your main story are great selling tools. Sometimes they even earn you more money.

I once wrote an article about helping your child get over his fear of the doctor. At the last minute, the editor who was planning to run the article called to say she had a bit more room in the layout, and could I provide a small sidebar of tips? I called the pediatrician I had interviewed for the article and got "Five Things to Look for in a Pediatrician." I got an extra twenty-five dollars for the sidebar, which took about ten minutes and was maybe 50 words. That's fifty cents a word ... or about $150/hour.

The Giveaway

Ready for the big leagues? If you can get REAL freebies given away with your article, it'll be very hard for an editor to pass. These might include first-come, first-serve products or service vouchers; a set amount of free products or service vouchers; a coupon code for use on the Web; or a limited-time giveaway. Need a few examples?

- A profile of a famous author could be accompanied by a box at the end offering free autographed copies to the first ten readers who opt in to his e-mail list.

- An article on organic food could include a limited-time offer for a trial-size box of organic cereal (or whatever other offer you find on the Web). Most companies will be thrilled for the free publicity—especially if they're paying to advertise the free trial in other publications. Just be sure the timeline works. You don't want to offer a product through a giveaway that ends in February only to find out your article won't run until March.

- An exposé on the dangers of lead paint in important toys could include a five-dollar-off coupon code to a company that sells lead testers on its Web site.

EXAMPLE 1.6 GOOD ARTICLE QUERY

July 2, 2004

Eva Leonard, Editor
Business Traveler U.S.A.
225 Park Ave. South, 7th floor
New York, NY 10003

Dear Ms. Leonard,

A chocolate stain in Chile? Mosquitoes in Melbourne? Downpours in Dublin?

As business travelers, we've learned to expect the unexpected. We pack bug spray, stain remover, three pairs of black pants, and an umbrella that wards off everything— from hail to 120-degree heat. But despite our best efforts, it's impossible to think of everything. Luckily, clothing manufacturers are thinking for us.

- Headed to the tropics? Buzz Off ™ offers apparel that uses a process to bond insect repellent to the fabric. Available in everything from hats and socks to pants and shirts.

- Is your destination known for pickpockets? How about a pair of ten-pocket pants with zippers and buttons? The manufacturer even claims that one pocket is so top secret you won't know its location till you buy the pants.

- Need to travel super light? Convertible clothes range from shorts-to-pants combos to three-in-one reversible skorts.

- Think you're up-to-date on stain-resistant, rain-repellent, and wrinkle-free clothes? Today's fabrics will knock your (waterproof) socks off.

I'd like to write **"Clothes Quarters: The Latest in Business Travel Apparel"** as a 1,200-word piece.

CREDENTIALS
Formerly the editor of Colorado Springs' largest business newspaper and now a full-time free-lance writer, my credentials include more than 500 published pieces. My work has appeared in such varied publications as *Front Range Business Magazine, Family Circle, Pizza Today,* Blue SuitMom.com, *Woman's Own,* SharpMan.com, *The Business Informant,* and *The Colorado Springs Business Journal.* I have also written two nonfiction humor books for McGraw-Hill.

Thank you for your time. I look forward to hearing from you.

Best regards,

Wendy Burt-Thomas
(address, phone, e-mail)

Don't be afraid to offer more than one "extra." An editor won't reject your piece because you're offering too much. He will just use what he can, but he'll appreciate the option to fill space at layout if needed.

VIII. THOU SHALT NOT PROPOSE THE IMPOSSIBLE

You know that old expression "It's easier to beg for forgiveness than to ask for permission"? This isn't the case in the editing world.

What does this mean for you as a writer? Don't pitch something you can't follow through on.

Failure to Deliver

One of my biggest pet peeves as an editor is getting pitched an idea, accepting it, and then having the writer fail to deliver. Sometimes this means getting a crappy article. Sometimes it means getting an e-mail right before deadline: "Sorry, I forgot" or "Sorry, I got too busy." The worst was when I received no forewarning at all. I'd called a writer to ask where the article was and he said, "I've been meaning to call you about that ..."

The inability to follow through can take several forms. It might entail pitching a story about a celebrity or expert only to find out your star witness isn't willing or able to be interviewed. Unless you share a family tree with Stephen King, don't assume he'll be falling over himself when you tell him you'll be writing a profile on his childhood. (And even if you *do* share genes, get him to agree *before* you query.)

Short Turnarounds

Unless an editor specifically assigns you a piece that she needs immediately, don't promise the world. This is especially true with lengthy features that require interviews with busy, important people, or extensive research and evaluation. And anything that requires waiting to hear back from the government ... well, don't even go there. There are exceptions to this rule. If, for example, a new bankruptcy law goes into effect at the first of the year, you could pitch a timely article and promise to get it completed immediately in order to make the January (or December) issue.

Impossible Word Counts

Here's another surefire way to let it slip that you're new to the game: Pitch a serious, in-depth exposé ... to be covered in 800 words. Nothing says, "I don't have a clue what I'm doing!" like a promise to fit in a few pages what needs to be covered in ten. Even if you *could* write the piece in 800 words, how good could it be? You're barely touching on a subject that needs to be expounded upon in further detail. Personally, I'd rather not write a 9,000-word piece anyway—especially on spec (short for "on speculation," which means you write the entire article before you find someone willing to publish it). That's a lot of work for something that might not run anyway, and unless you've got a lot of credentials already, your chances of being given the assignment are low.

IX. THOU SHALT SHOW CREDENTIALS

Here's another oldie but goodie that I get from people who take my class: "What do you put in a query if you don't have any published pieces?"

To be honest, there's a lot of disagreement about this. I've read query books that have advocated not mentioning anything unless you've got clips from national magazines. I've read others that have said include writing samples on the same topic you're pitching, even if they're not published. The two things everyone seems to agree on are (1) Don't include a list of everything you've ever published; and (2) Don't spill your guts that you've never had anything published.

Here are my suggestions for those who have few or no published pieces.

Option A: Say nothing. Just pitch your idea and say that you look forward to hearing from them. Just be prepared: An editor may e-mail you and ask for clips. If he does, offer to send samples of your writing—even if they're unpublished. If an editor is still hesitant, you can offer to write for an even earlier deadline, allowing him plenty of time to find a replacement article (or writer) if your work isn't up to par.

Option B: If you've never published anything but are writing on a topic you know a lot about, focus on your expertise. If you were a teacher for ten years and are writing an article about education, mention your experience.

If you've seen *The Phantom of the Opera* seventeen times, few could argue that you're not an expert (albeit in a somewhat freaky, deranged-fan sort of way). Use your obsession to your advantage. One of the best ways for new, unpublished writers with children to break into a market is to pitch an idea on parenting or kids. Who's going to argue that you're not an expert on, say, feeding a big family on a budget when you raised four boys? Or perhaps you quit your job to have a baby and have discovered a fun new world of decorating a nursery on a budget. Tell the editor and she might not even notice you don't have clips.

Option C: If you've never been published and don't feel you're a true expert in anything (No kids? No dogs? No travel? No budgeting?), find someone who is to "co-author" your article (even if you do all the writing). I once had a friend who taught music lessons to children. I sat down with her to brainstorm on an article on the subject and then queried, listing us as co-authors. See **Example 1.7**. You'll note that—for the sake of this commandment—I don't mention any of *my* credentials, or lack thereof. What we *did* offer, in addition to my friend's experience as a music teacher, was to compile a list of local businesses that offer music lessons. This proved to be a great benefit to the small local parenting magazines, which appreciated our effort in helping them sell advertising. (This actually required little more than a search on the Internet.)

Experts are rarely more than an arm's length away if you know where to look, and who doesn't love to see his name in print, especially as a co-author? Consider the people you see on a regular basis: your daycare provider, your hairdresser, your therapist, your doctor, or your acupuncturist. Even better, make it someone you frequently chat with in person or on the phone: your lawyer husband, your sister-in-law the chef, your dog-groomer neighbor, or your father the more-than-a-hobby carpenter. Pick their brains, write a draft, and then have them review it for accuracy. If it gets published, you can give them a framed copy or offer to split the payment with them.

Option D: If you have a few clips—no matter how small the publication—mention them. Again, this approach will have its opponents, but I've been an editor for several publications and I can honestly say that I'd *much*

EXAMPLE 1.7   GOOD CO-AUTHOR ARTICLE QUERY

January 1, 2005

Cathy Jones, Managing Editor
ABC Parenting
888 Kiddy Place
Manitou Springs, CO 80904

Dear Ms. Jones,

Jancy Wendell has been teaching music lessons to children for five years. She has offered to share her expertise with me to collaborate on an article entitled, **"Music to Your Ears: Is Your Child Ready for Music Lessons?"**

The 800-word article will cover such topics as:

- Is your child ready to play an instrument?

- What instrument is appropriate for your child?

- What about music lessons?

- How can you tell if your child is really interested?

We would also be happy to include a sidebar of local businesses that offer music lessons. (We could provide this immediately in order to assist your salespeople in selling advertising.)

Thank you for your time. I look forward to hearing from you.

Best regards,

Wendy Burt-Thomas (and Jancy Wendell)
(address, phone, e-mail)

Encl: SASE

---

rather see someone with a few small credits to her name than none at all. There is some logic to my reasoning:

- *Someone* liked her writing enough to publish it. Unless the writer was published by a vanity press (e.g., an anthology in which everyone gets published in hopes that their egos will drive them to purchase a copy for $49.95) or wrote for their church newsletter because no one else volunteered, clips demonstrate to me that your writing is not horrible. (Hey, it's a starting point!)

- This writer is familiar with the submission process and therefore may have queried in the past, or at least read some books on writing.

- This writer might know how to meet a deadline, which is more than some writers. Worst-case scenario, I give her an earlier-than-needed deadline to allow myself plenty of time to find filler—or ask for a rewrite—if her piece isn't up to par.

- Maybe this writer is just starting her life as a freelancer and I'm the lucky editor who has found a (cheap) diamond in the rough. By all means, let her build her writing clips with my publication for a measly five cents a word before being scooped up by a dollar-a-word magazine. (About this five cents a word: Don't shoot the messenger. I just worked there; I didn't set the budget.)

- If she's written for very small publications, she won't be disappointed when I tell what we pay writers. In fact, this writer might be in it for the clips, not the money.

- If she's looking for good clips for her portfolio, this writer might be more likely to provide me with photos, sidebars, good interviews, etc.

- If she's pitching the article as a freelance writer—not, for example, as a business trying to get free publicity—there's a greater chance that I'll be able to actually use the piece. (Business owners are notorious for pitching advertorials under the guise of articles.)

- If she's pitching the article as a freelance writer, not as a business owner, there's a good chance I can give her more assignments. On the contrary, an insurance agent who pitches an article on how to protect your home might get the assignment, but I'm not going to ask him to write an article on insurance for every issue. His focus is just too narrow and he probably has no interest in writing about topics outside his expertise—or that don't give him a relevant by-line with contact information.

- This writer may not be listing all the places she's been published. Maybe she forgot a couple or is only listing the few titles that are relevant to the story she's pitching. A friend once told me that the word *including* doesn't mean "all-inclusive"; it can imply that there's more. So try this approach: "As a freelance writer, my credentials include work in *The Cavalier Courier, Building Business,* and *The Financial Wizard.*" You don't need to indicate whether "include" means "that's it" or "there could be more." Don't ask, don't tell. I may not have heard of the publications, so how do I know how small (or big) they are? I might skim the list and see that you've been published in *The Cavalier Courier, Building Business,* and *The Financial Wizard.* What I *don't* see is that *The Cavalier Courier* was your college newspaper, *Building Business* is your women's networking group e-newsletter, and *The Financial Wizard* is an e-zine with a circulation about the size of a soccer team. Who cares? Send me the best tear sheet of the three and pitch a good query. Then follow through with a great story—by deadline or sooner—and we're both happy.

If you don't have any clips but do have other types of writing experience (editing, copy writing, copyediting, tech writing, etc.), go ahead and mention it. I have a friend who worked as a copy editor at the city's largest daily newspaper for more than a decade. Even if she had no published (writing) pieces to her name, do you think I'd give her a shot? Of course! She knows what good writing sounds like and how to create a concise piece of writing. Best of all, she knows correct grammar.

X. THOU SHALT HAVE FUN

Like it or not, you're going to be writing a lot of queries over the course of your career as a freelancer. So why not find ways to have fun with them? We've talked about all the ways you can appease an editor, but what about yourself?

I once asked my parents a question from the game, Would You Rather … ? The question was: "For the same pay, would you rather work twenty hours a week at a job you hate, or sixty at a job you love?" Without hesitating, and in unison, they responded, "Sixty hours."

At first, I was shocked. Who wouldn't love to work less—even if it means you're miserable? Twenty hours a week is less than three days' work. But the more I thought about it, I realized that I would *never* give up what I do to go back to a nine-to-five job. Even on the weeks when I work sixty hours to meet pressing deadlines, I'm happy and having fun. Don't you deserve the same? I mean, you didn't get into freelance writing for the money, right? (This is an old joke. The truth is, you can actually make very good money as a writer. Plus, you can work in your pajamas and catch up on reality TV between assignments.)

If you don't find ways to make writing queries fun, one or more of the following will happen:

- It will become such drudgery that you'll stop doing it
- It will take forever just to get one completed
- Editors will be able to tell you're not really into your article

Don't believe me? Just feel the difference in these two opening hooks:

Dear Mr. Corey,

On a recent trip to Las Vegas, I had the pleasure of meeting the cast of *Ocean's Thirteen*. Because my brother-in-law was the assistant director for the movie, I was also invited to dine with them. Needless to say, it was incredibly exciting and the conversations during the meal provided me with good fodder for my article, "Dining With the Cast of *Ocean's Thirteen*."...

The only thing this person has going for him is good grammar. Granted, he's just eaten dinner with some of Hollywood's biggest leading stars, but that alone might not be enough to save this piece. If his article is as bland and stoic as his query, even Fabio's fan club will be bored by the likes of Brad Pitt, George Clooney, and Matt Damon. Unsexy.

Now try this on for size:

Dear Mr. Corey,

I have to wash my brother-in-law's car for a year, but it's worth it. As the assistant director on *Ocean's Thirteen*, he allowed me to tag along to a four-hour dinner with three of the hottest studs (um, that's according to my wife) in Tinseltown: Brad Pitt, George Clooney, and Matt Damon. The three were forewarned that I was a freelance writer and they didn't disappoint. From kissing Julia Roberts and visiting Cambodia to attempts to launch Matt as *People*'s "Sexiest Man of the Year," I've got dirt to dish and the photos to prove it. At just over 2,000 words, "A Dud Among Studs" is a humorous piece about a night that was nothing less than hysterical—and humbling—with the three Hollywood hotties. (I did mention I'm married, right?)

Can you feel the difference? The second query's opening was probably as much fun to write as the article itself. The writer is enticing the editor with not only the topic, but also the voice he'll use to write it: a fun, funny, self-deprecating style that's hard to find, and therefore, hard to pass up.

Of course, you don't have to dine with the Hollywood elite to write a fun and enticing query. The trick is to find the stories that fascinate or entertain you—and then make that interest contagious in your query.

With these basics under your belt, hopefully you've got a solid understanding of the query process. But now we're going to get even more specific. And while the next chapter on article queries may send some of you aspiring authors jumping ahead to the chapters on book queries, take note: There's a lot of money to be made on shorter pieces. In fact, some writers make as much money from one or two feature articles as they do on a book advance. Indeed, writing is the great equalizer: It's not the size of the manuscript but how—and to whom—you sell it. Besides, you need something to pay your rent while you work on that Great American Novel. Remember, Rome wasn't built in a day (but that forklift sure would've helped!).

CHAPTER 2

ARTICLE QUERIES

Query letters can be intimidating. Sure, you could picture the editor in his underwear (heck, it got you through that speech in 1996!), but it might be just as easy to overcome your fear by reminding yourself that queries are nothing more than fancied-up letters. Letters aren't scary, right?

COMPONENTS OF A QUERY

Remember when you were in elementary school and you had to learn the basic components of letter writing? There was a salutation ("Dear Santa"), the introductory paragraph ("Thank you for the Easy-Bake Oven"), the body ("Mom says she's gained fifteen pounds from sampling all my cupcakes"), and the complimentary close ("Sincerely yours")?

A query letter is like the grown-up version with a twist. You'll still have the salutation and complimentary close, but between those two bookends are the four meaty parts:

1. The opening hook (one paragraph)
2. The supporting details (two or three paragraphs)
3. Your qualifications (one paragraph)
4. The thank-you (one paragraph)

The Opening Hook

The opening hook can be taken right from your article's first paragraph ("citing the lead") or can be a completely new grabber. It should include something fascinating, intriguing, controversial, funny, or outright bizarre that immediately makes the editor want to request or assign your article.

Example: Cathy Cacowski thinks worms taste delicious, and she's not alone. In fact, when the Denver chef took them off her menu at her restaurant, Gourmet Grubs, customers complained. *A lot.*

The Supporting Details

The supporting details will provide information about some of the "five Ws"—who you'll interview (the chef and some customers), where you'll go (watching a worm stew being made), what people order (worm chowder, anyone?), or tidbits to let the editor see why it's such an interesting story. You can include bullet points of things you'll cover, offer to send photos (or a menu), suggest a word count, offer a match to a certain section of the magazine, or even offer a timely tie-in, such as a January deadline in order to coincide with the publication's June edition on "New Trends in Dining."

Your Qualifications

Your qualifications paragraph doesn't necessarily need to be a long list of published pieces. It simply needs to explain why you're the perfect person to write the piece. ("I'm a gourmet cook myself," or "I live right down the road from Gourmet Grubs," or "I've already been granted a backstage pass to the kitchen.")

The Thank-You

Your thank-you paragraph should thank the editor for her time and let her know you are enclosing an SASE.

IDENTIFYING YOUR MARKET

Now that you know what, when, how, and why to query, let's talk about *whom* to query. There are five major considerations when looking for a magazine to query:

1. Does it serve my article's audience?
2. Does it represent my article's market?
3. Does it run my type of article?

4. Does it accept freelance material?

5. Does it pay? (If you happen to be one of those independently wealthy writers who say, "Writing is about the craft, not money," you can have your editor make the check out to me.)

First, the **audience**. If you're writing an article about, say, understanding reverse mortgages for yourself or your aging parents, your audience will likely include senior citizens or baby boomers. Who are you missing? What about people who are somehow tied to that industry? If you used to work in the mortgage industry and are pitching a complicated, technical article about reverse mortgages, you may be able to target mortgage brokers, bank loan officers, real estate agents, and financial advisors.

How does this translate to finding your **market**? For a more basic article, the obvious focus should be on *general consumer magazines* read by baby boomers and seniors. And there are also unique demographic or niche magazines (with titles like *Senior Living* and *Senior Times*). But for the more technical version of your article query, you'll want to aim for *trade magazines* read by professionals in the industry. Again, these readers are mortgage brokers, bank loan officers, real estate agents, and financial advisors.

A third target will be *specialty magazines* read by senior citizens and baby boomers. These might include RV magazines (because a great majority of RV owners are retired), membership magazines (think *AARP The Magazine* or that quarterly magazine your health insurance company mails you), and in-flight magazines for travelers.

And of course, don't rule out online publications, local and regional magazines, and even the senior, real estate, or financial section of newspapers.

One easy way to get a quick list of markets is to break out *Writer's Market*, the research bible for freelancers. Skim the table of contents for a list of publication categories (fitness, trade, parenting, etc.). Here's an example of how to use it:

I wrote an article called "Getting Your Kids to EAT YOUR VEGGIES!" and after skimming the *Writer's Market* table of contents, I sold it to magazines in all the following categories:

- Health
- Parenting
- New Age
- Vegetarian
- Women's
- Fitness
- Gardening
- Food

One tip: Don't make the mistake of assuming that any financial article can only go to a financial magazine. The competition is incredibly stiff and there are plenty of writers pitching who have more experience than you. Look for the diamond that's just waiting to be mined, the publication that other financial writers never thought to pitch (like the RV magazines), and you'll greatly increase your chances of seeing your name in print.

Next on your list of criteria: Does it run my **type of article**? For this, you'll need to look at the publication's writer's guidelines. You can start your search in *Writer's Market* or online at www.writersmarket.com. If your publication isn't listed, search its Web site. Many list writer's guidelines (or "contributor's guidelines"). Still don't see them? E-mail the editor to request them. If the editor doesn't respond, try calling to request them from the receptionist. If the publication doesn't offer them, ask if they **accept freelance material**. If they do, but don't have guidelines, review a back issue (or two) to study the publication's tone, voice, and style. You can also get an estimate of word count for features or particular sections.

Note that some publications do not use freelancers at all. Don't waste your time on trying to convince them otherwise. There are plenty of fish in the sea.

And finally, does the publication **pay**? In general, the larger a publication's circulation, the more money it pays. The exception is often found in your favor: A few smaller publications will pay because they have good funding. It's rare to find a very large magazine that doesn't pay its freelancers.

There are a few other—in my opinion, less important—reasons to consider which publications to pursue. They include:

Circulation. Is the magazine a local rag printed out of the publisher's basement? Chances are that even if five hundred copies are printed, not all are picked up and read. But if you're OK with smaller circulations just to get your name in print, go for it.

There are, of course, some small-press publications that are very popular. I once edited a small magazine (literally run out of the publisher's basement) that focused on all the fringe elements of society: extraterrestrials, government conspiracies, making clothing from hemp, how to legally avoid taxes, etc. The magazine had an opt-in list, probably made up of mostly expatriates. I don't know what the circulation was, but because it was a very targeted market and people asked to receive the magazine, I knew it was being read. (Probably by the government.)

If the magazine is published online. This is a tricky one. The good news is, more and more magazines that publish an online version are paying extra money for electronic rights. The bad news is, because more people will have access to viewing your piece, you'll have a much harder time reselling it. Not every magazine that runs an online version runs ALL the print stories on the Web. This means that your story might get into *The New York Times*, but not www.nytimes.com. (Read details about electronic rights later in this chapter.)

Prestige. You've got a triangle of people to impress with your publications: yourself, your friends, and your editor. I stopped trying to impress the first two years ago. Getting into a well-known publication is no doubt an ego boost and a conversation piece, but if you plan to do this for a living, you'll need to value this nugget for what it is: a medal on your uniform. Just having a medal doesn't automatically make you a general; you've still got to sell yourself to the committee. Editors do like to see national publications on your list of credentials because it's a sign that someone with experience liked your writing. So go ahead and pitch to the big names. Just remember that five or six published pieces in small magazines can carry as much weight as only being published once in the *New Yorker*. (Besides, most people don't "get" half the stuff published in the *New Yorker*.)

DECODING WRITER'S GUIDELINES

Writer's guidelines can be intimidating, but think of it this way: They are there for two reasons, both of which are to help you. They'll either increase your chances of getting published ... or save you from wasting your time.

While writer's guidelines can vary greatly, most contain the same basic components. The following are the most common you'll encounter. We'll use this sample listing from *Writer's Market* to illustrate the points. (I took this from the 2003 edition so I could justify keeping it when my husband was cleaning out the attic.)

$$ THE NATION, 33 Irving Place, 8th Floor, New York, NY 10003. (212) 209-5400. Fax: (212) 982-9000. E-mail: submissions@thenation.com. Web site: www.thenation.com. **Contact:** Peggy Suttle, assistant to the editor. **75% freelance written.** Works with a small number of new/unpublished writers each year. Weekly magazine "firmly committed to reporting on the issues of labor, national politics, business, consumer affairs, environmental politics, civil liberties, foreign affairs, and the role and future of the Democratic Party." Estab. 1865. Pays on other. Buys first rights. Accepts queries by mail, e-mail, fax. Sample copy for free. Writer's guidelines for 6 × 9 SASE.

Nonfiction: "We welcome all articles dealing with the social scene, from an independent perspective." Queries encouraged. Buys 100 mss/year. Pays $225 300. Sometimes pays expenses of writers on assignment.

Columns/Departments: Editorial, 500-700 words. **Pays $100.**

Poetry: *The Nation* publishes poetry of outstanding aesthetic quality. Send poems with SASE. Grace Shulman, poetry editor. **Payment negotiable.**

**The online magazine carries original content not found in the print edition and includes writer's guidelines. Contact: Katrina Vanden Heuvel, editor.

Tips: "We are a journal of left/liberal political opinion covering national and international affairs. We are looking for both reporting and for fresh analysis. On the domestic front, we are particularly interested in civil liberties; civil rights; labor, economics, environmental and feminist issues; and the role and future of the Democratic Party. Because we have readers all over the country, it's important that stories with a local focus have real national significance. In our foreign affairs coverage we prefer pieces on international political, economic, and social developments. As the magazine which published Ralph Nader's first piece (and there is a long list of *Nation* "firsts"), we are seeking new writers."

Whom to Contact

Some guidelines list a publisher or editor at the very beginning, only to later give you another person's name as the contact. Follow that instruction. You'll notice in the above piece that there are actually three contacts listed: one to whom you should send articles and essays for the print magazine, one to whom you should send poetry, and one for submissions to the online publication. Don't assume that the editor at a print magazine is also the editor of the online version. In larger publications especially, there are often two separate staffs. When in doubt as to whom you should send your query, choose a name in the *middle* of the masthead, such as an assistant editor. The editor-in-chief at a large publication rarely reviews submissions, nor do contributing editors.

How to Contact

Lucky you! *The Nation* accepts queries by mail, e-mail, and fax. Go for one of the latter two and save yourself the postage, envelope, and trip to the post office. It's rare to see publications that accept queries by fax now that e-mail exists. Unless the guidelines specifically indicate that it's OK to do so, don't fax a query or submission.

Remember, "how to contact" also includes whether the editor wants to see a query. Some will indicate, "Send complete manuscript." If they don't, send a query.

Web Site

The listing of a Web site tells you several things. There may be writer's guidelines available on the site; you may be able to view past editions—or at least parts of articles—to get a sense of the publication's style and voice; and it may offer an online edition. The latter could come into play if you're hoping to reprint your article with other publications that don't accept material that has previously appeared on the Web.

Preferred Word Count

Different sections of a publication typically require different word counts. (In this case, editorials range from 500 to 700 words.) Even features can vary greatly, ranging from 1,200 in one publication to 6,000 in another. As a general rule, investigative pieces will require more words to allow a writer to present in-depth reporting. A feature in a small parenting publication, on the other hand, might max out at 1,200 because (A) the magazine is smaller (in terms of page count); and (B) editors know that busy parents often don't have time to read several pages of an article.

Types of Material Accepted

Unless you read *The Nation* on a regular basis, you might be surprised to see that it accepts poetry. What might surprise you more is what magazines *don't* accept. *Woodshop News*, for example, doesn't want general interest profiles of "folksy" woodworkers or broad, general-interest themes about woodworking. Would you know that *Notre Dame Magazine* doesn't want nostalgia pieces or anything on sports if you hadn't read the guidelines? Or that *Photo Life* is "currently overflowing with travel articles"? If you did, good for you. Take one step forward ... past your competition.

Percent of Freelance Material Accepted

Obviously, you want this number to be high. The more freelance material a magazine accepts, the greater your chances of getting in. You can compete with other freelancers; you *can't* compete with staff writers.

Publication Frequency

This might not seem important, but indicating in your query that "this is for your February edition" (instead of, say, "your January/February edition") is a sure sign to an editor that you aren't familiar with the publication or haven't read the writer's guidelines. Long gone are the days of only month-ly magazines. Some magazines come out weekly, bimonthly, quarterly, or even annually. (I was the editor of an annual magazine and received un-timely queries, mostly from public relations people, right after we went to print. I'd say, "Sorry, we're an annual. Try us again next year—a lot earlier,"

---

knowing they had obviously never seen our publication.) Another example of an annual is *The Old Farmer's Almanac*.

Circulation

Although the example above doesn't list circulation, you can almost always find this number on the publication's Web site. That's because even if it's not listed in the writer's guidelines, it will be listed to show potential advertisers how many readers they'll reach. Look under any of the following on a Web site: "Advertise with us," "Information for advertisers," "Media kit," or "About us."

In addition to hinting at the prestige or payment offered by a publication, the circulation will sometimes help you decipher if a publication is national or regional. Of course, large circulation numbers could also indicate a large local or regional readership, such as a citywide newspaper, and small circulation numbers could be due to a national magazine's narrow niche, as with *Onion World*. (Not to be confused with the *Onion*, which is obviously much, much funnier.)

Founding Date

Because the *Nation* was founded in 1865, you know (A) it's probably pretty reputable; and (B) it's not going anywhere. That's not to say that long-established magazines can't go under (*House and Garden* folded in 2007 after more than a century), or that new publications won't be around for centuries. But I've learned the hard way that writing for a brand-new publication often means (A) they don't have much (or any) money to pay writers; and (B) there's a chance that any money I *am* promised won't make it to me before the publication folds. I've had checks bounce, publishers skip town, and worse—articles published on a Web site with no payment and no one to contact to request it be taken down. (You can contact the Web master or host site and threaten legal action, but sometimes it's more of a hassle.)

Let me be clear: I'm not advising you to avoid writing for start-ups; I'm just trying to share with you that an older founding date typically indicates stability—and less risk to you.

Pay Rates

Oooh, the good stuff. You'll notice the dollar signs before the *Nation's* listing. These are symbols that *Writer's Market* uses to indicate, at a glance, what publications pay, with one dollar sign being the lowest and four being the highest. If you look at the "Columns/Departments" section, you'll see that an editorial of 500 to 700 words pays one hundred dollars. That's fourteen to twenty cents a word. Not enough for my taste, but for brand-new writers, it's not bad, and being published in such a prestigious publication might make it worth the low pay.

Payment Terms

There are two types of payment terms: *pays on acceptance* and *pays on publication*. Although you don't typically have the option to negotiate, pays on acceptance is always better. First, you get your money sooner. Second, things can change between the time your piece is accepted and the time it's published. Magazines go under, editors quit or get fired (and the new editor may not like your essay on "How I Ran the Boston Marathon in Slippers" as much as his predecessor), and editorial lineups get changed—especially if something newsworthy happens that just *has* to get covered instead of your piece.

There's not much you can do, although I've heard of more experienced writers offering a discount for publications changing their pay-on-publication terms to pay on acceptance. Personally, I'd wait it out. (But be aware that a publication could buy all rights to your piece and never run it. So it had better pay you well, because not seeing it in print and not being able to sell it elsewhere can be hard to swallow.)

Number of Manuscripts Purchased Each Year

Although it's good to know the percent of freelance material used, the number of manuscripts purchased each year tells you specifics. How else would you know if "10 percent freelance" means that the magazine buys ten articles a year or one hundred? (I suppose you could count the number of pieces in a magazine and then do the math, but that would be time-consuming and incredibly annoying.)

Information on Photo Submissions

This information could cover one line or one page. A few of the things covered might include:

- Whether to submit the actual photos or to just indicate on your query that they are available
- Rights purchased (more on rights later in this chapter)
- Payment rates for photos (or "payment to be negotiated" or "no payment for photos that accompany manuscripts")
- How to submit (by e-mail, by mail)
- Format (dpi, black and white vs. color, size, prints vs. 35mm transparencies, TIF vs. JPG)
- Other expectations (if model releases, captions, or identification of subjects are required)

If the Magazine Has Online Versions

The Nation, like many other publications, has an online edition of the magazine that carries original content not found in the print edition. That tells you that (A) you could query just the online version; and (B) any article you submit to the print magazine could be picked up to run online. The latter of the two will need you to consider if you're willing to sell electronic rights.

Rights Purchased

This will become a crucial piece of the freelancing puzzle as you learn more about what rights a publication wants to buy, what you *want* to offer, and what you *can* offer. (Hint: You can't offer first North American rights if you've already sold the piece to another publication in North America.) Eventually, you'll be using this criterion to rule out magazines before you query.

Columns/Departments

Ideally, you will have reviewed a publication before you submit a query, noting in which columns or departments your piece fits. But just because a certain department appeals to you doesn't mean it's open to freelancers. In the writer's guidelines for *Bridal Guide*, for example, it clearly states, "The only columns written by freelancers cover finance and wedding-planning

---

issues." And to think that you were going to waste your time pitching a fashion feature on choosing your veil.

Notes From the Editor

Many of the entries in *Writer's Market* include specific notes from the editor that can help you tailor your query or article, or rule out a publication even before you pick up a copy of the magazine. Here are a few general tips from magazine guidelines:

- From *Sport Fishing*: "salt water only"
- From *Western New York Family* Magazine: "We ... need more material on preteen and young teen (13-15) issues."
- From *DAC News*, Official Publication of the Detroit Athletic Club: "We also welcome articles on Detroit history, Michigan history, or automotive history."
- From *Toastmaster*: "Avoid sexist or nationalist language and 'Americanisms' such as football examples, etc."
- From *Cineaste*: "We dislike academic jargon, obtuse Marxist terminology, film buff trivia, trendy 'buzz' phrases, and showbiz references."

Sometimes, tips are more specific, offering fabulous details about what *not* to send, what section of the magazine is most welcoming to freelancers, and what topics are sorely underrepresented. Tips for breaking into a publication should be heeded to greatly increase your chances of seeing your byline in an upcoming edition. Just look at these juicy bits of advice:

- "*Grit* is looking for articles about how ... baby boomers are planning for retirement and how children are coping with aging parents."
- "[*Complete Woman*] ... reports a need for more relationship stories."
- *FellowScript*: "Please do not swamp us with inspirational articles (e.g., "How I Sold My First Story") as we receive too many of these already."
- *American Forests*: "We're looking for more good urban forestry stories, and stories that show cooperation among disparate elements to

protect/restore an ecosystem. We do not accept fiction or poetry at this time."

- *The Saturday Evening Post*: "Areas most open to freelancers are Health, Fitness, Research Breakthroughs, Nutrition, Post Scripts, and Travel."

General Information About the Magazine

These quick summaries are essential in shedding light on what a magazine is all about—before you even head to the newsstand (or library) to pick up a copy. Here are a few examples that offer great insight into lesser-known publications:

- *MetroKids Magazine:* "Monthly tabloid providing information for parents and kids in Philadelphia, South Jersey, and surrounding counties." (Would you have known it was a regional publication from the title? Would you know what region?)
- *School Mates:* "Quarterly magazine of chess for the beginning (some intermediate) player." (I would have thought it was a magazine about school.)
- *Genre*: "America's best-selling gay men's lifestyle magazine." (Definitely didn't see *that* one coming, did you?)

If Byline/Bio Is Given

Have a book to promote? A blog that needs traffic? An e-book for sale? Look for magazines that offer a bio—a sentence or two about the writer—or at least a byline (your name appearing with the piece) for better "proof" that a clip is yours. Bios come in several forms and can appear at the end of an article or at the front of the magazine on the contributors' page (often with your photo). I've had editors ask for one line, one paragraph, and even a page on my "advice for new writers and theories on writer's block." It's also common to read contributors' page bios that include some tie-in to their experience while writing the article, often with direct quotes from the writer. Here are four very different versions:

- **SIMPLE:** Wendy Burt-Thomas is a freelance writer in Colorado.

- **DETAILED:** Wendy Burt-Thomas's credentials include more than one thousand published pieces in such magazines as *Family Circle*, *The Writer*, and *Home Cooking*. She lives in Colorado Springs, Colorado, with her husband and two children.

- **ADVERTORIAL:** Wendy Burt-Thomas's books, *Oh, Solo Mia!* and *Work It, Girl!* can be purchased through www.burtcreations.com.

- **CONTRIBUTOR'S PAGE:** "I had no idea that pigs could be so much fun," says Wendy Burt-Thomas, who wrote our feature article, 'Hog Wild: A Family Trip to the Farm.' "My daughter loved it when they rolled around in the mud—and it made for some great photos." A frequent contributor, Wendy is looking forward to finishing her third book and writing a follow-up piece for us on chickens. She can be reached at WendyBurt@email.com.

Lead Time

This is the time needed to review manuscripts for a particular issue. In general, the larger the publication, the longer the lead time. *O, The Oprah Magazine*, for example, will likely be organizing its Christmas issue for 2009 in December of 2008. A small local monthly tabloid, on the other hand, might accept pieces up to a week before an issue goes to print.

If Simultaneous Submissions Are Accepted

A simultaneous submission is a query or manuscript sent to several editors, agents, or publishers at the same time. Some publications (and agencies) refuse to review these, as it can lead to complications down the road. (One example: You submit to two publications, and Magazine A wants to use the piece. Unfortunately, Magazine B [direct competition] just contacted you and said they, too, want to run it or have just run it.)

How to Receive a Sample Copy

In *The Nation*'s guidelines, it states that sample copies are free. This often requires you to pay for postage, though not always. In most cases, you'll have to at least submit an SASE. Other publications will list a set amount (such as four dollars) to include the magazine and/or shipping and handling.

Kill Fee

Despite its horrible-sounding name, a kill fee is a good thing. Typically accounting for 25 to 50 percent of the original fee you were promised, a kill fee is monetary compensation for a completed article that was scheduled to run but was subsequently cancelled. I once wrote a piece for a company that folded before it really got started. My editor called to share the bad news and asked me where to send my $250 kill fee. (At the time, that was more than I made for most articles that were actually published. I feigned indifference but I think he heard me dancing.)

Visits Per Month

Similar to circulation, this number refers to the number of online readers who visit the publication's Web site each month.

Special Issues

Publications often print special issues (usually designed to attract new advertisers and readers). Sometimes these are merely theme issues (such as dedicating the July issue to party planning). Other times, it's a completely separate edition—a supplement to the regular issues. *Country Sampler Decorating Ideas*, for example, used to run the following special issues: Decorate With Paint (February, July, and November); Kitchen & Bath Makeovers (May); Window & Wall Treatments (August). Likewise, *Jacksonville Magazine* delivers a supplemental publication twice a year called *Home*.

Response Time

This will let you know how long to hold your breath on a query. As with lead times, a general rule is that the larger a publication, the longer the response time (due the number of submissions it receives). If you haven't heard back on your query from a publication that says, "Responds in one month," go ahead and follow up at the beginning of the second month.

If Reprints Are Accepted

Reprints are exactly what they sound like: pieces that have been previously published. Some magazines don't use reprints. Some only use reprints that

---

have appeared in print, but not online. Some don't care. And *Reader's Digest* is known for about two-thirds of its articles being reprints. (In fact, the guidelines for *Reader's Digest* even state: "Send tear sheet or photocopy with rights for sale noted and information about when and where the material previously appeared.") Personally, I'm all about reprints. I've sold several parenting articles ten to twelve times because most small regional parenting publications don't care if you sell out of their region. It's a noncompetitive market for them. I may only get forty dollars a piece, but multiply that by ten and it adds up.

Famous People Who Have Contributed

You'll notice that *The Nation's* guidelines allude to "discovering" Ralph Nader's writing abilities. Name-dropping is perhaps more common in literary magazines that scare writers off by listing heavy hitters. (Luckily for me, I didn't recognize most of the names when I started, so I wasn't afraid to submit.)

If the Publication Pays for Writer's Expenses

Don't get too excited. They're not paying for your postage. In fact, the publication isn't paying for anything—especially your trip to Maui to write about that ocean-side resort—until the piece has been assigned and accepted.

OTHER MARKET RESOURCES

In addition to *Writer's Market* (and www.writersmarket.com) and actual writer's guidelines supplied by the publication, there are some great resources available. Here are a few of my favorites:

1. **WritersWeekly** (www.writersweekly.com): In addition to a great weekly newsletter for writers, Publisher Angela Hoy lists original, up-to-date writer's guidelines on the Web site each month. Other general market databases can be found on www.writerswrite.com, www.freelancewriting.com, www.writersdatabase.com, www.read ersread.com, and www.writefordollars.com.

2. **Worldwide Freelance Writer** (www.worldwidefreelance.com): This Web site offers two databases of writer's guidelines that include *international markets*. The free version offers more than five hundred mostly

lower-paying markets, and Markets Plus (access from $1.25/month) offers more than two thousand mostly higher-paying markets.

3. **Wooden Horse Publishing** (www.woodenhorsepub.com): One of the largest databases in the world, this site goes beyond writer's guidelines, offering two huge advantages: editorial calendars and news about brand-new magazines.

4. *The International Directory of Little Magazines & Small Presses*: For beginning writers, this directory is great for finding smaller markets with much less submission competition. Information on more than five thousand presses and journals from around the globe covers the same type of info as the *Writer's Market* guides.

5. *Writer's Market*—**by genre**: Did you know that in addition to *Writer's Market* there are genre-themed versions? If you specialize in a particular type of writing, it'll be worth investing in one of the guides to help you sell your fiction, poetry, or writing for children.

KNOWING WHAT EDITORS WANT

Since you don't want to hear that "trial and error" works best, I'll start by encouraging you to hear feedback right from the horses' mouths.

Bob Andelman, otherwise known as "Mr. Media," offers a wonderful line-up of interviews with magazine editors on his Web site, www.mrmedia.com. You can read the transcripts online or download the audiocasts to your MP3 player to listen while you're stuck in traffic, walking on your treadmill, cooking dinner, or otherwise avoiding writing. These aren't tiny e-zines, either. We're talking about interviews with editors from *Playboy, Cooking Light, Consumer Reports, Smithsonian* magazine, and *Reader's Digest*, just to name a few. Get your fill of some insider tips and then crank out a few great queries, mentioning to the editors that you heard their interviews.

Mediabistro.com has a regular featured called "How to Pitch" that gets inside major (paying) magazines and tells you how to break in. You have to become an AvantGuild member (fifty-nine dollars a year), but the membership has incredible benefits for freelancers.

Here's another idea for those who want a double whammy: Pitch a query to the editor of a magazine or e-zine for writers about interviewing a major magazine editor, like *Cosmopolitan* or *Men's Health*. (Just make sure the big-name editor agrees to be interviewed *before* you query.) If everyone agrees (and you do a good job—which is hard not to do with a basic Q&A format), you'll get a notch on your credentials belt and a prescreening of the editor's advice on how to break into her magazine.

In the meantime, here are some thoughts on what editors like.

Impress an Editor With ...

These are somewhat different than the Ten Commandments you read about earlier. In fact, you might find that some of these even contradict each other. That's because every publication is different and—I think this bears repeating—editors are people too. We have different opinions, histories, preferences, personalities, and procedures. Your job is to figure out what works best for each editor; not an easy task, but well worth the effort.

Humor—or at least personality

Nobody thinks the increase of euthanasia (or youth in Asia) is funny, but an article on this century's most influential comedians just begs a funny query letter.

Compliments

I'm not talking about praise to us personally (unless we wrote a piece you liked or gave a talk you enjoyed), but about the magazine in general. These shouldn't be fake or forced—or long; just a quick sentence about how you made a copy of the piece on "Manners at the Dinner Table" for your brother-in-law or that you were grateful for the in-depth reporting on how to negotiate with a used car salesman because it saved you two thousand dollars. Even if you don't become the editor's new favorite writer, you'll be her new favorite reader.

A specialty

Everybody can't be good at everything and writers are no exception. While some writers are good at writing about a wide range of topics (which can come in handy), editors like to see that, when it comes to assigning an article on an important piece, you're the perfect person for the job. Even if you don't have a lot of published clips, you can mention in your query that you "specialize" in health, fitness, parenting, etc. You may even want to mention that you're a member of a reputable organization that relates to your topic. (When pitching parenting articles, I often mention that I'm a writer-member of Parenting Publications of America.)

You could also state that you subscribe to media alerts on the latest developments in (insert topic of choice), or that you frequently attend conferences on the topic. Of course, only use these options if they're true.

Sympathy

If you've ever heard the horror stories about a day in the life of an editor, you know that many are overworked, underpaid, and under extreme duress at any given moment—including lunch, which is often (A) a Three Musketeers bar; (B) day-old doughnuts at the staff meeting; or (C) skipped. Editors don't like pandering, but they also appreciate when someone understands that it was difficult for them to have to cut your piece at the last minute. Or that you never received your check because it's still sitting on someone's desk. Or that you only received two contributor's copies because the warehouse flooded.

Experience

Sorry newbies, that's not what you want to hear, but experience makes editors' lives easier. And it's not always about clips. A query that cites your experience as a former assistant to an editor would be greatly welcomed if for no other reason than you know the industry. Someone who worked for an editor probably knows about deadlines, rewrites, and strong leads—not to mention all the terminology that might get thrown your way.

Pieces that affect change

While journalists, editors, and publishers like to win awards, the next best thing is changing the world through their work (or yours). If you can pitch an in-depth article on new research in preventing SIDS, or share a personal essay on your experience as a soldier in the Middle East, the editor will be sorely tempted to at least give you a shot—even if you don't have a lot of credentials. Give him a story that can change a life—or save one—or make people think twice. And make sure you reveal the power of your story in your query.

Patience

Guidelines are just that. If a publication states that it typically takes a month to respond to queries, don't call us on day thirty-two asking why you haven't heard yet. Ditto with articles that we are "hoping to run soon." Granted, that's a vague response, but the polite way to demonstrate patience is with a nice note, like:

Dear Ms. Swan,

I'm so pleased that you've chosen to accept my article on "Hand Knitting the Perfect Wool Sweater." Although I had estimated that the piece would appear in your fall crafters' guide, perhaps you've now slated it for the winter edition. When it's convenient, could you drop me a quick e-mail to let me know when it will run so I can pick up several copies for friends and family? Thank you in advance. I know you're very busy.

Patience can mean waiting for a response to your query, your manuscript, your publication date, your e-mail questions, your contributor's copies, your check, or even acknowledgement that an editor received your assignment. Now, when I turn in articles, I'll include an e-mail that says: "I realize you probably won't have time to read this immediately, but would you mind hitting reply and just confirming that you received it? I'd hate for you to think I missed my deadline because my e-mail got lost in cyberspace or your spam folder. Thank you!" Editors will appreciate that you're aware they don't always have time to review submissions—even assigned pieces—the second you turn them in.

A new voice

While some editors would like to be the next Hemingway, many are just as happy to be the one who discovers him. Imagine being the agent that got Stephen King's first novel published, when everyone else had turned it down. Jackpot! Sure, the money was great (I'll take 15 percent of what Stephen King makes), but the bragging rights are priceless.

Loyalty

Parenting vs. *Parents*. *Woman's Day* vs. *Family Circle*. *Men's Health* vs. *Men's Fitness*. They may not be archrivals, plotting each other's doom in secret underground meetings, but you can bet that no one wants to be "scooped" by the other. If you've gotten your foot in the door with *Men's Health*, good for you. Give them a first look at your exclusive interview with former President Clinton on his new, post-McDonald's workout. If they choose to pass, head to *Men's Fitness*.

When I worked at a local business newspaper, I was always amazed at the number of people to whom we gave free publicity (mentioning their company in an article they pitched to us), who then turned around and *paid* for ads in our competitor's newspaper. Granted, any publicity you get (or in your case, any clips you get) shows you're doing your job as a marketer for your company. But do you think we ever let them write for us again? Or that we went to them when we needed a source to quote in our lead story? Never. Yes, sometimes editors *do* hold a grudge.

Perfection

So now you know editors aren't perfect. But *you* should be. We know perfection when we see it, and we will love you for it. Dream writers are those who turn in assignments early. Who go above and beyond to get fabulously clear, up-close photos. Who do extra legwork to track down interesting facts about Nicole Richie's macaroni and cheese fetish or Karl Rove's stint as a male cheerleader in high school. (I made these up. These are not true. To my knowledge.)

Perfect writer's queries are concise, interesting, insightful, energetic, and tailored to the magazine. They are clear indications of how great your article will be, and they smell like roses, puppies, and homemade chocolate chip cookies, all rolled into one. Now is that too much to ask?

Depress an Editor With ...

Now, the stuff to avoid.

Not enough details

If you're hoping a vague query will either protect you from having your idea stolen or encourage the editor to choose a direction toward which you should aim, think again. For one, editors rarely "steal" ideas to assign to other writers. That's because your idea isn't that great, it was just covered in a recent edition, or they were already planning on covering it in an upcoming issue. Pitch a solid, narrowed query and even if you're off a bit, an editor who sees potential may give you the assignment with a slightly revised angle.

Say, for example, you send a query indicating that you've just returned from a family safari in Kenya with your husband and two young children (and seven hundred digital photos!) and would like to write about how the local children raise elephants as if they were family pets—washing and feeding them daily. An editor might not want that exact story, but she knows from your well-written query that you'll be a strong writer and wants to seize the opportunity of someone with an entire database of photos to choose from. She may write back to ask if you can work on a piece about how the Kenyan children related to American children, and vice versa, and if you have any photos of them together.

See? If you had just pitched a story about traveling to Kenya, she might not have known that you took your kids, that you interacted with local children, or that you had photos of the two together feeding an elephant bananas and Fritos.

Threats

No, I'm not talking about threats of bodily harm if an editor doesn't publish your piece. (Although who hasn't fantasized about getting into a no-holds-barred Ultimate Fighting Champion match with those editors who write snide comments in the margins of your manuscript? In my fantasy, they have their hands tied behind their backs to ensure a fair fight.) I'm referring to the timeline threat: "If I don't hear from you by June 1, I'll assume you're not interested and will submit it to your competition."

I can guarantee you that even if an editor *loves* your idea, he'll gladly pass it up just to avoid having to work with you. (And he'll secretly revel in the fact that his competition—and every other well-known magazine—will also turn you down.)

Submit your query (sans threat), wait the appropriate response time (as indicated in the writer's guidelines), and then follow up. If you still don't hear back, *then* send your query to another publication.

Bragging

This is a personal favorite of mine among new writers when referring to their manuscript or idea: "My mother loved it!" Guess what? Your mom loves everything. She also thought you were a cute baby—even when you were an hour old and looking like a cross between a plump raisin and one of those short-legged dogs with layers of wrinkles. "But my friends loved it too! They all said I should get it published." That's why they're called friends. Now give me a testimonial from your archenemy and we'll talk.

If your piece is good, don't say it—show it. Editors have way too much experience and confidence to be convinced that a crappy piece doesn't stink because your hairdresser said so.

Clichés

Unless you're querying for a piece on clichés, don't open with one. On second thought, even if you *are* querying about them, don't do it, because an editor may not even read far enough to realize that's what you're doing.

If you don't know what a cliché is, look it up. I'm not just talking about clichéd phrases like "It was a dark and stormy night," but also clichéd ideas. These include spin-offs of anything to do with *The Wizard of Oz* ("You're Not in Kansas Anymore! The Ten Most Devastating Tornadoes to Hit Missouri") or the phrase "on a budget" ("Cleaning on a Budget," "Decorating on a Budget," "Raising a Family on a Budget"), among others.

You'll also want to stay away from opening your query (or manuscript) with famous quotations, poems, and otherwise generally corny and formulaic snoozers like dictionary definitions (e.g., "scam (n.) a fraudulent scheme, especially for making money quickly").

Come up with an original title and opening paragraph and save the cheesy sentiments for your grandmother's birthday card.

"On spec" offers

If you've never heard this term, great. It means you won't use it in your query. Offering to write "on spec" (short for "on speculation"—meaning an editor agrees to review your completed manuscript with no promise to publish it) is a tip-off to an editor that you're new to the game. If an editor likes your query, she'll request the manuscript. If she likes the manuscript, she'll probably use it. You don't need to tell her how to do her job.

Hesitation

Let's say you see a job in the newspaper for a receptionist. You don't really have any job experience in such a position, but you type 60 words per minute, have a good phone voice, know how to file, and consider yourself a good multitasker. Would you apply for the job but blurt out in the interview, "I've never done this! I'm not even sure I'll be good at it, but I'm two months behind on my cable bill ..."

If you've got half a brain—(and a serious addiction to HBO)—you'll keep your mouth shut. And instead of hoping the interviewer will convince *you* that you'll be good for the job, you look for ways to convince *him* that you'll be good. I'm not talking about lying, but rather focusing on your strengths.

The same is true for a query. You can't show any hesitation that you're not ready for the assignment. None of this, "I've never written a feature-length piece, but my father thinks this could be a good article." (He gets that from your mother.)

Instill us with great confidence that you'll write a brilliant piece, even if you don't believe it yourself yet. Fake it till you make it. (I am breaking my own rule about clichés.)

Badgering

Take a hint, kid. Before you send *Veggie Life* your nineteenth query in as many days, realize that maybe the problem is on *your* end. Did you follow the writer's guidelines? Did you write a fabulous query? Have you had luck with lots of other publications but just can't seem to crack this nut? If you answered yes to all three questions (of course, the middle one is a matter of opinion), it may be time to move on. You can always keep a watchful

---

eye on the editor to see if she changes positions or leaves the magazine, giving you an opportunity to start from square one with a new editor.

Your other option is to write a short but genuine note pointing out that you enjoy *reading* the magazine, but have failed to pique her interest enough to also be *writing* for it. Ask if she can offer any solid tips on how to break in—such as a certain department, a less-covered topic ... or taking a basic grammar course.

Phone calls or drop-ins

Because most of the publications I edited were local or regional, I expected to get some calls because people felt I was approachable—and I was. The editors of national publications, however, don't have that kind of time, nor do they depend largely on ideas (from businesses or new freelance writers) to keep their publication afloat. In most cases, a phone call to an editor is a last resort after e-mail and snail mail—and only in the following circumstances:

- The editor has indicated that phone queries are okay
- You're calling to speak to the editor's assistant to confirm the editor's name, gender, title, etc.
- You're calling with specific questions once a story has been assigned— and only when e-mail has been attempted first

My ultimate pet peeve as an editor? Drop-ins. On any given day, especially close to deadline, I could have twenty hours of work to squeeze into an eight-hour day. Dropping by to "just run some ideas by me" or saying you were "in the area and thought you'd take me to lunch" is almost always out of the question. If you really want to impress me, respect my time— and my workspace.

Militant rule-following

First, let me say that it is possible to be *over-informed* when it comes to writing queries. By this I mean too "by the book." My good friend Christina Katz, author of *Writer Mama* (Yes, this is a plug for her book. When you get your own book deal you can plug your uncle's CPA business) and I have discussed this increasing phenomenon. We've seen it in the classes we teach:

new writers who read every single book on queries and work so hard to follow the rules that their queries end up feeling like cardboard.

As Christina explains it, "Sometimes new writers are so eager—even impatient—to succeed that they spend more time reading every single thing on the topic at the expense of applying what they've learned and integrating it into their process. They read every book on query writing then try so hard to follow every rule that their writing just lies flat on the page. It's like they are so worried about writing a proper query that they forget to write a readable one. I try to teach writers to apply what they learn a little bit at a time as they go along so they can integrate skills into their practice."

Cluelessness

While the Type A new writer is common, the worst thing you can say about his queries is that they're boring. The uninformed newbie, on the other hand, produces queries that are either maddening or outright hysterical. (See **Example 2.1** [pg. 61] for an extreme—though frighteningly near-true—example of a query that might get posted in the staff lounge.)

Asking "How should I get this piece to you?," not enclosing an SASE, or discussing payment in your query are signs that you're neither experienced nor willing to do the slightest bit of research to learn about the industry. Hopefully, if you're reading this book, being uninformed no longer applies to you. Just watch out for the *over-informed* trap.

Pitching too many ideas

In most cases, separate ideas require separate queries. A shopping list of topics can indicate that you're (A) not confident enough in one particular idea; or (B) too lazy to pitch them separately. Either way, an editor probably won't want to work with you.

This isn't to say that a solid idea has to be set in concrete. For your article on pregnant brides, you can offer to get quotes from a bride about how she feels about shopping for maternity gowns—focusing on the emotional side of things. You could also mention that you know a minister who frequently marries expectant couples—focusing on the moral/religious angle. If you're really creative, suggest an interview with a fertility expert who can talk about the number of women choosing to get pregnant without

---

being married—some of who end up finding Mr. Right before they give birth. Present a narrowed query, but leave a bit of wiggle room.

As for the laundry list of unrelated ideas, skip it altogether. One exception to this rule: if you're pitching a column. While a column should have a general theme to unify the articles or essays, it can be rather broad (parenting, pet care, marketing, living on a budget, etc.). In order to demonstrate the topics you plan to cover, you'll need to provide an outline of *specific* topics. (Trust me, writing to tell an editor you want to write "a marketing column" without listing what exactly that entails will get you nowhere.) See **Example 2.2** (pg. 63) for a good column query.

As with any list of dos and don'ts (except in relation to airport security), there's wiggle room. You may develop a relationship with an editor who *loves* to be pitched multiple ideas, appreciates that you keep reminding her about your article-in-waiting, or thinks that clichés are the best thing since sliced bread (insert groan). The important thing is that you understand the general rules and then adapt your style with each publication you approach. If you want to succeed as a writer, IQ is very important, but so is EQ (emotional quotient). EQ will allow you to interpret editors' preferences and respond in kind. Read between the lines and adapt. It's not selling out—it's survival … and success.

ARTICLE QUERY FAQS

Still have questions? You should. It's impossible to cover every aspect of writing in one book, let alone one chapter. (But don't blame us for trying!) Here are some frequently asked questions when it comes to article queries.

1. WHAT IS THE BEST WAY TO SUBMIT A PHOTO? WHAT ELSE DO I NEED TO INCLUDE?

Many writer's guidelines will state how the editor prefers to receive photo submissions. The guidelines might just ask that you simply indicate in your query that photos are available upon request, or they might go so far as to list a method for sending them (by e-mail as an attachment or via snail mail). If you can't find this information in the writer's guidelines, simply indicate that you can provide

EXAMPLE 2.1   BAD ARTICLE QUERY

Ⓐ

Dear Wendy, Ⓑ

Everyone tells me what an interesting life I've had Ⓒ and that I should write about it. Ⓓ
Luckily for them, I've been writing in my journal for over ten years and am looking for a
publisher who will make it a bestseller. Ⓔ

    I know you don't do books, but I think your readers will be fascinated to read an
excert. Ⓕ It's got sex, drugs, and lots of excitement. Just to give you a taste, one time
my uncle took me hunting and almost shot me by mistake. The near-death experience
has made me a better person, and a better writer. Ⓖ

    You can call me at home at 719-555-1234 Ⓗ to discuss the article Ⓘ and how long
you want it to be. I've got boxes full of journals so don't worry about asking for too many
words! Ⓙ If you're not sure exactly which part would be best, I can stop by with some of
my favorite journals to go over them with you. Ⓚ

    Thank you.

John Myran Campbell Ⓛ
Author Ⓜ
Ⓝ
P.S. Maybe you could make this an ongoing column! Ⓞ

WHAT'S WRONG: EDITOR'S COMMENTS

Ⓐ No date, no editor's name, title, magazine, or address. Ⓑ Do I know you? He refers
to me by my first name. Ⓒ They're being nice. People with really interesting lives don't
need reinforcement. Ⓓ Because they want you to stop talking. Ⓔ Good luck with this
one! Publishers don't run biographies of "regular" people and they certainly can't make
it a bestseller. Ⓕ I think he means "excerpt." Ⓖ Almost being shot is a near-death experience? I'd hate to see what kind of writer he was BEFORE! Ⓗ Thanks. Now I know what
number to block. Ⓘ He refers to excerpts as an "article"? Ⓙ I was going to suggest we
fill the entire magazine with nothing but this guy's life story, but now I realize we'll have
to dedicate an entire year of issues to it. Ⓚ You could stop by with boxes of journals OR
I could just save you the trouble and jump off the roof now. Ⓛ Don't serial killers always
have three names? Ⓜ Seriously? Ⓝ I love how he excludes his address and e-mail, and
doesn't include an SASE, so we have no way to reach him except by phone. So he'll never
get a response from us. Ⓞ Let me give you the name of a good therapist.

photos upon request—if the subject matter is obvious. A profile on author Julia Cameron will most likely include her photo (and perhaps some jacket covers of her books), while an article on preparing for a marathon leaves room for interpretation. In the latter case, you'll need to indicate if you'll be supplying photos of rain gear, running shoes, someone training for a marathon, or a crowd of people actually running a marathon.

You'll always need to include a photo caption (even if the editor chooses to rewrite it) and, in the case of a nonpublic photo of a person or people, you'll need to include a model release. (You can easily find one on the Web by doing a Google search.) If the photo is supplied (that is, taken by someone other than yourself), indicate if you need to print a photo credit and to whom the photo should be credited.

Photos can be submitted in many different formats: JPGs, TIFFs, slides, transparencies, and prints. Some magazines only use color or only black and white, so find out in advance what the publication's needs are.

For those not already familiar with the acronym dpi (dots per inch), it refers to the measurement density of resolution. Most publications will require that your photos be "high-resolution," that is, at least 300 dpi. A lower resolution will look fuzzy when printed—even if it looks good on your computer screen—so make sure your camera is set to take high-resolution pictures or that the person providing you with photos understands what you need. (Most Web-only publications will accept 72 dpi.)

2. SHOULD I INCLUDE CLIPS—EVEN IF THEY'RE ON TOPICS THAT MIGHT OFFEND THE EDITOR?

If your only clips are irrelevant to the topic you're pitching but do show your writing style, I'd say include them. If, however, you're pitching *Christianity Today* and your only published pieces were with *Playboy,* you'll need to find a way around that. Here are a few options:

• If the pieces you wrote for *Playboy* were clean (such as an in-depth feature on why divorce is still on the rise and a how-to piece on personal grooming) but you don't want the editor to know where they ran, include the articles as clips by printing them off (or e-mailing the Microsoft Word documents) from your own computer (as opposed to sending the tear sheets that have *Playboy* printed on

EXAMPLE 2.2   GOOD COLUMN QUERY

January 1, 2008

Mary Conner, Assistant Editor
Women's Business Magazine
1234 Main Street
New York, NY 12345

Dear Ms. Conner,

I just read an announcement on MrMedia.com about your soon-to-launch publication.

As a full-time freelance writer and marketing specialist, I feel that I could contribute a strong marketing column to assist your readers in promoting their businesses. My one-page column has been running in New Zealand's *Her Business Magazine* for three years now, and the editor reports that she receives numerous (positive) letters from her readers on its usefulness. I have retained all rights to offer the column outside New Zealand.

I'm attaching a PDF of the most recent column (as it ran in *Her Business Magazine*) for your review. The topic was networking. Other topics have included:

1. Ten marketing mistakes
2. The DOs and DON'Ts of customer feedback surveys
3. Cross promotion
4. Ten tips to run your business more effectively
5. Building loyalty
6. Catering to moms
7. Organizing your business
8. Stealing the spotlight (getting free publicity)
9. Choosing a group (networking vs. accountability vs. industry-specific)
10. Selling on the Internet
11. Choosing the right home-based business
12. How your addiction affects your business (smoking, workaholic, stress, complacency)

If you would like to review the pieces to see if they'd be a good fit for *Women's Business Magazine*, I could provide an entire year's worth immediately by e-mail.

Thank you for your consideration.

Best regards,

Wendy Burt-Thomas
(address, phone, e-mail)

Encl: SASE

the bottom of the pages). Then, just indicate in your query that you've included published clips—but don't indicate where they ran. (Heck, if you're good enough to get published in *Playboy*, you probably won't have a hard time demonstrating your skills!)

• Use a more general approach, ending your query with a paragraph about how you're "a full-time freelance writer whose work has appeared in local and national publications."

• Use a more general approach, citing the *types* of material you've had published with something like, "I'm a freelance writer whose published pieces range from short how-to pieces on personal grooming to in-depth reporting on the decline of marriage."

Remember the old adage: "When in doubt, leave it out."

3. WHAT ARE THE BEST MARKETS TO BREAK INTO?

That depends on a lot of factors, including who you are, what you write (essays, articles, tips, short stories), what you write about, what you read, and where you live. Assuming all things equal (i.e., no writing clips):

• **Who you are:** If you're an African American mother of three, for example, you'll have an advantage to query for a publication like *Black Woman and Child* magazine. Likewise, a former jewelry store owner is going to have a better shot than most at breaking into *Modern Jeweler*.

• **What you write:** Are you big into personal essays? Look for the national consumer magazines (*Woman's Day, Family Circle, The Sun*) that designate a specific page (or section) for personal essays. These are often sent in by "regular people" (nonfreelancers) but are paid. Short fillers like news briefs and tips are also a great way to crack a big market if you don't have writing credentials. Big magazines like *ePregnancy* and *Men's Health* often uses upwards of one hundred per issue, so there's always a market.

• **What you write about:** Obviously, there are a lot more markets for health writers than those who write about helicopter safety or teaching theatre. But that's not to say you'll have a hard time getting published if you're the latter. In fact, you may have an easier time breaking in because there's so much less competition and always a need for new ideas in niche markets.

- **What you read:** Who better to keep tabs on what stories have run—and what still needs to be covered—in a magazine than its die-hard fans? Subscribers or long-time readers of a publication should indicate so in their query. Editors like to hear from their readers, and readers who can fill the gaps on missed coverage by suggesting articles—especially if they can write them—are always welcome.

- **Where you live:** The good news about living in a huge metropolitan area is that there are always plenty of publications to query. The bad news is, there are often plenty of local wannabe writers doing the same. The reverse can be said about small towns: fewer publications to pitch, but fewer writers to compete with. Of course, the Internet allows, to a certain extent, for all writers to be equal in terms of proximity to a publication, but it's a lot harder to break into *Atlanta Parent* if you live in Denver because the editor will know you're not reading the publication regularly.

If you're just starting off, query a local or regional magazine and let them know you'll be including quotes from the locals, photos from the area, or local events. Those are big promises to live up to for your out-of-state competition.

4. HAVE YOU EVER HAD SUCCESS PITCHING MORE THAN ONE IDEA IN A QUERY?

I have, but it's not something I recommend for new writers. I have a multiarticle query that I frequently send to start-up parenting magazines that are on a limited budget. Because the articles have all been previously published, any money I receive for them is essentially gravy.

I mention that the articles are reprints and that they're available for a set amount of, say, thirty dollars each (plus a contributor's copy for my portfolio), and most of the publications I approach end up buying at least one, if not more.

You do have to be cautious with this approach, keeping careful track of where you submit (so you don't hit up two parenting publications in Dallas, for example) and that you're not infringing on any contract agreements. If you sell an article to *Miami Parent* with a contract clause that says "author will not resell the article to any other publications in the state of Florida for one year," you'll need to wait a full year from publication before approaching any Florida publications.

See **Example 2.3** (pg. 67) for this type of query.

5. HOW CAN I SELL AN ARTICLE MORE THAN ONCE?

Of all the things you'll learn about freelancing, this might be the trickiest.

When you create a piece (article, essay, poem, short story, etc.), you automatically hold all the rights to said piece. When you agree to allow a publisher use your work—in print, on the Web, or both—you are granting the publisher certain temporary or permanent rights. In general, the more rights you sell, the less potential you have to continue making money off your piece. Therefore, aim to keep as many rights as possible, whenever possible. Sometimes, you'll be able to negotiate with a publisher on what rights you're willing to sell. Other times, as with large-circulation consumer magazines or online publications, there's no room for haggling.

Here are the rights you'll encounter most when selling an article:

• **One-time rights:** A favorite among writers, one-time rights (aka *simultaneous rights*) allow you to license rights to more than one publication at a time (unless there is a specific clause indicating that you won't sell the piece to other publications in that city, region, or state for a set period of time). The term *one-time* means that the publication can only print it once—unless they specifically ask your permission to run it again in a future issue.

• **First serial rights:** Another good one. These rights allow a publication to be the first to use your piece. Once published, all rights revert back to you. You cannot sell first serial rights to more than one publication (only one can be the first to use it) unless there is a regional qualifier, such as "first *North American* serial rights." In that case, you could sell first rights to a magazine in North America and, say, Europe, at the same time (unless the publication in Europe asked for all rights, first *world* rights, or first *English-language* rights).

• **Second serial rights:** Also known as *reprint rights*, this is where you make your icing on the cake. Although most publications pay quite a bit less money to license reprint rights, you've probably already made money by selling first rights, making any income from reprint rights feel like "extra" income for virtually no work. (Sure, you had to query the publication, but you didn't have to write a new article or revise it.)

• **All rights:** Ugh. Selling all rights means you are signing away any rights to ever use the piece again. If you sold all rights to a poem, for example, you couldn't

EXAMPLE 2.3   GOOD MULTIARTICLE QUERY

January 1, 2008

Don Daniels
Kennedy Parents Magazine
123 Maine St.
Kennedy, MA 12345

Dear Mr. Daniels,

I'm not sure if you were at the national Parenting Publications of America conference in March, but I had a flyer listing the following reprints. Each is available for just thirty dollars:

1. "Getting Your Kids to EAT YOUR VEGGIES!" (485 words)

2. "My Kids Are Driving Me Crazy! Ten Tips for Staying Calm When Your Kids Aren't" (1,132 words)

3. "Music to Your Ears: Is Your Child Ready for Music Lessons?" (845 words)

4. "What's the Number for 911? The Essential Assume-Nothing List for Your Babysitter" (845 words)--Good for dotted-line cut-out for refrigerator

5. "It's Your Move, Kid! Helping Your Child Prepare for the Family Move" (638 words)

6. "The First Day of School: Helpful Hints and Money-Saving Tips" (560 words)

7. "Dealing with Dr. Phobia: When Your Child Is Afraid of the Doctor" (749 words)

8. "Raising Polite Children in Impolite Times" (975 words)

9. "The Season of Superwoman: Surviving a Kryptonite Christmas" (1,097 words)

10. "Growing Up Online: A Parent's Guide to Reinventing the Lost Art of Play" (1,000 words)

11. "Twenty-five Tips for a Safe Holiday Season" (short and long versions available)

12. "Birthday Brilliance" (869 words + sidebar)

CREDENTIALS

- More than 500 published pieces, including articles in *Family Circle*, *The New York Times*, *Woman's World*, *ePregnancy*, *Nashville Parent*, *Vermont Parent and Child*, *The Parent Planner*, *Complete Woman*, *Christian Parenting Today*, *Woman's Own*, *American Fitness*, and on the Nemours Foundation's KidsHealth.org

- Former editor, columnist, staff writer, and regular contributor (now full-time freelancer)

- Author of two women's nonfiction humor books for McGraw-Hill: *Oh, Solo Mia! The Hip Chick's Guide to Fun for One* and *Work It, Girl! 101 Tips for the Hip Working Chick*

I'd be happy to send any or all of the articles for your review. Thank you for your time.

Best regards,

Wendy Burt-Thomas
(address, phone, e-mail)

---

even use it in your own self-published book of poetry unless you asked for—and were granted—permission by the publisher.

Why would a writer ever sell all rights? Inexperience, desperation, money, or prestige. At least the latter two can help you. After all, it's hard to pass up the opportunity to have Time magazine on your résumé, and even harder to pass up three thousand dollars when your rent is due.

• **Electronic rights.** Sometimes referred to as *e-rights*, these cover a variety of electronic media, including online publications (like www.nytimes.com or www.salon.com), blogs, public and private Web sites, e-zines, and streaming media. A good contract will specify exactly what type(s) of electronic rights are being purchased. If a magazine editor doesn't seem to know what rights he's asking to license, take the reins and offer one-time print rights (or in the case of online publications, aim for a specified time frame, such as one year of archival, in order to have your article offline for good).

You'll find that many small publications don't even bother with contracts. That's because The Copyright Law of 1978 states that unless the publisher and author agree on licensing rights in writing, it's assumed that the publication is only purchasing one-time rights. Just be forewarned: I've received checks and contributors' copies in the mail with no previous indication that the publications had chosen to accept the articles I had sent them. While it's nice to receive unexpected checks, you don't want to have sold infringing rights to another publication in the meantime.

6. HOW DO I PROTECT MY IDEAS?

You can't. Ideas can't be copyrighted, only pieces of work. New writers often complain that they pitched an idea that was rejected only to later see it in the maga-

---

zine. Chances are, the publication was planning to run the article before the writer queried, and that's why the idea was rejected—not the other way around.

And while some publication may have "lifted" your idea to give to a more qualified writer, it's rare. Some do offer "idea fees" to writers, though again, that's rare.

As for publications stealing your actual writing, the odds are next to nothing. No reputable publisher wants to worry about an expensive lawsuit, not to mention the bad publicity that comes with such a fiasco. If you're really worried about it, feel free to register your work with the United States Copyright Office (www.copyright.gov). A basic online filing is only thirty-five dollars.

7. HOW MANY QUERIES CAN I SEND AT ONCE TO ONE PUBLICATION? TO MORE THAN ONE?

It's not recommended that you send a publication more than one query at a time. Wait to hear back from the editor regarding the first idea. If it's rejected, feel free to send her another query, taking into account why she rejected the first idea (if indicated in the editor's response). If the first idea is accepted, wait until your article is published before sending her another query.

There is no limit on the number of simultaneous submissions (or queries) you can send to multiple publications. Just be forewarned that if you get multiple acceptances, you'll have to be very cautious about what rights you can offer. If one magazine offers you one hundred dollars for first North American serial rights and you accept, what will you do if a second publication offers you five hundred dollars the very next day? While it's possible to withdraw your agreement with the first publication (if you haven't signed a contract yet), you'll most likely be burning a bridge with that editor. Remember, sometimes money isn't the only thing to consider. A long-term relationship with an editor can take your career a long way.

8. HOW DO I ESTIMATE WORD COUNT?

While I'd argue that with today's computer technology there's really no excuse for lacking an exact word count, there is a simple way to estimate your article's length. Assuming a one-inch margin, double spacing, and a 12-point font (like Times New Roman), multiply your pages by 250 words. A ten-page feature, then, would be 2,500 words.

9. CAN I SEND A QUERY FOR AN ARTICLE BEFORE I'VE LINED UP MY INTERVIEWS?

Yes, although you should be cautious about mentioning specific names if you haven't yet confirmed that the person is willing to speak with you. In your query you could mention that you'll be interviewing "a pediatrician, a single mom, and a teacher" (rather than specific names) to allow you to find replacements if your first picks don't come through.

If the person you're interviewing is famous or prominent, you should have permission to speak with him (or e-mail him questions) *before* you query. This will serve two purposes: It will protect you from having to scrap the story (and tick off your editor) if the interviewee declines the opportunity, and it will likely increase your chances of landing the assignment in the first place. After all, what editors would turn down the opportunity to scoop their competition with a celebrity interview for which you've already received the go-ahead from his publicist? Just be very clear in your query that the interview is already approved.

10. HOW DO I GET INTERVIEWS?

While getting an interview with a celebrity will likely require you to contact her publicist or agent, interviewing a noncelebrity will probably require little more than a nice e-mail or phone call. Most "regular" people are delighted to be a resource and see their name in print. Even better—they don't expect to be compensated for their quotes or information, although many will ask for at least one copy of the publication to show friends and family.

The key to contacting a noncelebrity for an interview is to keep your letter simple. You don't need to go into detail about the piece, the publication, or that you've never had anything published. What you might want to include is why you chose him, that you're still in the query stage (if you are), and that you're flexible in terms of how and when to interview him. Here's a short example:

Dear Mr. Philips,

I am a freelance writer working on a story about successful family-owned franchises that I will be pitching to numerous local and national magazines. A friend recently told me about your company making *Entrepreneur*'s Top 500 franchises and I would love to ask you a few questions about your business.

If you are open to the idea, I could send you five or six questions via e-mail, or we could set up twenty minutes or so for a phone interview.

Thank you for your consideration.

Sincerely,

Wendy Burt-Thomas
Phone/e-mail

Not everyone checks e-mail regularly, so be prepared to follow up with a phone call if a week passes with no response.

11. IS IT EVER OKAY TO JUST SEND A RESUME AND ASK FOR AN ASSIGNMENT?

I wouldn't even send a resume with a query. Most editors don't care about your education, work history, or accomplishments (unless you've won the Pulitzer)—only your writing credentials. A summary of your writing experience (if you have any) should be included near the end of your query. Sending just a resume and asking for an assignment is a sure sign that you're either (A) inexperienced; or (B) too lazy to query.

I hope you're feeling pretty good about submitting article queries because the next chapter is a natural progression for nonfiction writers. If you've ever thought about writing a nonfiction book, there are three bits of good news: (1) writing a nonfiction book is a lot like stringing together a bunch of articles; (2) you can sell a nonfiction book simply on the IDEA; and (3) you can make some great money. Stick with me, Kid. We'll make you glad you quit your job. (Minus the finger gestures to your boss on the way out.)

CHAPTER 3

NONFICTION BOOK QUERIES

If you've been toying with the idea of writing a nonfiction book, you'll be happy to know that unlike novels, nonfiction books can often be sold on not much more than an idea. Much like the article queries discussed in the previous chapter, the first step in selling a nonfiction book idea (usually) requires a query letter. If some cases, you'll be advised to just skip the query and submit an entire proposal, though that's not as common. For the purpose of making you the most informed writer on your block, this chapter will cover both.

QUERY VS. PROPOSAL

As with an article query, a book query is a one-page, single-spaced pitch. In this case, however, you're pitching to get an agent or editor to request your book *proposal*, not your entire book manuscript.

Your query will break down into a paragraph following a similar format to that of the magazine query discussed in the last chapter:

1. The opening hook (one paragraph)
2. The supporting details (two or three paragraphs)
3. Your qualifications (one paragraph)
4. The summary (one paragraph)
5. The thank-you and request to send the proposal (one paragraph)

The Opening Hook

This will be very similar to what you might write on a book flap to get readers to buy your book. It should set the tone for your book's voice and style using something fascinating, controversial, hilarious, or newsworthy.

Example: Just as I've been explaining to Christians in my congregation for more than thirty years, being gay is not a "choice." In fact, as of August 7, 2008, we have proof: Scientists have just discovered the "gay" gene. With proof that homosexuality is as genetic as skin color or hair texture, the anti-gay community has a lot of thinking (and apologizing) to do. As a minister, writer, and brother to an openly gay man, I've got some ideas on how to get started.

Fascinating? Check. Controversial? Oh yeah. Newsworthy? Definitely. (Hilarious? Not so much.)

The Supporting Details

Much like a magazine query, the supporting details paragraph (or two) of your book query will provide information on how you'll research and gather information for your book. It's the time to mention the generalities of your resources, such as who you'll interview (conservative Christian and Jewish clergy, gay and lesbian ministers, leaders in the gay community); what you'll discuss (how they feel about the news and what this means to the Christian and gay community); why the book will make an impact (will it change the way Christians view homosexuality?); and how it will be used (a book of opinions from both sides—and those in the middle—to foster conversation).

You don't need to go into specifics (like the number of people you'll interview or their names—unless it's Rev. Jesse Jackson!) but there should be little room for the agent or publisher to guess how you'll gather your information, what approach you'll take, or how the book would be categorized. (Is it a religious personal opinion piece? A political how-to book for church groups? A pro-gay biography with resources?)

Don't worry about things like marketing, detailed readership demographics, or competitive books. Save that for the proposal.

Your Qualifications

This is the time to impress, if you can, or fake it till you make it, if you can't. If you don't have a lot of published pieces, don't worry. Just focus on why you're the perfect person to write this book. In my case, *The Writer's Digest Guide to Query Letters* had my name all over it (figuratively) before it had my name on it literally. With more than a thousand published pieces (about a quarter of which required queries), years of experience being pitched article ideas as a magazine editor, and two previous books for McGraw-Hill (which required agent queries and book proposals), the acquisitions editor knew I was familiar with several types of queries (including bad ones). It didn't take much convincing on my part, making the process both ironic (no query for a book on queries?) and relatively easy.

Don't lie about your experience—focus on your sources. (Do you have access to a lot of ministers in a wide variety of denominations because you live in a metropolitan area? Are you networked with leaders in the gay community? Have you spoken on the topic at national conferences?) Feel free to include a bit more about your education or career, if it's relevant, or any awards you've received (if they're specific to writing or the topic you're pitching). Mentioning that you won the Edward R. Murrow Award for your exposé on the Vatican is impressive. Mentioning that your haiku won best place at the PTA meeting might be best kept a secret.

The Summary

The information in your final (or near-final paragraph) can vary greatly. It could include possible spin-off ideas (i.e., a book on pet-friendly restaurants and hotels in San Francisco could easily branch out into tour books in other cities); a few sentences about which groups of readers will enjoy—and buy—the book ("Pet owners are willing to spend gobs of money on their animals. Surely they'll shell out $12.95 for this!); or even how the book will fit perfectly with that particular publisher's new line ("Your new line of travel books has yet to include a piece for animal lovers.").

A good book query takes a sandwich approach: strong lead, filler details, and strong finish. You might lose the editor a bit in the middle filling, so be sure to end strong. Mention the name of your book again and the (large) readership that's waiting for it. ("I hope you'll agree that the ten million baby boomers are ready for *The Senior's Guide to Dating Etiquette.*")

Remember, the only job of your query is to get the editor to request a full proposal. You don't have to sell her the book with this letter—just leave her wanting to learn more. Then deliver.

The Thank-You and Request to Send the Proposal

This is the time to not only thank the agent or editor for her time, but also mention that you have a full proposal available upon request. Don't expect that you can whip up a great proposal if it's requested. Have a polished one ready to send so you can respond while the editor or agent is still enthusiastic about your query.

BOOK PROPOSALS

A book proposal is a much more detailed and therefore much lengthier (usually thirty to forty pages) pitch. It covers more ground than just a basic idea, including additional components to what you covered in your query, like:

- Your competition
- What you'll do to market the book
- One or two sample chapters

But again, most agents and publishers want you to start with the query letter, asking you for a proposal only if the query sparks their interest.

While it may seem redundant to require a three-step process (query, proposal, manuscript), the method actually expedites the process for you and the agent or publisher. That's because it's much faster for an agent or publisher to review thousands of one-page queries to choose the few that hold promise than it is to review thousands of thirty-page proposals.

Take note: Getting a bite on a query will send you to the front of the class (or at least the second row) when you *do* send your proposal. That's because the agent or editor will most likely remember your name and that he's requested the proposal—unlike the hundreds of unsolicited (not queried) proposals that he has yet to review—if he does at all. (Some agents and publishers are very strict about unsolicited proposals if their guidelines specifically state to send a query first. In the case of the big publishing houses, they generally only accept agent-pitched proposals.)

Key Components of a Nonfiction Book Proposal

Now that you've mastered the art of query writing, you'll need to perfect the craft of writing a genius book proposal. The good news is, you get more than one page. The bad news is, you need to kick butt for fifteen to thirty pages. The query was the sprint. The book proposal is the endurance challenge. (The book will be the marathon.)

There are five basic components to a nonfiction book proposal:

1. The synopsis (one to two pages)
2. The table of contents (one page)
3. Chapter summaries or sample chapters (ten to twenty pages)
4. The market analysis, including competition, platform/promotion, demographics (two to four pages)
5. Your qualifications (one page)

While there are sometimes additional components (e.g., supplements of published clips on the proposed topic, relevant news articles about you, copies of your self-published book), none of the original five should ever be omitted.

The synopsis

Think of the synopsis as you would the hook of your query. Although it's not exactly the same (a hook might be just a paragraph while a synopsis is typically a page or two), it serves much the same purpose. It's your (second) sales pitch to the acquisitions editor.

Unlike your hook, which will be more of an enticement than full summary of your book, the synopsis will detail your book's content, structure, tone, and design (if needed). You'll have a bit more room to talk about the unique elements of the book, examples you'll use, the solutions the book will provide, the reader takeaway, the voice and tone (serious, funny, helpful), and the timeliness or timelessness of the topic.

Your best bet is to start your synopsis strong *immediately*, then fill in the details later. Starting slowly and building momentum may cause the editor to toss your proposal into the rejection pile before he even reads the second paragraph. To understand a successful synopsis, imagine the news, sports, and entertainment story links you get on your homepage when you sign on to check e-mail or if you subscribe to any electronic newsfeeds. If you're like most of us, you'll skim the headlines and only click on the link to read more if something sounds intriguing—otherwise you'll just go about your day. Surf news sites on the Web and dissect these little article blurbs. What makes them enticing? What do they all have in common? Start your synopsis with a similar punchy grabber and use the rest of the paragraphs to support the opener.

Remember the advice from your article query: Open with a question, anecdote, interesting fact or fascinating comparison, e.g., "Dolly Parton and Pamela Anderson have more in common than their cup size. Both attended Harvard Medical School before pursuing careers in entertainment." (My sources tell me this is not true. They do not have the same cup size. The Harvard part is a bit questionable too.) Your synopsis is no place to drone on about how it took you ten years to get up the nerve to query.

Because your synopsis will only be one or two pages, you'll need to cover the important elements in order to show that your book has both readability—and salability. Mention its relevance to a hot topic or current movement. (Current trends are okay if they're not likely to be headed out before your book gets published.) Discuss its value to the reader. (This isn't necessarily the same as demographics, which we'll cover soon.) Use the writing in the synopsis itself to demonstrate—rather than tell—what your voice will be throughout the book. Will you be entertaining? Funny? Informative? Authoritative?

Although my synopsis for this book was mostly verbal, my discussion with the acquisitions editor at Writer's Digest was similar to what I would have put in a written version. We talked about the readership for this book (mostly beginning and intermediate writers), what it would cover (article, agent, and publisher queries), why it was needed (last Writer's Digest guide to queries was a decade ago), and what would make the book stand out among a shelf of other query how-to books (humor and plenty of examples of real queries that landed agents, articles, or book deals).

My synopsis probably would have focused on the fact that things have changed since Writer's Digest's last book on queries came out a decade ago. A lot more agencies and publishers accept e-mail queries, for example, which require special sections on electronic submissions. Self-publishing has become easier and cheaper than ever, making it necessary to at least touch on the issue. There are also many more online publications, requiring a book on article queries to examine electronic rights. And with the ever-changing writing-related books, Web sites, and e-zines, it's vital that Writer's Digest have a book with updated resources.

Not everyone is doing an updated version of a book that's already out there. Your selling point might be timeliness, a true niche, humor, entertainment, or controversy. Don't just know *what* you're pitching in your synopsis—but *why*.

The table of contents

While it's tempting to crank out a simple table of contents by listing mere chapter subjects, most editors would prefer to see a more detailed one. This might include one to two sentences per chapter, explaining what will be covered. In addition, the book proposal is the perfect place to let your creativity shine with more engaging chapter titles. Just look at the difference between these chapter titles and summaries for a book on horse care:

> Chapter Seven: "Caring for your horse's teeth"—dental care

> Or

> ✓ Chapter Seven: "Straight from the horse's mouth"—This chapter will cover the basics of horse dental care, including how to brush a horse's teeth, removing objects from between teeth, spotting a dental infection, identifying jaw and tooth pain, post dental-care issues, and removing baby tooth "caps."

Chapter summaries or sample chapters

If you're writing fiction, your book will be complete, making it easy to include sample chapters in your proposal—if required. There are varying opinions as to which chapters to include (first and second, first and last) but perhaps the best advice is to include a chapter that showcases your best writing. Of course, many agents or editors won't give you a choice, specifically asking for "the first fifty pages" or "the first chapter only."

If you're writing nonfiction, you'll need to include chapter summaries or, more likely, sample chapters. The bright side of this is that of all the components required for a book proposal, your chapter summaries (or sample chapters) will be the most useful to you later. They'll serve as an outline of sorts and will help keep you on course as you write the book.

It's important to note that sample chapters are not rough drafts. They are actual chapters that you'll be turning in as part of your manuscript. Take your time to make them stellar; they can make or break your shot at a book deal.

The market analysis

Your market analysis section will include four basic components: your competition, your existing or soon-to-be-created platform, your promotional plan, and demographics.

Most first-time writers expect to produce a few of these above components. However, over my years of teaching new writers, I've found that many are surprised—and somewhat depressed—at the prospect of having to produce a platform. (A platform is essentially your reputation and visibility as an author and/or expert.) The thought of having to do promotion of any kind often fills new writers with anxiety. (Some writers even find it beneath them, believing that marketing a book takes away from the craft to focus on the commercial. These people are generally poor. And unpublished.) In a profession in which solitude and privacy are relished and introversion is so prevalent, promotion can feel like a violation or bait-and-switch. "I've got to write a four-hundred-page book and then do *what*?"

Perhaps now more than ever, publishing houses expect authors to do most—if not all—of their own marketing and promotion. There's little room in the publicity budget for new authors, and those that do get funds or the help of an in-house publicist are usually getting it *after* prepublication buzz or early sales show huge potential.

Competition. Why would you want to list your competition? Because you want to show that there's a market for your work. Granted, you don't want to show that a book *exactly* like yours sold well (unless the book is old and you're doing a much-needed updated version). You want to convey that there is indeed a *readership* for your work, but your book takes a slightly different twist on what's already out there—and you're just the person to write it.

Your competition should include at least four or five books. If you can get sales numbers (good luck—these are hard to find!) or at least mention that the books hit a best-seller list or went into a second (or third) printing, all the better.

Be cautious about mentioning books that didn't sell well. Trying to persuade an editor that your book on the same topic will "do better because it's better written" is like saying that your lead boat will float better than your competition's lead boat because it's better built. If there's no readership, there's no book.

Platform. Your author platform is your immediate visibility. This includes things like speaking engagements (to writers' groups and conferences), newsletters, blogs, or workshops. If you don't already have these things, you'll need to begin building them immediately—preferably before you create your proposal—because these demonstrate your ability to target potential buyers.

There are a lot of great resources out there to review *before* you work on your book proposal's marketing plan, including:

- *Get Known Before the Book Deal* by Christina Katz
- *1001 Ways to Market Your Books* by John Kremer
- *Guerilla Marketing for Writers* by Jay Conrad Levinson, Rick Frishman, and Michael Larsen
- *The Complete Guide to Book Marketing* by David Cole
- *Publicize Your Book!* by Jacqueline Deval
- *The Savvy Author's Guide to Book Publicity* by Lissa Warren
- *The Frugal Book Promoter* by Carolyn Howard-Johnson
- *The Web-Savvy Writer: Book Promotion With a High-Tech Twist* by Patrice-Anne Rutledge

- Fiction Factor (www.fictionfactor.com): This Web site has a great piece by Lorna Tedder called "Your Book Promotion Countdown Checklist."
- Author & Book Promotions: (www.freewebs.com/authorpromotion): This Web site has a great collection of promotional resources, book reviewers, marketing tips, and articles on promotion.

Promotional plan. Your promotional plan is a list of things you intend to do to market your book. This could include radio and TV appearances, book signings, sending press releases to the media, attempts to get columns or articles on the subject published in newspapers, magazines, and Web sites, audio/Webcast interviews, teaching online classes, attending book expos, direct mail promotions, etc.

You'll need to be very specific, mentioning how many newspapers you'll contact, who you'll ask to write your book flap blurbs, how much money you'll invest in your promotion efforts, how many talks you'll give (and to whom), and any partnerships you'll try to build with other authors, businesses, colleges, and/or nonprofits.

The promotional plan should be written in third person: "Author will contact forty national radio shows that specialize in parenting-related topics" and should be realistic. Mentioning that you will contact your cousin who produces *Good Morning America* is believable. Stating that you'll *be* on the show is not.

For a great example of how to write a promotional plan, visit Michael Larsen's Web site at www.larsen-pomada.com.

Demographics. Your demographics represent your audience. You'll need to clearly define your group of target readers, including characteristics like gender, age, income, education, nationality, religion, and/or political views—if relevant. This is the time to be specific. Offer recent facts and figures and quote your sources. Saying "this book is for everyone!" is a sure sign of naiveté.

You'll also need to offer a theory on the motivations of your target market to buy the book. Saying "Five million American men over the age of fifty are divorced" is good, but saying that a recent AARP survey found that half of them would like to remarry would certainly lend itself to your book about finding the woman of your dreams late in life.

You can cite recent articles or studies pertaining to your readership, include information about other successful media targeted to your target group (such as magazines, TV channels, or radio shows), and/or point out new publishing subsidiaries (even if you're not pitching that particular publisher).

Qualifications

For new writers, this is often the most worrisome component of a book proposal. There's a fear that not having a lot of published pieces will automatically cause an editor to decline. But as with your initial query letter, you can focus on other qualifications that might lead an editor to believe you're the right person to write the book. These could include your expertise on the topic, your personal experience with the topic, your education (degrees in the field), your "following," public speaking, and media or industry contacts.

If you do have published pieces—especially if they're relevant to the topic—mention them. Pertinent clips (such as articles or columns on the subject) should be included with your proposal. These can be copies of tear sheets or articles printed from Web sites.

Remember: Publishing houses are in the business of selling books to make a profit. Use your proposal to help the publisher see why your book will sell, and you'll both make money.

CHOOSING A PUBLISHER

Chapter five covers the details of finding and working with an agent. In the meantime, here's some information for those of you confident enough to approach publishers on your own. Just remember, once you choose to approach publishers on your own, there's no going back. If you get a hundred rejections and then decide to ask an agent for help, chances are she won't be willing to represent you because you've already used up all her options!

Step one: Make a list of publishers that represent your subject area. In nonfiction, this could include anything from children's/juvenile to reference and humor, how-to to biography, and cookbooks. Start by picking up a copy of *Writer's Market* or *Jeff Herman's Guide to Book Publishers, Editors, & Literary Agents.* These are updated annually, so make sure you have a recent copy. Be sure to rule out any publishing houses that don't accept unagented submissions.

Another effective method for making a market list is to visit your local bookstores and browse the sections and shelves that contain the books most like yours. Look at the spine and the title page to see who published the books. When you get home, use one of the market guides mentioned above or search the Internet for writer's guidelines to determine if any of these houses accept unagented submissions.

Step two: Do some research and consider some important numbers that may help determine your chances of getting picked up by that publisher. These include percentage of books from first-time authors, number of queries and manuscripts that are submitted each year, and number of books that are published each year.

Step three: Rule out publishers that don't take simultaneous submissions, or be prepared to wait to hear back from each publisher before pursuing another.

Step four: Head to each publisher's Web site to review its submission guidelines. If no guidelines are posted on the Web site, contact the company to request them. You may also want to request a publisher's catalog (or browse the one on their Web site, if available) to be sure you're not duplicating an existing book.

Step five: Submit a professional query or proposal, tailored to each house and acquisitions editor.

Step six: Wait.

Catch a Book Editor's Eye With ...

The rules of the game are very similar to what magazine editors want: professionalism, experience, and a fresh approach. But there are specifics to pitching publishers that go beyond the magazine query, which should come as no surprise. You are, after all, trying to get a publishing house to shell out thousands of dollars; countless staff hours; and some publicity time, energy, and money, not to mention its reputation. It's a bigger gamble than the one a magazine editor takes on publishing your 600-word article on "How to Groom Your Dog." You don't need to be intimidated by the prospect, but you do need to understand that getting a book deal means far more than bragging rights at your class reunion.

Using close to the same Ten Commandments from the chapter on magazine queries, here are your goals:

Cross your Ts

We're back to the importance of looking like a professional—before you even need to *sound* like one. While a properly addressed and formatted query with an accompanying SASE doesn't get you a guaranteed request for a proposal, a query that's *not* professional on first glance won't even give you a running start. In the case of publishers, this will require you to review the writer's guidelines carefully for each house. Some have unique rules and conditions. Here are a few I've seen:

- "No registered, certified, return receipt submissions accepted!"
- "We will not open anything without a return address."
- "Query by e-mail preferred."
- "Query with synopsis and SASE."
- "Query with SASE or submit first page of manuscript."
- "Paragraph query only with author's vita and SASE."
- "Does not respond unless interested."
- "Query via Web site."
- "Request guidelines to receive Project Appraisal Form Questionnaire."
- "Query by e-mail only. No attachments."
- "No submissions between April and August."

See how fickle the industry can be? Guidelines are in place to make an editor's life easier and to immediately catch the nonprofessionals.

Open with a strong hook

Left hook, right hook—it doesn't matter. Hit the acquisitions editor right between the eyes with a lead he can't resist. If you've got a particularly "punchy" title, capitalize on it by using it early in the query.

If you've got part (or all) of the book written, use a trick an old friend once shared with me: Talk about the book in present tense. There's something about present tense that just makes the book seem that much more, well ... *finished.*

Another hint toward writing a good lead is to use as descriptive and specific a word as possible, whenever possible. I'm not advocating that you overwrite—hyperbole and purple prose are big turnoffs to editors—but examine each of your sentences to see if you've painted a clear picture in as few words as possible. Economy of language is the key here.

Here are two examples to allow you to compare these tips yourself.

Instead of:

A *Ghost in the White House* will recount numerous stories from those who have sworn they've seen the specter that has supposedly haunted the first families' house.

Try:

With more than thirty accounts from former staffers, housekeepers, and even a former first lady, A *Ghost in the White House* reveals the never-before-published stories of 'The Pink Lady' that haunts the mansion.

See how the energy of the sentence changes just by replacing *specter* with *The Pink Lady*? The latter shows you've done that little bit of extra research already and it creates a sharper, more compelling image in the reader's mind. And doesn't "more than thirty accounts" sound more journalistic and credible in comparison to "numerous stories"?

Even the slight rewording of "has supposedly haunted" to "that haunts the mansion" removes the speculation (which helps keep the book's energy) and keeps the prospect of an *existing* ghost in play.

No matter what style of hook you use, remember that your job is to present not only a book that will make the publisher money, but also one that the acquisitions editor herself will want to read.

Make sure your queries fit like a glove

If you haven't skimmed a list of publishers yet, you'll quickly learn to identify some of the genres they represent just by their names. Here's a fun little quiz to show you what I mean. Can you guess what type of books these publishing houses print?

A. Saint Mary's Press

B. New England Press, Inc.

C. Intel Press

D. Beaver Pond Publishing

E. Passport Press

F. The Mysterious Press

G. Westernlore Press

Answers:

A. Saint Mary's Press: Titles for Catholic youth and their parents, teachers, and youth ministers

B. New England Press, Inc.: High-quality trade books of regional northern New England interest

C. Intel Press: Reference, technical; subjects include computers/electronics, software

D. Beaver Pond Publishing: Subjects including nature/environment, photography (outdoor), sports, hunting, fishing

E. Passport Press: Practical travel guides on specific countries

F. The Mysterious Press: Crime, mystery, and suspense fiction

G. Westernlore Press: Scholarly and semischolary Western Americana

With literally hundreds of publishers in existence, learning to distinguish the genres they represent at a quick glance can be a useful time-saver. That doesn't mean you'll automatically weed out those that don't fit your topic. (How could you know that Michael Wise Productions only publishes how-to books for professional film and video makers?) You'll need to narrow the field, and then narrow it again, and again. Don't try to fit a square peg into a round hole. Trying to convince a mystery publisher to consider your how-to book on building an outdoor sauna is a waste of everyone's time; you could be using that energy to pitch a tailored query to ABC Publishing, which just launched a new line of do-it-yourself books.

To really impress ABC Publishing, you'll need to (A) make sure they haven't already covered the topic in another (recent) book; and (B) convince them you're the writer for the job.

Impress them by mentioning you read an article about their new line, that you studied their frontlist and backlist and didn't see anything about outdoor saunas, that you tried to find a book about the topic for yourself when you first started building your own sauna (but found nothing).

Make the pitching glove fit so tightly there's no room to argue a case *against* you writing the book.

See **Example 3.1** (pg. 88).

Show them why it's timely

As an editor, I'm often shocked at how fast newsworthy story ideas end up in my e-mail box. A famous sixteen-year-old entertainer announced she's pregnant? Within minutes I'll have four e-mails:

- "Story idea: Helping your preteens choose good role models"
- "Interview opportunity: Relationship author offers advice on how to talk to your kids about sex"
- "Reverend Jones available for the media to discuss the importance of abstinence"
- "Article for consideration: Taking the glamour out of teen pregnancy"

It might seem easier to be timely when you're pitching magazine articles, but the truth is, you're only pitching an *idea* for a book, not the book itself. What's to say you can't e-mail a query for a book idea within twenty-four hours of a major news story or fast-moving trend?

There are countless sources providing you with "news of the now" and at the risk of sounding gimmicky, you can capitalize on being in the know. With the Internet, twenty-four-hour news coverage, and newswire services, information is now an equal-opportunity commodity.

And remember, you don't have to be an expert to write a book. You can *interview* experts. Just take a look at a hot topic in the news and brainstorm spin-off book ideas and whom you could interview:

Topic: A new study has found that for the first time in history, there are more female college graduates than male.

> **Idea #1:** *The Hip Chick's Guide to Surviving Dorm Life*
> **Idea #2:** *The Soccer Mom's Guide to Going Back to School*

EXAMPLE 3.1   GOOD NONFICTION BOOK QUERY

September 5, 2006

Mark Modden, Acquisitions Editor
ABC Publishing
123 Main St.
New York, NY 10001

Dear Mr. Modden,

I just finished reading about your new line of do-it-yourself books in the recent issue of *Publishers Weekly*. As a former construction foreman turned freelance writer, I was especially drawn to your comments about the need for more "original outdoor projects."

Last year I built two outdoor saunas—one for my family and one for our neighbor (who, frankly, was using ours a bit too much!). Word spread among friends and I was eventually contacted by a magazine editor who asked me to write a how-to article about the project. The 4,000-word piece, complete with photos, seemed like a drop in the bucket, leading me to begin writing **THE TWO-WEEK HANDYMAN: PROJECT OUTDOOR SAUNA.**

As I began research for the book, I was surprised to find virtually no competition. While other books cover repair, indoor saunas, or multiple projects, I have yet to discover one that dedicates itself to one project.

THE TWO-WEEK HANDYMAN: PROJECT OUTDOOR SAUNA covers the process of building, using, and maintaining an outdoor sauna from start (choosing location, buying materials, do I need a permit?) to finish (staining the wood, maintaining the interior, replacing the thermometer) and includes more than sixty photos along the way.

This could be the first in a series of books on two-week projects, as I've also built dollhouses, canopy beds, two-story playhouses, and a small gardening shed.

If you're interested, I'm prepared to send you a complete proposal, including the first three chapters.

Thank you for your consideration.

Sincerely,

Dave Douglas
(address, phone, e-mail)

Idea #3: *The 2009 Guide to Scholarships for Women*
Idea #4: *Finding Your Calling: The Girls' Guide to Choosing the Perfect Career for Your Personality, Interests, and Goals*

Your query would mention the study, statistics about the number of girls heading off to college in the next few years (or the number of moms going back to school), the ever-increasing cost of college (for the scholarship book idea), and statistics on the number of times women change careers (for the "finding your calling" idea).

You've probably figured out that most of these topics aren't *pressing* in terms of timeliness. (That is to say, they're "evergreen.") But timeless and timeliness don't have to be mutually exclusive. You're not always trying to beat your competition to the punch as much as you're trying to find a timely factor (a study, a news brief statistic, a hot trend) to help support your query.

Hit the target (market)

Using the above topic of women graduating from college, do you think you could convince a publisher that you're hitting a good target market? You bet!

Some of the issues relating to target market will already be obvious to publishers, like the fact that women read more books than men (especially self-help). Your job will be to cite specific examples for a target market by citing statistics, like:

- The number of girls expected to head off to college next year (book idea #1 and book idea #3)

- The number of women expected to graduate from college next year (book idea #4) or expected to hit the workforce

- The number of women (e.g., soccer moms) expected to go back to school next year (book idea #2 or book idea #4)

- The number of women expected to go back into the workforce (when their kids are old enough to go to school full time, or when they become empty nesters) (book idea #4)

- The number of female retirees or senior citizens who have decided to go back into the workforce next year out of boredom or financial need (book idea #4)

Any statistics you can provide to show your book will target a large number of readers will demonstrate you've put some thought into marketing.

Make sure your focus is narrowed

It's hard to write a book for everybody, and you shouldn't try. If Stephen King can't do it, neither can you. Besides, the broadly focused nonfiction books (*Work Less, Live More*; *PCs for Dummies*; the *Betty Crocker Cookbook*) have all been done before.

A narrowed query is the sign of a true professional. If you think you've got a focused idea, do a quick search on Amazon.com to see if it's been done before. Chances are, you'll need to put it through the strainer again.

Remember the article idea about traveling in style? We had to whittle that topic down to its lowest common denominator. Now do the same with your book idea.

Your book idea for throwing a fun kids' birthday party sounds original enough, right? Let's head to Amazon.com to get an example of category narrowing.

Under Books, go to Parenting.

Under Parenting, go to Family Activities.

Under Family Activities, type in "birthday."

Guess how many results you'll get? 248.

In your defense, not all of the books are "how to throw a fun birthday party" exactly. Some are general craft books that were snagged in the search because they use the word "birthday" somewhere in the text. But by and large, the majority of the books are about throwing a fun birthday party.

So how could you narrow this focus—and your query—even more? How about:

- Birthday games for children with developmental disabilities
- Throwing a birthday party for twins
- Hosting an Afrocentric birthday party
- The untacky guide to throwing your own birthday party

In your proposal, you'll need to name your competition and explain how your book will be different. While some overlap in material is to be expected, there's got to be something special enough about your book that separates it from the pack. That special something is what will sell your query, too.

Be thorough

Have you ever thought of a brilliant idea for an article, pitched it to an editor, and then noticed a week later that the magazine ran the same topic last month? Oops. A little research goes a long way to save you time, energy, and face.

Before you even begin to craft your book query, you'll need to invest substantial time in thorough research—not so much to write the book, but to make sure the material you're using to pitch it is accurate. Imagine the disappointment (and blacklisting) in learning that the new study on which you based your entire book concept was flawed. Or fake. Or at the least, a grossly exaggerated marketing ploy (e.g., "Fifty percent of smokers surveyed say they've never felt better." Of the four smokers in our survey, two were under twenty-five and drunk at the time.)

Thorough research will either disprove the brilliance of your book idea or lead you to impress an editor so much that he can't resist requesting your proposal.

Example 3.2 (pgs. 93–94) shows an actual query that (after requesting the proposal) landed me an agent. You'll notice that although this isn't a proposal, within the first two paragraphs I managed to squeeze in:

- Three books that might be competition (all about how to be a successful freelance writer)
- Why my book was different (*don't* quit your day job!)
- Why my book needed to be written (nothing like it on the market)
- A huge target market (84 percent of writers don't make more than thirty thousand dollars a year)

If I hadn't been thorough in my research and had just submitted a query that said "here's my book idea," the agent might not have known that 84 percent of writers (and possibly the other 16 percent) would qualify as potential readers. That one statistic alone probably helped him see the light.

Keep it real

Guess who's going to write the authorized biography of Jack Nicholson? Probably not you.

Because authorized biographies require you to obtain permission from the famous person, your chances of writing his authorized biography are slim to none. And while unauthorized biographies are more research- than permission-heavy, they are generally written by a member of one of three groups:

- Seasoned journalists
- Scholars (for the less "sexy" bios)
- Tattlers (former loose-lipped employees, lovers, friends, or confidantes. They represent the classic chicken or the egg dilemma: Are they telling all because they're no longer employed, or no longer employed because they're telling all?)

They're called "kiss-and-tell" books for a reason. So unless you frequently shared a bottle of wine (or a bed) with a celebrity, don't expect to be writing about it.

The same goes for saturated expertise topics. If you have no experience as a realtor, investor, or millionaire, don't pitch a book on how to invest in real estate to make millions (unless you have a co-author who does). There are just too many writers out there who *do* have experience in these areas. Ditto for books on medicine, psychiatry, and serious legal matters, most of which will require you to have some string of letters after your name.

A realistic query presents a realistic book idea that you can realistically write. It won't require you to take multiple trips to Switzerland, interview Bono's wife, or break into top secret government files. It should be something you're qualified to write (*uniquely* qualified is even better) and the research should be accessible and realistic. Make the query believable … and the book *unbelievable.*

Demonstrate credentials

Ah, yes. We're back to the touchy area of why you're qualified to write the book. Although your query should ideally wrap up with your writing credentials, other information can help: writing awards, experience in the field of which you're writing, and access to the subject matter. Here's an example of a qualifications paragraph for a book on wheelchair fitness from a writer with very few published clips:

The Writer's Digest Guide to Query Letters

EXAMPLE 3.2   GOOD AGENT QUERY

July 8, 2004

Michael Larsen
Larsen-Pomada Agency
1029 Jones St.
San Francisco, CA 94109

Dear Mr. Larsen,

Everybody wants to be a writer, and there are lots of books on the market that encourage writers to quit their day jobs:

- *Secrets of a Freelance Writer: How to Make $85,000 a Year*
- *Achieving Financial Independence as a Freelance Writer*
- *The Well-Fed Writer: Financial Self-Sufficiency as a Freelance Writer in Six Months or Less*

Realistically, however, only 16 percent of working writers make more than thirty thousand dollars a year.* Where does that leave the rest of us who struggle to write while juggling a full-time job?

THE WRITER'S GUIDE TO KEEPING YOUR DAY JOB is a how-to guide and workbook for the beginning or struggling freelancer who can't afford to leave the security of a forty-hour-a-week job.

The book offers practical tips on everything from "Finding Time to Write," "How and When to Tell Your Boss You're Moonlighting," and "Setting Up Your Creative Space" to "Writing in Traffic," and "A Novel Idea" (finishing a novel within six months on the job).

THE WRITER'S GUIDE TO KEEPING YOUR DAY JOB is littered with Web sites, specific hints, creative exercises, brainstorming sessions, and concrete examples of what works and doesn't, as well as short exercises for writing fiction, the Five-Minute Character, sample cover letters, query letters, personal experiences, and (what some might consider) humor.

Beginning and intermediate writers will learn step-by-step tips to help them begin and maintain their career as writers—whatever their interests—without the pressure to quit their "day jobs" in hopes of striking it rich as an overnight success.

ABOUT THE AUTHOR

As the subject line of this e-mail indicates, I am the daughter of one of your clients, Steve Burt. My father suggested I send you my (thirty-plus-page) proposal for **THE WRITER'S GUIDE TO KEEPING YOUR DAY JOB,** therefore I am querying first.

Nonfiction Book Queries   **93**

Formerly the editor of Colorado Springs' largest-circulated business newspaper, I know firsthand about the commitment it takes to be a successful freelancer.

In addition to my full-time job, I managed to teach writing, sell my freelance articles, stories, and greeting cards, write monthly columns, run a two hundred-plus-member women's creative group, speak to writers' groups and conferences, and market my first book, *Oh, Solo Mia! The Hip Chick's Guide to Fun for One* (April 2001, McGraw-Hill). My second book for McGraw-Hill, *Work It, Girl! 101 Tips for the Hip Working Chick* hit bookstores in June 2003.

At 33, I have published more than 1,000 articles, short stories, essays, and greeting cards, and have been teaching "Breaking Into Freelance Writing" for six years. My writing club memberships have included PEN Women, Front Range Fiction Writers, and the National Writers Union, and I am the founder of Just CAWS (Creative Alliance of Women's Support), a two hundred-member creative women's group.

I was one of the youngest faculty members to teach at the 2001 Pikes Peak Writers Conference—the sixth largest writers conference in the United States—and have won various writing contests, most notably, first place for fiction in PEN Women's "Soul-Making Literary Contest" and "The Dabbling Mum's Short Fiction Contest."

I have appeared on the Oxygen network's Pure Oxygen talk show, have been interviewed on numerous TV and radio shows including iVillage.com, and my books have been excerpted/quoted in *Cosmopolitan, Woman's Own, Complete Woman*, and countless other publications.

In 2001, at the age of thirty, I was named one of the "Twenty-five Most Dynamic Business Women" of Colorado Springs—a city with a population of half a million.

Now a full-time freelance writer and editor, I still teach "Breaking Into Freelance Writing."

For years, my students have been asking me, "How do you balance a full-time job and a freelance career?"

This book will tell them how.

Thank you for taking the time to read my query. Please let me know if you would like to review the full proposal.

Best regards,

Wendy Burt-Thomas
(address, phone, e-mail)

Encl: SASE

*SOURCE: National Writers Union

After a car accident left me paralyzed from the waist down, I went back to school and got my degree in physical therapy. I now teach Wheelchair Yoga at schools, fitness centers, and assisted living facilities and am currently competing to be in the 2012 Paraplegic Olympics.

If the query itself were well written, the acquisitions editor would be hard-pressed to question the writer's lack of clips before requesting the proposal.

Show me the money

Don't be fooled into thinking that the publishing world is all about literary genius and scholarly writings. Cover your ears, Gutenberg: Today's publishing houses are about making money.

The potential for a book to make a publishing house (or agent) money goes far beyond its original sales. Book ideas are sometimes catalysts in multimedia successes, and the more spin-off potential your idea has, the more possibilities for big bucks for everyone involved. Here are some well-known examples:

- Martha Stewart's catering book *Entertaining* spawned a new book every year for several years. These led to her own TV show, *Holiday Entertaining With Martha Stewart*, high-end seminars, *Martha Stewart Living* (magazine and TV show), and her own line of products (first for Kmart and now for Wal-Mart).

- J.K. Rowling's Harry Potter books unleashed not only a fury of blockbuster movies, but also a merchandising phenomenon. The wizard and his sidekicks appeared on everything from jellybeans and clothing to games and collectors' cards.

- First created in 1926, A.A. Milne's Winnie-the-Pooh character has since spun off into TV cartoons, videos, feature-length films, and video games—not to mention stuffed animals, collectibles, clothing, toys, and home décor.

This said, your query isn't the place to mention spin-off ideas. Save the "extras" for your proposal. And if/when you do mention a particular idea in your proposal, keep it realistic and focused. Don't talk about your vision of a

Furpy the Cat doll and cartoon character to accompany your book on *Raising Healthy Cats*. What you could suggest might include your availability to use your textbook as a required material in a class you teach, or the fact that your annual convention's director has already committed to purchasing five thousand copies for attendees if your book on healthcare reform is published. Another idea is to suggest a workbook (if applicable) that could accompany the book. Examples of similar book/workbook pairings have included:

- Julia Cameron's *The Artist's Way*
- *Japanese for Busy People*
- Dr. Phil's *Family First*
- Sean Covey's *The 7 Habits of Highly Effective Teens*
- John C. Maxwell's *Your Road Map for Success*

Anything regional just begs to be made into a series (for other cities), as do many self-help books in which the gender or target (children, teen, adult, parent) can be changed. The best example of this is Jack Canfield and Mark Victor Hansen's Chicken Soup series. A search of Amazon.com for "Chicken Soup for the" turns up 19,681 results, but here are a few of the super-targeted spin-offs:

- *Chicken Soup for the Preteen Soul*
- *Chicken Soup for the American Idol Soul* (Unless TV suddenly becomes obsolete, there is no end in sight for the Chicken Soup series. On second thought, even if TV does disappear, we'll someday see *Chicken Soup for the MySpace Soul*.)
- *Chicken Soup for the Soul: Children With Special Needs*
- *Chicken Soup for the Prisoner's Soul*
- *Chicken Soup for the Mother and Son Soul*
- *Chicken Soup for the Veteran's Soul*
- *Chicken Soup for the Writer's Soul*
- *Chicken Soup for the Nurse's Soul*

Another collection that encompasses several of the spin-off ideas I've mentioned (age, gender) and more (audio, discussion guide, large print) is from Shaunti Feldhahn. In just three years she launched:

- *For Women Only: What You Need to Know About the Inner Lives of Men*
- *For Men Only: A Straightforward Guide to the Inner Lives of Women*
- *For Young Women Only: What You Need to Know About How Guys Think*
- *For Parents Only: Getting Inside the Head of Your Kid*
- Plus discussion guides to accompany each of the above, audio versions, large-print versions, multibook sets (which doesn't usually work with regional guides), and even one Spanish-language version.

Again, don't be too concerned about presenting a spin-off idea (especially if you're a first-time author). This approach should only be taken if you've already got a strong "lead" (required reading for your class, the convention, a strong workbook idea).

Ensure an Editor Will Overlook You By ...

Although the rules are a bit more set for what you *should* do in a nonfiction query, it's trickier to generalize what *not* to do. That's because acquisitions editors are so overwhelmed with queries that sometimes it's okay to break—or at least *stretch*—the rules in a way that helps you stand out in the slush pile.

Still, it's good for you to have a general idea of things to avoid. After all, how will you break the rules if you don't know what they are?

Not including enough details about the idea

Don't assume that the title of your book will be "enough said." Even a narrowed-down topic doesn't give the publisher enough info. You might be able to guess that my book, *Oh, Solo Mia! The Hip Chick's Guide to Fun for One* (McGraw-Hill, 2001) is for women who want to have fun alone, but a query would need to detail more. Is this a serious or light-hearted book? Are the activities indoor or outdoor? How would the chapters be broken down? Are the ideas all things to do at home or do some involve going out in public? (See **Example 3.3** on pages 99–100 for a version of the actual query that sold this book.)

While a query is no place to get into *all* the details of the book's topic, format, or outline (save that for the proposal), you will need to bait the hook with more than a title and your credentials.

Comparing yourself to big authors

It's okay to mention that your book is similar in style/tone/voice to another (especially if the publisher you are approaching published the book), but don't blacklist yourself by jumping on the Ego Express. Comparing yourself to Hemingway, Erma Bombeck, Mark Twain, or Jane Austen (or comparing your book to theirs) is just outright embarrassing. (See **Example 3.4 [pg. 101]**.)

Using a cliché or sappy title

Admittedly, there are times that sappy titles work. A book about overcoming grief might need a phrase like "healing the heart" rather than "moving on" or "getting over it." But in most cases, nonfiction books do better with titles that entertain or inform. Look for original ways to use humor; a play on words; motivational words (especially for self-help), such as *change, reverse,* or *unleash*; or power words (*successful, rich, influence, forever*) while identifying your target reader in the title with positive (fit/healthy), negative (addiction/loss), or neutral (parents/dog lovers/nurses) words.

Don't get too attached to your title, as often it will change, but do put some time into coming up with a good one to catch a publisher's eye.

Trying to convince a publisher to print a subject outside its genres

Any sentence that begins, "I know you don't represent this genre, but ..." is a turn-off to an editor. Don't waste your time trying to convince an editor that yours should be the first cookbook he publishes, and don't assume that a publishing house that printed a book on Buddha buys religious books. It could mean that they're a Buddhist (read: not Christian) publisher or that they print biographies. (In case you weren't aware, there's already a pretty well-read biography on Jesus.) You wouldn't go to a podiatrist and try to convince him to look at your deviated septum, would you? The same is true with publishing specialties.

EXAMPLE 3.3 GOOD NONFICTION BOOK QUERY

June 2, 2000

Dana Vincent, Acquisitions Editor
McGraw-Hill
1333 Burr Ridge Pkwy
Burr Ridge, IL 60527

Dear Ms. Vincent,

Forty million women are single, divorced, or unattached. Add to that the number of married, engaged, and cohabitating women seeking quality "alone time" and you've got nearly half the world population.

While some of these women know how to celebrate the solo life, too many lone ladies are still sitting home on Saturday nights watching *Walker, Texas Ranger* reruns in lieu of living it up alone. Be it fear of being seen alone or lack of creative ideas, these women need a guiding light to show them the way to a celebration of singledom. Enter our book ... **PARTY OF ONE: 99 SOLO EXCURSIONS AND OTHER DIVERSIONS FOR WOMEN**.

Savvy singles know you don't have to be paired up to have a great time and would probably love a few tips on doing the solitary scene in style. **PARTY OF ONE** offers women hilarious and helpful hints ranging from mild to wild. With rapid-fire fun suggestions ranging from silly to scandalous, **PARTY OF ONE** offers tongue-in-cheek advice to help women bring out their inner vixen.

Feeling artsy? Try on idea number thirty-three and "Linger Over a Book at the Local Beatnik Coffee Shop."

Contemplating motherhood? You may think twice after number twenty-three's "Coaching a Kiddie Sports Team."

Feeling naughty? Number forty-four's "Posterior Posterity" suggests baring it all and getting racy photos taken of yourself.

Other ideas include:

- "Thelma and uh ... Thelma"—Road Tripping in a Rented Convertible
- "Hello Mudda, Hello Fadda ..."—Summer Camp for Big Girls
- "Self-Steaming Your Windows"—Park at Inspiration Point on Friday night. Contemplate the city lights—you'll be the only one not arrested for public nudity.

PARTY OF ONE is the collaborative effort of Erin Kindberg and Wendy Burt, professional freelance writers with a combination of more than 300 feature articles, essays, short stories, and greeting cards. When they're not slaving over a hot keyboard or living lives of lone ladies of leisure, they're brainstorming together in a party of two.

To request a proposal, please contact the authors at any of the numbers or e-mail listed below. Thank you in advance for your time.

Sincerely,

Wendy Burt-Thomas   Erin Kindberg
(address, phone, e-mail)   (address, phone, e-mail)

[Note: Right before publication, due to a title conflict with another book, the title of this book was changed to *Oh, Solo Mia! The Hip Chick's Guide to Fun for One*.]

Skipping research

This goes back to the lack of proposal. Research might seem time-intensive but it'll save you more time in the long run. Just imagine your surprise that your brilliant idea for a self-help book on clearing your heart and mind by cleaning out your house was already a (recent) book. A simple search on Amazon.com for keywords like "de-cluttering" or "organizing your life" would have turned up Kathryn Porter's *Too Much Stuff: De-Cluttering Your Heart and Home* or Julie Morgenstern's *When Organizing Isn't Enough: SHED Your Stuff, Change Your Life*. The time you wasted could have been reinvested in coming up with a slightly different angle that would have landed you a book deal.

Acquisitions editors have their finger on the pulse of most recent and upcoming releases, and if they like a query, they may turn it down after a quick search reveals the idea has been done to death (or someone else beat you to the punch). While you can't possibly know all the books that are waiting in the publishing wings, Amazon.com is a great resource for a lot of them. Take advantage of such a simple tool.

Submitting only self-published material

Advances in technology have allowed for anyone to self-publish. For those who have a great book and an even greater marketing platform, this can mean more money in your pocket because you're not sharing the proceeds with a publisher or agent. For most, however, self-publishing is merely a vanity move. Publishers often look down on books that are self-published

EXAMPLE 3.4   BAD NONFICTION BOOK QUERY

March 13, 2008

Attn: Publisher
Try Again Books
555 Notachance Pass
Reject, MN 12345

Dear Sir, **A**

Tired of reading through the slush pile of boring book ideas? I'm here to break up the monotony! **B** As the author of *Laughter Makes Everything Better*, **C** I've been called "the male Erma Bombeck of the twenty-first century." **D** Just check out the reviews of my book on Amazon.com—all five stars! **E**

The book teaches people the importance of laughing every day and gives them tips on how to heal their hearts with humor. **F** I've already sold 50 copies **G** myself, but because I'm so busy with my job, **H** I'm looking for a publisher who is ready to make this a bestseller. **I** I could also see this turning into a morning TV show, similar to the Dr. Phil format, **J** in which I would help people heal broken hearts (from divorce, loss, depression) by teaching them to add more humor to their daily lives.

If you think you'd like to publish my book, I'll send you a copy immediately.

Thank you for your consideration.

Neil Noway
FunnyMan@email.com **K**

WHAT'S WRONG: EDITOR'S COMMENTS

A If he had taken the time to look up the acquisitions editor's name, he would have learned that he was a she. **B** This is presumptuous. **C** Horrible title. Generic and boring. **D** Who compares him to Erma Bombeck? His mother? I'd love to see proof of this from a reputable magazine or he could mention the publication in this query if it's true. **E** Amazon reviews don't tell me much. They could be written by friends and family. **F** This is cliché. "Healing their hearts" is tired and overused. He doesn't seem to have any awareness of established books on the topic, like Norman Cousins's *The Healing Heart*. **G** Fifty copies isn't much at all and there's no way to verify these sales. **H** He's got a job, so he's not a full-time writer. It's not a requirement, but it helps. **I** It's not our job to make his book a bestseller and we couldn't if we tried. **J** Now he's comparing himself to Dr. Phil and he thinks he deserves his own TV show. **K** He only lists his e-mail, no phone number or address.

because in most cases, it means your material wasn't good enough to land an agent or publishing house.

If you've self-published a book exactly for this reason, you're probably better off not mentioning that you've done so. "No agent would represent me so I decided to move forward on my own" just screams "I dropped three thousand dollars for a major print run and my basement is full of books I can't sell."

If, on the other hand, you sold out of a print run or can indicate in your query that you've won awards with your book or had relative success with marketing due to a strong platform, you should say so. (See **Example 3.5** for a successful self-published book author pitching a publisher.)

Special Nonfiction Book Considerations

Different genres of books call for different types of query letters. For example, a memoir might rely more on how well you can summarize an interesting life in one paragraph, while a textbook might rely more on your industry expertise or college degrees. Although all pitches will share common components, here are a few book genres that will require you to branch off the standard query tree.

Memoirs

By definition, a memoir is the story of an event or period of your life or family history. Because the writing itself must be incredibly strong and creative in a memoir (as opposed to, say, a cookbook), you'll need to demonstrate that you've mastered your craft—right in your query letter. Yes, that's a tough hill to climb in a paragraph or two—but no matter how exciting your life story is, no one's going to buy it (publishers *or* readers) if it's not well written. And by well written I don't just mean technically proficient: You must master voice, tone, pacing, and other nuanced fiction-writing elements.

If you're not sure what makes for a good memoir, pick up any of the following, noting the ways in which the story presentation resembles a novel:

- *Animal, Vegetable, Miracle: A Year of Food Life* by Barbara Kingsolver
- *A Long Way Gone: Memoirs of a Boy Soldier* by Ishmael Beah

EXAMPLE 3.5   GOOD NONFICTION BOOK QUERY FROM
SELF-PUBLISHED AUTHOR

July 18, 2008

Shelley Wolf, Submissions Editor
The Globe Pequot Press
Morris Publishing Group
725 Broad St.
Augusta, GA 30901

Dear Ms. Wolf,

As the first self-published author in history to win the Bram Stoker Award (tying with Clive
Barker for the 2005 Young Readers' Award), I've had a busy year. The honor, coupled with
my 2004 Bram Stoker nomination and three Ray Bradbury Awards for previous books in my
Stories to Chill the Heart series, has left me traveling New England for countless book signings, school and library talks, book fairs, and media interviews.

  Unfortunately, the constant travel has taken its toll on my fifty-eight-year-old body
(not to mention that my wife of thirty-eight years is barely speaking to me!). I've been
offered a part-time position as a pastor near our home (the media calls me "The Sinister
Minister") and would like to use the opportunity to get back to writing.

  To minimize my travel time, I'd like to find a publisher for my four-book series of
scary tales for young adult readers. I'm a big fan of your Campfire Stories series by William Forgey and think my style will also appeal to that series' readership.

  I'd be happy to send you copies of all four books, all of which are in extended (second, third, or fourth) print runs. They include:

- *Odd Lot: Stories to Chill the Heart*
- *Even Odder: More Stories to Chill the Heart*
- *Oddest Yet: Even More Stories to Chill the Heart*
- *Wicked Odd: Still More Stories to Chill the Heart*

You can read summaries, reviews, and testimonials on www.burtcreations.com. The site also
details my other books (some with traditional publishers) and audiobooks (one was a finalist
for the 2001 ForeWord Award Audio Book of the Year), thousands of published pieces (articles, essays, poems) and other nicknames I've garnered from the media.

  Thank you for your time and consideration. I look forward to hearing from you.

Sincerely,

Rev. Dr. Steve Burt
(address, phone, e-mail)

- *Eat, Pray, Love: One Woman's Search for Everything Across Italy, India, and Indonesia* by Elizabeth Gilbert
- *Angela's Ashes* by Frank McCourt
- *The Liars' Club* by Mary Karr

As for what makes for a good memoir query, see **Example 3.6.**

Prescriptive/How-To books

Though few may have heard the term *prescriptive nonfiction*, many can identify such books once the word is defined. Put simply, a prescriptive book lays out the rules for something, such as grammar or etiquette. One particularly successful example can be found in (what could have otherwise been a boring book) *Eats, Shoots & Leaves: The Zero Tolerance Approach to Punctuation* by Lynne Truss. (Don't laugh. The book became number one in the United Kingdom. Of course, they also gave us the Spice Girls.)

Prescriptive books sometimes teeter on that thin line between how-to and educational/textbook, and require special finesse when determining an approach to your query. In Truss's query (assuming she even had to write one), she likely set out to accomplish three things:

- Offer her use of humor on an otherwise dry (no, barren) topic
- Demonstrate her ability to explain complex terms and concepts in layperson's terms
- Allow her credentials to offer more-than-sufficient reason to demonstrate that she was the perfect writer for the job. (Truss was not only an experienced writer, journalist, novelist, columnist, and reviewer, but also presented *Cutting a Dash*, a well-received BBC Radio 4 series about punctuation. Can you imagine anyone better suited to write the book?)

For the "average" person's prescriptive book idea, you'll probably need the latter two from above. (The humor won't apply to most prescriptive books, although it's probably helped you get through this book on queries.) For an example of a sample prescriptive book query, see **Example 3.7** (pg. 109).

How-to books leave a bit more wiggle room in terms of credentials, especially because their topics can vary so greatly. *How to Raise a Snob of a Cat*

EXAMPLE 3.6   GOOD MEMOIR BOOK QUERY

November 21, 2007

Sarah Smith
The Great Agency
444 Bookseller Dr.
New York, NY 10001

Dear Ms. Smith,

I am a psychiatrist, published author, optioned screenwriter, and expert for the national media seeking representation for my memoir entitled, **QUEEN OF THE ROAD: THE TRUE TALE OF 47 STATES, 22,000 MILES, 200 SHOES, 2 CATS, 1 POODLE, A HUSBAND, AND A BUS WITH A WILL OF ITS OWN** for which I have a proposal and two sample chapters. Because you are interested in memoir and women's stories, I thought we might be a good match.

When Tim first announced he wanted to "chuck it all" and travel around the country in a converted bus for a year, I gave this profound and potentially life-altering notion all the thoughtful consideration it deserved.

"Why can't you be like a normal husband with a midlife crisis and have an affair or buy a Corvette?" I demanded, adding, "I will never, ever, EVER live on a bus."

What do you get when you cram married shrinks—one in a midlife crisis, the other his materialistic, wisecracking wife—two cats who hate each other and a standard poodle who loves licking them all, into a bus for a year? **QUEEN OF THE ROAD** is a memoir of my dysfunctional, multispecies family's travels to and travails in forty-seven states.

As millions of baby boomers reach middle age, they reflect back on their lives, as well as look ahead to what retirement will bring. **QUEEN OF THE ROAD** is a much-needed tale about not settling: in life, at work, or in relationships. It is about choosing the unconventional road and surviving the ruts and wrong turns along the way. It is a sassy, heartfelt account of married, mid-forties psychiatrists (and polar opposites) who seem to have it all, only to squeeze it all into 340 square feet. It is not only a memoir of adventure and misadventure (fire, armed robbery, and finding ourselves in a nudist RV park, to name a few) throughout America, but the story of a Long Island Princess becoming less materialistic, in spite of that never being one of her life goals, while her Type A husband toils relentlessly to become mellow. The transformational aspect of our trip will resonate with a diverse audience and as psychiatrists, readers will especially love getting into our heads and marriage, hopefully gaining insight into their own lives along the way.

As a psychiatrist, award-winning author (*I Know You Really Love Me*, Macmillan/Dell), book review editor (*Journal of Threat Assessment*), optioned screenwriter, national lecturer, faculty member (University of Colorado Medical School), and frequent media expert on psychiatric topics, (including *Larry King Live*, *GMA*, *48 Hours*, *The New York Times*, and *People* magazine among many, many others), my life has centered on introspection, analysis, and storytelling. Yet I count among my greatest accomplishments that last year, our bus was featured as the centerfold of *Bus Conversions Magazine*, thus fulfilling my lifelong ambition of becoming a Miss September.

The story of our yearlong adventure is already garnering interest in the media and has been mentioned in *American Medical News* (circulation 250,000, and this journal of the American Medical Association has already agreed to review the book with an author interview when it comes out), *Woman's Day*, *Quick & Simple*, Match.com and *Best Life* magazine. An upcoming *Parade* magazine article on the growing phenomenon of midlife career breaks (who knew I was a trendsetter?) will include a photo of Tim and me, along with our story. My blog of our trip has also been mentioned in Andy Serwer's Street Life e-column (*Fortune* magazine).

I hope you are interested in seeing the proposal and if so, would be most happy to send it to you.

Doreen Orion
We didn't just dream of the road ...
www.queenoftheroadthebook.com
(address, phone, e-mail)

[Note: This book sold to Broadway.]

---

will no doubt require little more than humor, cat ownership, and a handful of cat-related writing clips. A more prescriptive book, say *Caring for a Cat With Type O Blood*, would probably require some letters after your name (not to mention an army of seriously devout feline worshippers).

How-to books can take on many formats so you'll need to be specific in your query. Will you be including quizzes, illustrations, photos, or instructions? Will your piece be serious, funny, or a bit of both? Will it consist of one hundred mini-chapters or twelve long ones? What will and won't be covered? A book titled *101 Outfits to Make Yourself* doesn't identify if the book will include patterns, tips on how to use a sewing machine or how to choose fabric, or if the outfits are for men, women, or children.

One great way to create a summary paragraph of what your book offers readers is by reading the book flaps (or summaries on Amazon.com) of other how-to books. Here are a few examples:

20 Master Plots (And How to Build Them) **by Ronald B. Tobias**

This book shows you how to take timeless storytelling structures and make them immediate, now, for fiction that's universal in how it speaks to the reader's heart and contemporary in detail and impact. You'll find lots of practical 'how-to' and 'what-to-do' advice, rather than a lengthy academic discussion of plot. Each chapter includes brief excerpts and description for fiction from many times and many genres, including myth and fairy tale, genre and mainstream fiction, film plots of all types, short story and novel.

How to Write Science Fiction & Fantasy **by Orson Scott Card**

You'll learn how to:
- wield story elements that "define" the science fiction and fantasy genre
- build, populate, and dramatize a credible, inviting world your readers will want to explore
- develop the 'rules' of time, space, and magic that affect your world and its inhabitants
- construct a compelling story by developing ideas, characters, and events that keep readers turning pages
- find the markets for speculative fiction, reach them, and get published
- submit queries, write cover letters, find an agent, and live the life of a writer.

And a simple one:

The Girlfriends' Guide to Surviving the First Year of Motherhood **by Vicki Iovine**

Wise and witty advice on everything from coping with postpartum mood swings to salvaging your sex life to fitting into that favorite pair of jeans.

Getting the idea? See **Example 3.8** (pgs. 111–112) for a how-to book query.

Educational/Textbooks

Much like prescriptive books, textbooks and educational books require you to be somewhat of an expert in your field. This doesn't mean you have to have worked as a teacher or professor. As an auto mechanic, you're probably qualified to write a vocational textbook on car repair (though you'll probably need to indicate that you've got *some* published clips as the industry is not known for its writing skills). Other expertise that may help you qualify to write a textbook with little writing experience: fluency in a foreign language, advanced degrees in a topic, business ownership, combined experience with a co-author (you as the writer, co-author as the carpenter/musician/chef), or awards/accomplishments (a perfect score on your SATs certainly qualifies you to write an SAT study guide).

Your query will need to indicate the topic of your book, what it will cover, and what it will prepare students to do. Be specific. Will students who finish using your textbook be able to perform all major repairs on any domestic vehicle? Will they obtain the knowledge and understanding to use all pieces of diagnostic equipment? Will they develop skills to repair all foreign cars and trucks, including vehicles with computer chips?

Some publishers will also require you to list the top few competitive books right in your query, including what makes your book unique or updated from the current version.

To indicate that you've researched the publisher's guidelines, you may also want to indicate exactly for whom the book is written. While some publishers print textbooks for all levels (elementary, middle and high school markets, vocational schools, college), others are very specific. ICDC Publishing, for example, clearly states in its guidelines that it only accepts books aimed at the private postsecondary school market. One way to demonstrate that your textbook is a good match is by mentioning the exact target market and the reading level of the textbook. For example: "*Diagnostics and Repair for Non-U.S. Vehicles Built After 2005* is written on a ninth-grade reading level in order to be easily understood by those with only a high school education or GED."

Other things you may want to include in your query:

- Whether you could produce a workbook to accompany the textbook
- Whether the book includes photographs or diagrams (and if you can provide them)

EXAMPLE 3.7   GOOD PRESCRIPTIVE BOOK QUERY

July 15, 2008

Marilyn Quenton
The Light Lit Agency
333 Bestseller Ave.
New York, NY 10001

Dear Ms. Quenton,

What if you had to start dating again after thirty years of being off the market? Would you know the new "rules" for dating? Do men still pay for dinner on the first date if both parties are retired? What if only the woman works? Can you join an online dating site if you're separated but not divorced? When do you introduce your date to your kids? Your grandkids? How soon is too soon to talk about your deceased spouse?

For the 56 percent of Americans over the age of fifty-three who have been divorced (or widowed), these are real concerns. Jumping back into the dating pool after decades in a relationship can be overwhelming, confusing, and downright scary. **THE SENIOR'S GUIDE TO DATING ETIQUETTE** is a prescriptive and informational book to help the ever-growing number of boomers (and beyond) grasp the "protocol" that is often unique to their age group. From introducing your grandchildren to your new "boyfriend" to discussing Viagra with a potential sex partner, this guide breaks down the often-taboo barriers of dating for a generation not known for its frank discussions on sexuality, "netiquette," and erectile dysfunction.

As a licensed clinical therapist and freelance writer, I've written on this topic countless times. My articles have appeared in *AARP The Magazine*, *Senior Living*, and *More*. Because you have represented similar books on relationship etiquette, such as *Dating for the Disabled*, I would be honored to call you my agent.

A full proposal is available upon request.

Thank you for your time.

Sincerely,

Marcia Brady
(address, phone, e-mail)

Nonfiction Book Queries   **109**

- Whether the book includes exercises, quizzes, or a glossary
- Possible shelf life of the book
- That a full proposal is available upon request

For a good sample textbook query, see **Example 3.9** (pg. 113).

Narrative nonfiction

Narrative nonfiction can encompass a pretty wide scope of material. This could include personal essays, food writing, biographies, or even travel pieces. You'll sometimes hear the genre referred to as "narrative journalism," "literary nonfiction," or "creative nonfiction," although the terms all do have subtle distinctions. For the sake of brevity, we're going to lump these together and say that this genre includes any presentation of facts (as opposed to fiction) that uses your own style/voice/perspective (as opposed to straight journalism that presents bare facts to describe news). Basically, it's storytelling of nonfiction accounts. (Memoirs often cross into this category.)

Now that you've finally got a genre classification for your book, you can work on crafting the perfect query. To properly express that your travel-related manuscript is narrative nonfiction (rather than how-to), you'll probably want to open with an actual excerpt from the book. That's because *showing* is always easier (and more demonstrative) than *telling* when it comes to this genre. Just look at the difference between these two introductory paragraphs from a query for a narrative nonfiction travel book:

> FLAT: I spent a year in Africa and have created a book about the experience to help other travelers make the best of their time. *Sleeping With Lions* is my personal account of 360 days in the open plains of the continent's most dangerous areas. In it, I'll advise readers about what to pack, what to avoid, and how to survive without the comforts of civilization.

> DYNAMIC: On day twelve, I was awakened from a deep-sleep dream by a four hundred-pound lion foraging through my backpack. She barely gave me a second look as she ripped the blue canvas to shreds in search of the half-eaten protein bar I had planned to finish for breakfast. I stayed huddled

EXAMPLE 3.8   GOOD HOW-TO BOOK QUERY

December 14, 2006

Jane Friedman, Editorial Director
Writer's Digest Books
4700 E. Galbraith Rd.
Cincinnati, OH 45236

Dear Jane Friedman,

Christina Katz suggested that I contact you. I'm an award-winning poet with an M.A. in creative writing from NYU and a B.A. from Brown University. My blog and Web site, sagesaid so.com, reflect a poetry platform cultivated through twenty years of publishing, teaching, and creating poetry communities—most recently in Portland, Oregon. Here's a poetry book concept I would like to propose for Writer's Digest Books.

Throughout most of human history, people have been seeking meaning through poetry. While it has waxed and waned in popularity over the years, today more and more people are turning to poetry to help us make sense of our lives and our world. *Poets & Writers* magazine reports a readership of seventy thousand poets. And according to the AWP, the number of degree-conferring writing programs has exponentially increased from 80 to 720 in the past thirty years, with creative writing ranking among the most popular classes in the humanities.

David Fenza, AWP Executive Director, offers this justification for such popularity: "Many students [today] feel that the world is not of their making, and not theirs to form or to reform; but writing classes often demonstrate the efficacy of the human will—that human experience can be shaped and directed for the good—aesthetically, socially, and politically." This impulse toward poetry as a lens of insight and influence is evidenced in Poets Against the War, a popular Web site that has received more than twenty thousand poetry submissions.

While these statistics may give us a sense of the number of people in the United States who consider themselves serious poets, they do not reflect the unnumbered masses that have some deep feeling they would like to express, but believe that poetry is out of their reach. My book, **WRITING THE LIFE POETIC**, is an empowerment-through-experiencing-poetry handbook for such people. Both practical and inspirational, it will leave readers with a greater appreciation for the poetry they read and a greater sense of possibility for the poetry they write.

The craft of poetry has been well documented in important books such as Frances Mayes's *The Discovery of Poetry* and Mary Oliver's primer, *A Poetry Handbook*. These books offer a valuable service to serious writers striving to become competent poets. Whereas **WRITING THE LIFE POETIC**, a gifty, contagious, 240-page reference adventure, will be written for readers who simply wish to test the poetry waters, as well as those in the courtship phase of their relationship with poetry. It will offer an entertaining mix of insights, exercises, expert guidance, and encouragement designed to get readers excited about the possibilities of poetry—and engaged in a beginner's creative practice.

I bring to this project two decades of education, experience, and expertise in the written word. I have published more than thirty poems in journals and anthologies including *Poetry Flash*, *Oregon Literary Review*, blueoregon.com, and *San Francisco Reader*. Recently, I was awarded first prize in the *Ghost Road* poetry contest, as well as a month's residency at Soapstone. My poetry manuscript *Like the Heart, the World* has placed as a semifinalist or finalist in four book award contests. Recently, I placed essays in the anthologies *A Cup of Comfort for Writers* and *A Cup of Comfort for Pet Lovers*, published by Adams Media (an F+W company). My short stories appear in the *Herotica 3* and *Herotica 4* anthologies, published by Penguin. You will find the full scoop on my history of creative writing success at sagesaidso.com.

For the past decade, I have built a thriving freelance marketing communications business (sagecohen.com) on referrals alone. As an author, I bring the deadline-driven writing and editing performance I cultivated in the corporate world, as well as the strategic thinking that connects objectives with audience. I work fast, perform well under pressure, smile pretty for the press, and am extremely organized and efficient.

It's time for a poetry book that does more than lecture from the front of the classroom.

WRITING THE LIFE POETIC will get readers leaping up out of their chairs, swaying to the rhythm of their own inner music. Leonard Cohen says: "Poetry is just the evidence of life. If your life is burning well, poetry is just the ash." My goal is that **WRITING THE LIFE POETIC** be the flame fueling the life well lived.

Thank you for considering this query. I'd be happy to speak with you about the possibilities that **WRITING THE LIFE POETIC** might have with Writer's Digest Books. If you are interested in **WRITING THE LIFE POETIC**, I can deliver a proposal by January 15. Please advise me if there is anything you'd like me to cover that I have not mentioned here.

Best wishes,

Sage Cohen
(address, phone, e-mail)

[Note: Although this query is longer than one page, it's incredibly well written and effective. In fact, the query landed the author a great book deal.]

EXAMPLE 3.9   GOOD SAMPLE TEXTBOOK QUERY

September 7, 2007

William Norm
Textbook Publishing
7654 Read Street
New York, NY 10001

Dear Mr. Norm,

As the Professor of Fashion Merchandising and Marketing at the Rhode Island School of Design for the past nineteen years, I tend to stay quite up to date on the latest textbooks for our industry. I have yet to find a post-2001 textbook on the topic, however, and feel that the emergence of Internet marketing and promotion alone necessitates a revised teaching manual. The good news for potential readership is that I am not alone. The need for such a textbook was the topic of lengthy discussion at the recent Fashion Merchandising Association's national expo. The two thousand-plus professors await **FASHION BRANDING & MARKETING IN THE INTERNET AGE** with bated breath ... and I think I'm just the person to write it.

In addition to my career as a professor, I've written more than sixty papers on the subject of fashion merchandising and marketing, including at least twelve in recent years that specifically relate to Internet tactics.

The book would address some of the specific advantages, limitations, and strategies that the Web can offer fashion merchandisers, manufacturers, and marketers and could be completed in six months. I could also supply a list of colleges and universities that have already shown an interest in purchasing the book as required course reading.

I have a full proposal ready to send upon request.

Thank you for your time.

Sincerely,

Professor Stephany Malachi
(address, phone, e-mail)

Nonfiction Book Queries   **113**

in my tent, fumbling equally fast for both my serrated knife and my camera. Luckily, I only needed one that night. Day thirteen wouldn't fare so well.

Which would capture *your* attention? Not only does version two evoke more emotion (danger, fascination) and demonstrate the author's ability to tell a story, it also implies that he has some incredible photos to include in the book. When was the last time you saw a lion up close?

Like other categories of nonfiction, you'll still need to explain the readers' "takeaway." This doesn't necessarily mean a bullet-point list of hardcore benefits ("I'll list the best hotels by price" or "I'll include an alphabetical listing of the must-see tourist attractions in Africa"), but rather a general summary of where your book takes the reader. What feelings does it evoke? Is it a day-by-day account of your journey through Africa or just the highlights? Does the story take place in one week or over several years where the reader will really get into the subject? What skills or lessons will it include? Be sure to mention if there's a geographic, cultural, or historical boundary to the book. Is the book of specific interest to African Americans? To survivors of World War II? Is it U.S.-focused or global? Don't assume that your title makes your angle obvious. Is *Travels to the Southeast* about Asia or Atlanta?

For a good narrative nonfiction query, see **Example 3.10** (pg. 116).

Cookbooks

Think you've got a new idea for a cookbook? Good, you're going to need a fresh approach. There are a limited number of publishers that print cookbooks and an endless number of cooks who think they deserve their own.

Because of this, a cookbook query letter will need to immediately catch the acquisitions editor's attention with a unique concept and self-explanatory title. Unlike other books, you probably won't be opening with an excerpt (at least, not a recipe). Also unlike other books, your credentials—as a writer or chef—may not play as strong a role. That's because (A) cookbooks tend to have much less writing than other genres, relying more on the recipes; and (B) a stay-at-home mom of six boys might have just as much to share about cooking as a gourmet chef at a five-star restaurant (the difference is all about market positioning).

So what would make an opening paragraph unique enough to spur an editor's interest in your cookbook? If it's:

- The first of its kind
- An updated version of an old concept
- A new twist on a "been-there, done-that" cookbook

Here are a few examples of hooks that could work:

1. An Olympic paraplegic shares his tips for cooking healthy and maneuvering around a traditional kitchen in *Cooking on Wheels*.
2. A bald BBQ fanatic puts a spin on Rhonda Levitch's *Cooking for Blondes* with his book *Barbecue for Bald Men* (at least there's never any hair in the food!).
3. A small-town yoga instructor combines the best of both worlds using breath work and still poses in *Burning Calories (Not Meals!) While You Cook*.

For an example of a good cookbook query, see **Example 3.11** (pg. 118).

Children's books

Everyone thinks they can write a children's book, and it may be the genre that more people try than any other simply because of the low word count needed to complete a book. This may be the reason the genre is so competitive—complete saturation from every wannabe author with a computer. Whatever the cause, breaking into children's books is difficult, so you'll need to be armed with a great query just to get your book read.

First you should know that not all children's book publishers are alike. What they print varies by reader age, fiction vs. nonfiction, picture vs. chapter books, educational vs. entertainment, and word count. This means your query will need to be even more detailed than if you were submitting, say, an adult mass-market romance novel, which would fall within specific parameters in terms of word count, target reader, and format. Here are the basics of what you'll need to cover in your children's book query letter, above and beyond the breakdown provided at the beginning of this chapter:

EXAMPLE 3.10   GOOD NARRATIVE NONFICTION BOOK QUERY

July 16, 2008
Doris Papileau
The Right Agency
222 Looney Loop
Ragland, AL 35131

Dear Ms. Papileau,

It's August 1986 in Ragland, Alabama, and at any given moment, fourteen-year-old "Disco Mike" has three things on his mind: girls, food, and music. Armed with an old, duct-taped boom box the size of a suitcase, he and his friends spend their days on the corner break-dancing to Michael Jackson's *Thriller* and waving to anyone they know. Which, in a town of a couple hundred black people—most of whom are related—is everyone. Sometimes they shoot hoops at the park, swim in the river, or leaf through the Sears catalog picking out clothes their single mothers can't afford to buy them. But mostly, they dance.

For a boy who has to share a room with five brothers, eat kidney bean sandwiches, and endure a blistering summer without electricity, Disco Mike is a pretty happy teen. So when his mother announces she's sending him to live with his father and white stepmother in Paradise, Iowa, Mike is anything but happy. For starters, the town is all white. Plus, he's starting high school this year. Who starts high school without any friends? Worst of all, everyone knows white people can't dance. Or play basketball.

But when Mike discovers he can be a star athlete, a magnet to the rebellious (and uninhibited) preacher's daughter, and the recipient of some ridiculous affirmative action in a town that's too politically correct for its own good, Paradise lives up to its name.

TALKING WHITE is a humorous real-life account of "Disco" Mike Carter's transformational summer. Although the 80,000-word narrative nonfiction book is written from a teen's perspective, the subjects of sex, community, love, poverty, friendship, racism (and "reverse" racism) are anything but juvenile. Despite the "heavy" topics, the book is written in a refreshingly light and funny tone that highlights the carefree decade that brought us Madonna, Pac-Man, Rubik's Cube, the jheri curl, and the pastels of the Miami Vice wardrobe. As Disco Mike learns, the combination of the latter two can quickly turn heads in small-town Iowa.

My published pieces span some one hundred short stories and essays in a wide variety of local, regional, and national publications, including *Utne Reader*, *Berkeley Fiction Review*, and *Beloit Fiction Journal*. I would be happy to send you the completed manuscript upon request.

Thank you for your time.

Sincerely,

Barbara Gordon
(address, phone, e-mail)

- Word count
- Age level (picture books are for preschool to eight-year-olds; "little books" or "first chapter books" are used by kindergarten and first-grade teachers to help emergent readers; "young readers" are five- to eight-year-olds; "middle readers" are nine- to eleven-year-olds; "young adult" or YA books are age twelve and up)
- Fiction or nonfiction
- Book title and one-paragraph synopsis
- Published clips
- A request to send the completed manuscript or proposal (for longer nonfiction)

Here's a sample of a nonfiction children's book summary:

> What kid doesn't fantasize about being stranded on a desert island with her friends? *Desert Island Survival for Kids* is a fun, fact-filled book for middle readers that introduces inquisitive young minds to fascinating tidbits on everything from what bugs are safe to eat and telling time with a homemade sundial, to identifying snakes and how to start a fire when you don't have matches.
>
> The book would have some similarities to David Borgenicht and Robin Epstein's *The Worst-Case Scenario Survival Handbook: Junior Edition*, but would be more specific to real outdoor survival and animal identification than theirs, which covers everyday topics like bullies, braces, chores, and school dances. The popularity of *Flight 29 Down*, a TV show about kids exploring an island, may be a good indicator that there is interest in this topic.

This nonfiction book summary requires quite a bit more detail than would a children's fiction book because there is no book excerpt. And because a similar book has been done, the author needs to identify it but then point out the differences. Mentioning the popularity of the TV show also helps demonstrate that there's a strong interest in this topic.

Be sure to read the writer's guidelines for each publisher. Some don't require queries at all and most have strict word counts.

The annual *Children's Writer's & Illustrator's Market* is your best resource for finding publishers by the genre, subgenre, and reader age they represent. The condensed writer's guidelines also offer glimpses into the

EXAMPLE 3.11 GOOD COOKBOOK QUERY

July 17, 2008

Harry Evans
The Evans-Herald Agency
111 Deal Dr.
New York, NY 10001

Dear Mr. Evans,

As the owner of The Kids' Fondue Bar, I'm always getting requests from parents to create my own cookbook. But now that we've begun franchising across the United States, I think it only makes sense to compile my two hundred best recipes to sell to an ever-growing audience. **THE KIDS' FONDUE BAR'S TAKE-HOME COOKBOOK** is just awaiting a publisher.

From Green Gouda Gouda and Monster Muenster Macaroni Dip to Cinderella's Pumpkin Poundcake, our ever-rotating do-it-yourself menu is anything but bland. We're constantly receiving testimonials (which I'm sure I can procure for the book) from parents who claim their once-finicky eater is now begging for broccoli and requesting radishes thanks to the fun and variety they encounter at The Kids' Fondue Bar.

My sister-in-law is a professional photographer and could supply some samples to accompany a full proposal, which I could supply upon request.

Thank you for your time.

Best regards,

Chef Jordan Smiley
(address, phone, e-mail)

---

acquisitions editors' minds, allowing you to avoid wasting time (yours and theirs) and helping you to craft a great query letter. Here are some interesting examples of advice from children's book editors:

- Jewish Lights Publishing: "Explain in your cover letter why you're submitting your project to us in particular. (Make sure you know what we publish.)"
- Charlesbridge: Wants "books that have humor and are factually correct."
- Greene Bark Press: "As a guide for future publications do not look to our older backlist."

- Lobster Press: "Do not send manuscripts or samples registered mail or with fancy envelopes or bows and ribbons."

Although market guides are very helpful, always review guidelines from the publishing house's Web site, request them by e-mail, or send an SASE. While market guides generally only cover a paragraph or two of basic information, detailed writer's guidelines can give you a much more specific look into the publisher's needs, preferences, and previous books.

NONFICTION BOOK QUERY FAQS

WHAT SHOULD I SAY IN THE BOOK PROPOSAL COVER LETTER?

For agents and acquisitions editors who allow you to skip the query process, opting instead to send a book proposal right up front, your cover letter will have to work as a query letter. This means that in order to get them to even *read* your book proposal, you'll have to use the cover letter to entice them to read the rest of the pages in your packet. Just refer to the rules for a good book query (less the paragraph about "Can I send you a proposal?").

In most cases, however, you'll be sending in your proposal based on the agent or editor's request. This means that your cover letter can be quite simple. There are a few things it should always include, such as a thank-you for agreeing to review the proposal, a brief reminder of the book's title, topic and market, and a request for representation (agent) or publication (editor). If you've written more of the book than is being represented by the sample chapters, say so. (It's less of a risk to publishers if a first-time author has completed a large percentage of the manuscript up front.)

Your cover letter should be no more than one page and should include all your contact information. See **Example 3.12** (pg. 120) for a typical cover letter for a book proposal.

CAN I GET FANCY WITH FORMATTING IN A BOOK PROPOSAL?

No. Truth be told, you don't want to. That's because doing so will likely earn you an automatic rejection.

Spend your energy making your words and ideas stand out from the slush pile—not the format. Don't try to make your proposal look like a completed

EXAMPLE 3.12   GOOD BOOK PROPOSAL COVER LETTER

August 19, 2007

Olivia Perea
The Emile Agency
543 Writer Blvd.
New York, NY 10001

Dear Ms. Perea,

Thank you for requesting my book proposal for **LOVE IN THE PRODUCE AISLE: THE 101 BEST PLACES TO MEET MR. RIGHT**.

As per my initial e-query on January 10, the book is based on my sixteen years as a professional matchmaker and includes advice for women who are ready to settle down but can't stomach the thought of another night at the singles' clubs.

Enclosed for your review is a forty-page proposal, including information about the number of single women in the United States (between the ages of twenty-one and fifty-five) who could benefit from this book. Please note that although I have only included one sample chapter (as per your writer's guidelines), more than half of the book is written.

Thank you again for agreeing to review my proposal. I hope that you will consider publishing **LOVE IN THE PRODUCE AISLE** with your 2009 line of relationship books.

Sincerely,

Joan Knightly
(address/phone/e-mail)

Encl: forty-page book proposal

book. Skip the mock cover, professional binding, or specially formatted layout. Agents and editors want professional-looking documents that are clean and easy to read. This means:

- Using a size 12 font, preferably Times New Roman
- Only printing on one side of the (plain white) page
- Justifying or left-justifying your text
- Including the page number, as well as your last name and (shortened) book title on each page

- Starting each element of the proposal (outline, table of contents, competition) on a new page

With so many books and Web sites available on the topic of book proposals, there's really no reason to submit a piece that uses unprofessional formatting. While your concept and writing can be profound, humorous, interesting, or intricate, the layout of your book proposal should be none of the above.

WILL I SEND THE SAME BOOK PROPOSAL TO AN AGENT AND AN EDITOR?

Essentially, yes. Obviously, the cover letter will change because you're now seeking publication, not representation. Also, don't be surprised if your agent makes recommendations to improve your proposal before sending it to a publisher.

Good agents often know what certain acquisitions editors' likes and dislikes are, what they might be working on in terms of a new line, or which genres are already saturated. A few simple tweaks can make the difference between seeing your book in print and heading back to the drawing board. It's OK to question—or even dispute—an agent's recommendations, but remember, she's much more in the know about the publishing world than you are.

It's also important to remember that you don't have to accept representation from any agent who offers it. Granted, it's difficult to pass up an opportunity when you're a first-time author and afraid no one else will bite. But if you and your agent don't mesh, find another one. A good agent can be a lifelong partner in the publishing world, so start off on the right foot.

CAN I SEND A PROPOSAL BY E-MAIL?

This one depends on the writer's guidelines. Some specifically state that you need to mail your proposal, while others will let you send it in by e-mail as an attached Microsoft Word document. But be forewarned: Some spam filters are set on high alert, snagging unknown e-mails—especially those with attachments. You might want to send a separate e-mail (with no attachment) indicating that you've e-mailed the proposal so they know to check their spam inbox.

CHAPTER 4

NOVEL QUERIES

For the same reason completed magazine articles require queries, so do novels. While it seems like completed manuscripts should speak for themselves, busy publishing houses and their staffs don't have time to slog through 80,000-word novels that may or may not contain a good story, great writing, and a topic of interest to readers.

Unless doing so is specifically stated in the writer's guidelines, skipping the query letter is not recommended. No matter how great you think your manuscript is (and it may be!), you could be shooting down your chance of publication by not following proper protocol. Sending a query is going to show that you're a professional, that you can follow directions (guidelines), and that you can write concisely. Your query is your first handshake with an acquisitions editor (or agent) and your first chance to make a good enough impression that he'll want to read your novel.

UNDERSTANDING THE FICTION QUERY

Your one-page query will contain some components similar to those found in a nonfiction query: a greeting to the correct editor or agent; the tentative title of your book, along with the genre and word count ("*Kiss & Tell*, my contemporary romance complete at 80,000 words ..."); the pitch or enticing summary of your book (generally three to five sentences long); information about your qualifications (if relevant); why you chose that editor or agent; a request for publication or representation; and your complete contact information.

As with nonfiction, you may or may not also need to mention:

- A strong current interest among readers on your topic or genre (e.g., "With the problem of global warming occupying more media attention, a story about a woman hell-bent on killing the CEOs of corporations that pollute may resonate with eco-conscious readers and generate some interesting publicity.")

- Any research you did for the book (e.g., "I lived with the Amish for six months to increase my chances of getting an accurate portrayal.")

- Any specific books on your topic or narrowed genre that have done well recently (e.g., "Thanks to Anne Rice's Lestat series, paranormal romance is now the second most popular subgenre, according to a recent Romance Writers of America reader survey.")

For examples of good novel query letters that landed book deals, see **Examples 4.1 (pg. 124)** and 4.2 (pgs. 126–127).

Remember, your query needs to be as compelling, interesting, and well written as your novel —just in a more concise manner. It's not uncommon for new writers to rush through a query after spending months (or years) completing a 90,000-word manuscript, only to find that no one will even request to *read* the completed novel (or parts of it). Take the time to write a great query. Don't shortchange yourself after putting in so much sweat and tears, or you'll never see your book in print.

The Credentials Question

There's good news and bad news about selling a novel and they're pretty much the same: The writing—not your credentials—will be what gets you the sale. The bad news is, this means you'll have to complete and polish the entire manuscript (no, 95 percent finished is not enough) to get a book deal. The good news is, as long as your writing is fantastic, it matters less whether you've had anything published in the past. Regardless, you should include a paragraph or so about your credentials (if you have them), and the more

EXAMPLE 4.1   GOOD NOVEL QUERY #1 (FANTASY)

January 5, 2007

John Helfers
Five Star Publishing
P.O. Box 8296
Green Bay, WI 54308

Dear Mr. Helfers,

Carnival is a part-time fortune-teller and occult troubleshooter and a full-time pain in the neck. Do you have a banshee that needs a tonsillectomy? Call Carnival. Do you need to give the yo-ho-heave-ho to some troublesome pirate-ghosts? Call Carnival. What about that mummy that thinks she's a rap artist? Call Carnival.

Carnival is a gypsy. His Poppa calls him a poshrat. That's Rom for half-blood. Carnival never listened to his Poppa when his Poppa was alive but these days he doesn't have much of a choice. It serves him right for sticking his Poppa so close to his heart. What a way to treat a dead relative, but that's Carnival for you. A real spontaneous kind of guy. Like when he gives that succubus a permanent case of lockjaw. Or when he invites a full-grown demon into the tub for a scrub-a-dub. Or when he falls in love with a vampire. Talk about your pain in the neck.

GYPSY BLOOD is an 85,000-word fast-paced, funny, and terrifying novel like nothing you've ever read before. The whole thing rolls like an avalanche of skateboards, building to a climactic battle royale between Carnival, his two-timing vampire lover, a she-demon with a mother complex, a social-climbing blood god, the collective spirit of the city and a mercenary mariachi band in a rickshaw.

That's right, I said a rickshaw.

I have been writing short genre fiction for over twenty years. My work has sold to such genre markets and magazines as *Horror Show, Cemetery Dance, Flesh and Blood, Horror Garage, Hot Blood XIII,* Tor's *The Year's Best Horror XIX,* and many others. **GYPSY BLOOD** is my first full-length novel. The main character, Carnival, is drawn a lot from my life as a full-time professional palm and Tarot reader. The novel is a standalone adventure that can easily be converted into a long-running series. I have already begun work on the second novel in the series, concerning Carnival's misadventures with a Humvee-driving werewolf.

That's right, werewolves drive Humvees.

Yours in storytelling,

Steve Vernon
(address/phone/e-mail)

[Note: *Gypsy Blood* sold to Five Star Publishing in July 2008.]

---

relevant, the better. For a novel, relevant information might include published short stories (to indicate you can write fiction), statewide or national writing awards or nominations (especially for fiction), serving as a judge in a fiction contest, or teaching experience in English or creative writing. See **Example 4.3** (pg. 128) for a novel query mentioning published short stories or judging fiction contests.

Another, and perhaps even more valuable, approach would be to mention your experience related to the topic of the novel. Here are a few examples:

- "As a private investigator for fifteen years, I like to think I have a slight advantage over other crime novelists..."
- "My twenty years as a prison therapist has certainly made me privy to gruesome stories—some of which I could barely stomach—until I channeled my experiences into the characters of my novel."
- "A runaway by fifteen, I know firsthand what it's like to live on the streets—always looking over your shoulder in fear."
- "Who better to write a novel about a serial divorcee than a woman who has been down the aisle five times? It was hardly a stretch to get inside the head of my main character. The tougher part was getting her out of mine."
- "When I was in college, I won a fortune at the blackjack table at the Mirage in Vegas. This was years before 'counting cards' would get you banned at a casino, and if the rules hadn't changed, I might have dropped out of Harvard to earn my living as a cheater."

The point is to use your life experience to demonstrate that you are the best person for the job of writing your novel. See **Example 4.4** (pg. 130) for a novel query mentioning life experience.

COMMON NOVEL QUERY MISTAKES

Now that you've looked at several successful query letters, let's take a look at what you *don't* want to include in your query. *Hint:* It's basically anything that shows you're inexperienced, boring, or incapable of good writing. This could include any of the following:

EXAMPLE 4.2   GOOD NOVEL QUERY #2
                       (FEMALE FANTASY DETECTIVE)

February 27, 2007

Kristin Nelson
Nelson Literary Agency
1732 Wazee Street, Suite 207
Denver, CO 80202

Dear Ms. Nelson,

I read on Publishers Marketplace that you're interested in female-oriented fantasy. I think that **THIEF OF SOULS**, the first novel in my fantasy detective series, might interest you.

What if you suddenly have a largely unknown, potentially unlimited power? What if that power just might eat your soul for breakfast, lunch, and dinner? What if every magical mobster and sicko sorcerer in town wants that power? And what if you can't get rid of it?

That's Raine Benares's problem. She's a Seeker—a finder of things lost and people missing. Most of what she's hired to find doesn't get lost by itself. It has help. Dependable help. Help she can depend on to use blades or bolts or magical means to keep what they went to all the trouble to get. When her sometime partner steals an amulet from a local necromancer, Raine ends up with the amulet and the trouble that's hot on its heels. What looks like a plain silver disk turns out to be a lodestone to an ancient soul-stealing stone, a stone that seemingly every magical mobster in the city wants—as well as a few heavy-hitters from out-of-town: goblins of the Khrynsani Order, their sadistic high priest, Guardians of the Conclave of Sorcerers, the goblin king and his renegade brother, and an elven spellsinger of dubious motives. People Raine doesn't want to have notice her, let alone have to outrun or outwit. She likes attention as much as the next girl, but this is the kind she can do without.

Then there's what the amulet is doing to her. New and improved magical abilities sound good in theory, but Raine thinks her soul is a little much to pay for resume enhancement. And when she tries to take the amulet off, the amulet tries to take her out. Soon Raine starts to wonder if her spells, steel, and street smarts will keep her alive long enough to find a way to get rid of the amulet before it, or anyone else, gets rid of her. And the worst part? She isn't even getting paid.

It's enough to make a girl consider a career change.

THIEF OF SOULS is my first novel. I'm an editor at an advertising agency, with prior experience in corporate communications and marketing.

I'd be glad to send you my complete manuscript for your review. Thank you for your time and consideration, and I look forward to hearing from you soon.

Regards,

Lisa Shearin
(address/phone/e-mail)

[Note: This book garnered the agent and sold to Ace.
The title was changed to *Magic Lost, Trouble Found.*]

- Addressing the wrong editor or agent or addressing them incorrectly (e.g., "Dear Mr. Smith" when Chris Smith is actually a woman) or generically (e.g., "Dear Editor"). This just shows you didn't take the time to research your audience, which communicates that you don't care enough about this editor or agent to treat her with respect. Make each editor or agent feel like she was your first choice.

- Spelling or grammatical errors. This is a no-brainer. In the minds of editors and agents, sloppy query = sloppy manuscript. No one in the industry has time for sloppiness, and your competition is too stiff to take such a cavalier approach to your query presentation. You're a professional writer now; act like one!

- Talking about how your friends and family love your novel and have been encouraging you to get it published. Even if it's true, saying so looks unprofessional and frankly, there's no guarantee that your family knows good writing when they see it. (Besides, they could be lying so as not to hurt your feelings. That's what friends and family do. Don't ask them. They will lie. Remember how your cousin said he'd pay you back that fifty dollars? Lie!) Let the work speak for itself.

- Discussing money, contracts, or TV and movie deals. You may think that discussing money and copyrights up front in the query will make you seem like a savvy businessperson, but instead it looks amateurish and pushy. The query is the place to worry about selling your story; you and your editor or agent will negotiate the terms once the manuscript is accepted. Your only job is to write a great query.

EXAMPLE 4.3   GOOD QUERY SHOWING PUBLISHED SHORT STORIES

February 27, 2007

Kristin Nelson
Nelson Literary Agency
1732 Wazee Street, Suite 207
Denver, CO 80202

Dear Ms. Nelson,

I'm a friend of the hilarious and fun Becky Motew, and she suggested I contact you about my novel, **REAL LIFE AND LIARS**. Here's a brief description.

As a wilted flower child, Mira Zielinski has never been one to follow orders. Not from her husband, not from her boss—not even from her oncologist. Mira has her own idea about handling her newly diagnosed breast cancer, and it does not involve hopping up on the operating table. Her grown children will no doubt object—when she gets around to telling them.

As they come home for the big anniversary party, her kids harbor some secret trials. Ivan's lifelong desire to be a songwriter is withering on the vine after years of futility, and youngest child Irina will walk in the door with a surprise groom, though she's already looking for the escape hatch in her shiny new marriage. As for Katya—let's just say that it would be a relief if her husband's big secret were just the affair she suspects. As these secrets come to light, will they shake Mira's resolve?

I'd love to send part or all of **REAL LIFE AND LIARS**, complete at 83,000 words. I'm a freelance journalist and published short story writer, plus I'm the co-editor for fiction at the e-zine *Literary Mama*, named one of *Forbes*'s "Best of the Web." My short story credits include *Cimarron Review*, *Net Author's E2K*, and *Espresso Fiction*. I served as a judge for the 2007 Carrie McCray Literary Awards in the short fiction category.

Besides your blog and Becky's recommendation, I'm also familiar with you as a member of Backspace, where I post (not as frequently as I'd like) as simply "Kris." I'll paste my opening few pages below. Thanks for your time and consideration.

Sincerely,

Kristina Ringstrom
(address/phone/e-mail)

[Note: This book landed the agent and sold to HarperCollins. The title was changed to *All Happy Families*.]

- **Threatening to take your book elsewhere.** Threats or demands scream "amateur" and "impossible to work with" and are a quick and effective way to get your manuscript rejected. Editors and agents are busy people with stacks of queries and manuscripts to read; if you think you can do better elsewhere and say so, the response will always be, "Go right ahead." No one wants to work with a diva.

- **Not giving enough information about your book.** Agents and editors can't make a decision about whether to request your manuscript (or parts of it) unless they fully understand its topic/voice/genre. Give them enough information to show them you know what types of material they typically represent and that your book fits that criteria.

- **Mentioning that the manuscript is not yet complete.** Don't pitch any piece of fiction that's not complete and ready to be considered for publication. No one can evaluate a novel that's incomplete! If you don't love your novel the way it is, work on it until you do. Agents want to be able to shop material immediately; editors want to be able to publish (after editing!) immediately.

- **Comparing its *quality* (not subject/style/readership) to a famous author.** If you're a great writer, your work will speak for itself. Telling someone you're as great a writer as Eckhart Tolle will be a red flag that you're (A) annoyingly conceited; and (B) not. Besides, there's already an Eckhart Tolle in this industry. Build a name for yourself.

- **Telling a publisher that you (A) couldn't get an agent to represent you; (B) fired every agent that agreed to represent you; or (C) had an agent who couldn't sell it so you're trying on your own.** It's really a toss-up as to which of these is the fastest way to send a publisher running for the hills. If an agent wouldn't represent you or couldn't sell your manuscript, chances are it's because your manuscript wasn't very good. If you managed to burn through several agents before deciding to represent yourself, you're likely giving off a "no wire hangers!" vibe. Unless there's a valid reason for firing your agents ("Both agents said they only had time to shop my manuscript to two publishing houses"), you may not want to bring that up.

EXAMPLE 4.4   GOOD QUERY SHOWING LIFE EXPERIENCE

February 27, 2007

Kristin Nelson
Nelson Literary Agency
1732 Wazee Street, Suite 207
Denver, CO 80202

Dear Ms. Nelson,

I must admit I hate Asian stereotypes. You know the ones. Good at math. Hardworking. We all look alike. Come to think of it, that last one might hold water. After all, my father once wore a button that read "I am Chinese" while growing up in Seattle's Chinatown during WWII. It was the only thing that separated him from the Japanese, at least in the eyes of his Caucasian neighbors.

Sad, but true. Which is probably why my novel has a little to do with that particular piece of history.

Anyway, the working title is **THE PANAMA HOTEL**, and when people ask me what the heck it's all about I usually tell them this:

"It's the story of the Japanese internment in Seattle, seen through the eyes of a twelve-year-old Chinese boy who is sent to an all-white private school, where he falls in love with a twelve-year-old Japanese girl."

But it's more complicated than that. It's a bittersweet tale about racism, commitment, and enduring hope—a noble romantic journey set in 1942, and later in 1986 when the belongings of thirty-seven Japanese families were discovered in the basement of a condemned hotel.

This historical novel is based on my *Glimmer Train* story, "I Am Chinese," which was a Top 25 Finalist in their Fall 2006 Short-Story Competition for New Writers. An excerpt was also published in the *Picolata Review*.

Think Amy Tan, but with a sweeter aftertaste.

Thank you for your consideration and time,

Jamie Ford
www.jamieford.com
(address/phone/e-mail)

[Note: This query landed the agent. The author and agent changed the title to *Hotel on the Corner of Bitter and Sweet* and sold the novel to Ballantine.]

- **Soliciting a manuscript idea that doesn't fit the agent/editor's subject representation, word count, or format.** Publishers have been around for decades (the houses, not the people). You're new to the industry. Don't irritate an editor (or agent, for that matter) by trying to convince him that he should suddenly start representing 120,000-word historical romances because yours is so great. It's a waste of everyone's time—including yours.

- **Soliciting a manuscript idea that has been done to death or covered very recently.** Check your local bookstore or Amazon.com to look for similar books. Don't assume that your deaf (done), Amish (done), lesbian (done), or wheelchair-bound (done) private investigator offers a fresh take on the mystery genre. Relying on one particular characteristic or even a blended genre (paranormal historic gay romance, anyone?) can be a mistake if you don't do your research.

- **Offering to rewrite before the person has even reviewed your manuscript.** (Rewrites are to be expected—even among the most prolific and experienced authors.) The only time you should offer to rewrite in relation to your query is if an agent asks you to "tweak" your query before she begins submitting it to publishers.

- **Dropping names (unless you have been specifically referred by someone).** No one needs to know who you know until it's time to market your book.

- **Going on at length about irrelevant details ("I had to do dishes for a month just to get my wife to type up my manuscript because I'm such a slow typist").** You've only got one page for your query. Use it wisely to share information that is pertinent to your book.

- **Submitting a query letter that is more than one or two pages.** If you ramble on and on in your query, an editor can feel nothing but dread for the state of your manuscript. A query any longer than a tight one or two pages might not get read at all.

- **Ignoring the submissions guidelines ("I know you say to query first, but ...").** Agents and editors post their writer's guidelines for your convenience and their own. Heed their advice and submit exactly as requested to increase your chances of getting representation/publication.

For an example of what *not* to do in a novel query, see **Example 4.5.**

COMPONENTS OF A NOVEL SYNOPSIS

The most significant difference between novel and nonfiction query letters is that, in some cases, your novel query will include (or be accompanied by) a synopsis. This is a more detailed summary of your book than appears in your query letter. If your query is your handshake (and smile, posture, and business attire), think of your synopsis as your first "conversation."

Ready to condense your 350-page novel down to a few pages? Good, because that's the definition of a synopsis.

Unlike the summarizing "pitch" paragraph in your novel query letter, a synopsis does more than tease; it tells the entire story of your book. Your synopsis will explain your entire novel from cover to cover—*including the ending.* You'll be describing characters, settings, major events, and plot twists, narrating the developments from start to finish.

Write in third person and use the present tense ("Clara finds her husband under the table").

Be cautious not to present a bare-bones outline (unless one is specifically requested), which may scare the publisher into thinking you can't write. Your synopsis should showcase your writing skills, voice, tone, and style as a reflection of your novel—not an aside to it.

As for what to actually include, you'll need to parallel your synopsis to your novel in terms of chronologically revealing things like the motivations, goals, and internal and external conflicts for lead characters, complicating events and emotions, life lessons learned, good/bad turning points, and happy endings.

Novels are typically plot-driven or character-driven. But even when a book is character-driven, you'll want to avoid putting too much emphasis on the characters' personal details. Avoid the temptation to describe your characters in any form of dating classified ad. Instead, find creative ways to introduce them in the synopsis, perhaps excerpting their entrance (or description) straight from the book. Compare the following examples.

EXAMPLE 4.5   BAD NOVEL QUERY LETTER

January 6, 2007

Acquisitions Editor **Ⓐ**
Randam House **Ⓑ**
1745 Broadway
New York, NY 10019

Dear Editor:

I know you typically only accept submissions from agents, but **Ⓒ** I have a book that might change your mind. **Ⓓ**

My dream has always been to be published by Randam House **Ⓔ** (I read a lot of your stuff growing up) and my book is now ready for the world. **Ⓕ**

You may want to stop what you're doing **Ⓖ** to read the enclosed book. **Ⓗ** It's got sex, drugs and rock 'n roll **Ⓘ** and everyone who has read it so far said they can see it being a bestseller **Ⓙ**.

I would love to talk to you about my idea for a miniseries **Ⓚ** based on the book, and maybe even a movie.

I'll call you next week if you don't call me first! **Ⓛ**

Ima Fullamyself
Phone only

WHAT'S WRONG: EDITOR'S COMMENTS

Ⓐ Thanks for taking the time to get my name. **Ⓑ** She couldn't even spell "Random" right. **Ⓒ** Here comes the "but"... This is exactly why we only accept submissions from agents! **Ⓓ** I highly doubt it. **Ⓔ** She's telling me why she wants to be published with us (we're perhaps the best-known name in publishing), but not why she's a match for us. **Ⓕ** Oh good. Now the world can exhale. **Ⓖ** You mean stop rolling my eyes? **Ⓗ** She sent the entire manuscript, even though our guidelines specifically say not to. **Ⓘ** This is cliché. I need a real description of what the novel is about. **Ⓙ** She's already talking about it being a bestseller? **Ⓚ** This is beyond ridiculous. **Ⓛ** Not only will I not call her, but I won't take her call.

Unsuccessful character description in a synopsis: Nanette is a tall, blond, thirty-six-year-old who used to model when she was younger. Now she's got three kids and is a "soccer mom" in the suburbs.

Good character description in a synopsis: Nanette knew the other moms well enough to sit with them on the bleachers, and well enough to know they talked about her when she missed a game. They resented her leftover good looks, the scent of her Lancôme perfume, and her ability to turn the coach's eye with a flash of her veneers. It wasn't that Nanette hated her life; on the contrary. She loved her husband and kids, but her bedside table of back issues of *Glamour* was a sad reminder of a heyday that no amount of plastic surgery could raise from the dead.

It's important to avoid going into too much detail about anything in particular—especially in a shorter synopsis. (The length of a synopsis can vary greatly—from one page to thirty pages. You'll have to read the agent or publisher's guidelines to get specifics for each submission.) While a thirty-page synopsis will allow for a bit more description, save the bulk of your adjectives for your actual novel. Skip elements like descriptive settings, physical appearances of characters (unless it's relevant—like the burn scars and mask from *The Phantom of the Opera*), and backstory unless they are absolutely crucial to explain what's going on. Remember: A synopsis should read more like a movie trailer than a poem.

A synopsis is also a great way to make sure you've got a strong plot *before* you write your book. It will help you create an outline of sorts and find holes in your plan. A quick read of your synopsis should immediately let the publisher know if your novel is plot-driven or character-driven. (This is your plot engine—what "drives" the story.) Examples of the five main plot-driven themes include:

- Man vs. man: e.g., anything James Bond
- Man vs. nature: e.g., *Jaws*
- Man vs. supernatural (or man's creation): e.g., *Frankenstein*
- Man vs. himself: e.g., *A Beautiful Mind*
- (Wo)Man vs. society: e.g., *Wuthering Heights*

If your plot isn't easily identified in your synopsis, go back to the drawing board. But before you do that, see **Example 4.6** (136–137) for a bad synopsis.

GENRE CONSIDERATIONS FOR THE NOVEL QUERY

Not all queries are created equal. Can you imagine reading a book flap for a crime novel that didn't mention the crime? Or a thriller that didn't build up suspense in its opening paragraphs? What about a romance novel that never mentioned the conflict that kept the two main characters from immediately living happily every after? There are some special things to consider when creating a query for a certain genre. If you write a great query, the agent or editor should know under what genre your manuscript will fall almost *immediately*.

Romance

When selling a romance, be sure your pitch description and synopsis include the "black moment." This is the point in the book when the hero and heroine believe their chance at happiness is gone. If your black moment isn't convincing to the publisher, your novel will likely come across as boring or emotionally unappealing. A bland black moment will make it hard to create a convincing happy ending because the publisher (and reader) won't have much invested in what happens to the characters.

Generally, this conflict happens about three-quarters to four-fifths of the way through the novel and is based on the lead characters' inability or unwillingness to resolve the issues that keep them apart. Sometimes, the less obvious you can make the resolution (to the characters or the reader), the better. You certainly don't want a reader yelling, "Why doesn't she just tell him that it was her *sister* he saw kissing Count VonSchnuzel?!" only to have the heroine do just that as a resolution in the final chapter.

The black moment can be based on an internal (e.g., one or both parties' reluctance to marry) or external conflict (e.g., physical distance between the lovers' hometowns).

Your synopsis will require you not only to present the black moment, but also to resolve it (the happy ending). Like the conflict that keeps them

EXAMPLE 4.6   BAD NOVEL SYNOPSIS

THE BUTLER DID IT Ⓐ

SCENE 1: Ⓑ The book opens with 10 dinner guests standing around in a big mansion trying to figure out who killed the woman on the floor in the living room. Ⓒ The woman, Mrs. Delacourte, was a rich socialite with four children, (two men and two women), who have all brought their spouses. The remaining two dinner guests are Mr. Delacourte and Mrs. Delacourte's attorney, Jonathan Stone, who was invited to the party to announce that Mrs. Delacourte had decided to change her will because she was sick of her family fighting over money. Mrs. Delacourte was going to ask each member of the family to tell her their favorite charity when the big storm hit and the lights went out. Ⓓ When the lights came on, that's when they found her body with a knife in her back.

SCENE 2: The police investigator arrives and starts to question everyone, including the maid and butler. He quickly learns that everyone had a motive, because no one wanted to be cut out of the will. Even the long-time maid and butler expected to get something, so they're suspects as well. The guests retire to their rooms after they're questioned, and start to discuss their own theories with their spouses about who killed Mrs. Delacourte. Surprisingly, no one seems that sad, except the maid. Ⓔ The investigator begins finding clues, like the fact that the killer was left-handed, though all of Mrs. Delacourte's children are right-handed. Also, Mrs. Delacourte's body was moved after she was stabbed (there's a blood trail on the carpet) and Mr. Delacourte is too old and weak to move the body. The lawyer had no motivation since he didn't stand to win—or lose—any money. That leaves the maid and butler, but the maid seems genuinely upset. Ⓕ

SCENE 3: The investigator sits the family down and presents all the clues. He explains to them that the butler killed Mrs. Delacourte. Ⓖ As he makes the announcement, the butler takes off on foot and a pursuit ensues. The entire family runs after him and finally one of the sons tackles him. But why did he kill her? The family wants to know. And if you do to, you'll have to request the book! Ⓗ

WHAT'S WRONG: EDITOR'S COMMENTS

(A) This title is already taken by a 2004 novel. The author couldn't be bothered to even do a quick search on Amazon. **(B)** This "scene" set-up is starting to read more like a play. A bad play. **(C)** This is about as cliché as "a dark and stormy night," which I fear is also right around the corner. **(D)** Did I call this one or what? **(E)** I have yet to see anything about character description, motivation, a strong moving timeline, or turning points, etc. **(F)** This is almost comical. It's cliché enough that the butler did it, but would someone seriously tell who the murderer was in the title of their book? **(G)** Why am I still reading???? **(H)** First of all, I couldn't care less why the butler did it. Secondly, a synopsis should reveal the ending of the book—among all the other plot twists, subplots, internal and external conflicts, etc., of which I see none. And finally, I would never request to read this book because the synopsis (if you can call it that) reads like a round of "Clue." Yes, the butler did it with the knife in the dining room. Now can we put the box away?

apart, the resolution can be due to internal (e.g., the heroine learns that the hero secretly did something to protect her when she thought he didn't love her anymore) or external (e.g., the hero kills the villain who has kept them apart). In either case, the characters need to come to a point of realization in which they admit that their love is more important than any problems they face individually or as a couple. And you need to explain this in your synopsis. Remember, everyone—including publishers—loves a happy ending.

To review a good romance novel synopsis that lead to a book deal with Harlequin, see **Example 4.7** (pgs. 140–141).

Literary

The term *literary fiction* is a relatively new category in book publishing, earning its own classification sometime in the late 1960s when more "experimental" forms of writing like narrative short stories and lengthier comic books (now called *graphic novels*) were popular. Today, this classification is often used to describe anything that falls outside prescribed genre conventions. It's sometimes referred to as "highbrow fiction," as it is particularly common to find book excerpts, short stories, and reviews of literary fiction in literary magazines, anthologies, and publications put out by well-respected universities.

Until recently, literary fiction wasn't known for crossing over well to a mainstream (commercial) readership. But in recent years, many literary novels have found their way onto best-seller lists, including Ian McEwan's *Atonement*, Khaled Hosseini's *The Kite Runner*, and Margaret Atwood's *The Handmaid's Tale*, all of which were made into movies.

Because literary fiction is such a broad category and an experimental genre (or non-genre), there are fewer guidelines by which a synopsis can follow. Most literary fiction is generally based more on a strong narrative (or characters) than a plot, with an in-depth focus on controversial issues, the human condition, or tragic circumstances. Still, your literary fiction synopsis will likely find you fleshing out some of the components found in genre fiction, including motivations, conflicts, resolutions, discoveries, backstory, and setting. (The synopsis for *Atonement*, for example, would need to open with the setting [1935, England] because it's relevant to the tone, mood, events, and fast-forward ending of the book.)

The motivation of one of the main characters also needs to be revealed early in the synopsis as it's a focal point for future events, conflicts, and resolutions. There are events throughout the book, though it is no doubt the characters that carry the book from cover to cover—and a good synopsis would let the reader know what to expect before he even picked up the manuscript.

Mystery

For centuries, mystery novels were confined to a certain chronological order: crime committed, crime researched, criminal discovered. But modern mysteries are taking new twists and turns—changing voices, timelines, and perspectives at any given moment.

In Sue Grafton's *T Is for Trespass*, for example, the reader is given a unique perspective: the point of view of the heroine in one chapter, and the point of view of the villain in the next.

Likewise, in Alice Sebold's *The Lovely Bones* (often classified as a mystery/thriller), the story is told from the deceased victim's point of view from heaven. As readers, we know early on who the killer is, yet we watch intently as the detectives and family members struggle to find clues to unveil the murderer.

Your job in writing the mystery synopsis is to write a strong plot. You'll need to open with the crime and quickly explain the motivations of the killer and the hero. A good synopsis will disclose motivations, internal and external conflicts, clues, and events through a chronological timeline that reflects that of the book. Remember, the reader (or in this case, the publisher) should always be just one step behind the investigating character when it comes to pursuing leads and discovering clues.

The ending will need to be strong, and you'll need to wrap up your synopsis with no loose ends. If the editor is left asking, "But what about the murder weapon?" or "So she found the knife but how did she tie it to the killer?" you haven't done your job.

One good guideline to help you write your mystery novel synopsis: Write the blurb for your book jacket. Then lengthen it to several pages and tell the ending. Save the cliffhangers and teasers for your book tour publicity.

Thriller/Suspense

The guidelines for a thriller/suspense synopsis are very similar to a mystery in terms of writing a strong plot and opening with a bang, or rather, an impending bang—such as a bomb that is scheduled to go off if the bus slows down (the plot from the 1994 suspense movie *Speed*). Like your book, the synopsis should offer a progressive buildup of suspense, including the roadblocks that your hero comes up against while trying to reach his goal (e.g., saving the passengers, disengaging the bomb, stopping the terrorists, or finding the would-be assassin). There should be at least one climax, although some suspense movies have two or more. (Think about movies in which the killer is shot and everyone is walking away and patting each other on the back. Suddenly, the killer uses his last breath to pull the knife from his chest and try to stab the heroine, only to have the hero shoot him again ... this time, for good. At least until the sequel.)

Speculative

Of all the definitions in the writing world, speculative fiction may cause the most arguments. For the sake of being all-inclusive, I'll use this label to

EXAMPLE 4.7   GOOD ROMANCE NOVEL SYNOPSIS

SAFE IN MY HEART

When the man that Katherine Whitman thought she would someday marry becomes engaged to another woman, Katherine is devastated. The blow is especially harsh because
Travis works at the same home-security company that Katherine does, and the woman
he's to marry is Sherry Osborne, the sister of Katherine's boss, Stephen Osborne, the president of the company. Despite her own strict rules for professional behavior, Katherine
turns for comfort to Stephen, and ends up spending the night with him. The next day, convinced that he stayed with her mainly because he felt sorry for her, and feeling that nothing
can preserve their professional relationship, she leaves the company and starts over.

A few weeks later, Katherine becomes ill. At first she blames heat and working conditions, but she soon realizes she's having morning sickness.

She informs Stephen of her pregnancy and is astonished when he suggests that they
do what people have always done when there's an unexpected baby on the way—get married. She agrees, though not without misgivings and distrust of Stephen's motives, because
she feels that the best thing for the baby will be for them to try to build a family.

But on their quiet weekend "honeymoon" Stephen makes clear that marriage does not
include any further intimacy. Katherine is confused until she realizes that there are other
reasons for his willingness to marry. A former girlfriend has been pressing him to marry her,
but by marrying Katherine he establishes a family-man image that will actually leave him
more free than being single, since Katherine owes him too much to make demands.

That understanding leaves her feeling trapped and she realizes that she loves him—
indeed, has loved him for a long time, but hid the fact from herself because it was unprofessional to fall for one's boss. Now she has few options—she can accept what she has
been offered and make the best of it, or she can walk out and be in worse shape than she
was before. She opts to stay, telling herself that nothing can keep her from loving him,
and perhaps if love sneaked up on her, it could happen to him as well.

When Sherry discovers her errant fiancé with yet another woman, she responds to
Katherine's sympathy with accusations that Travis is actually the father of Katherine's
child. Worse, it's immediately apparent to Katherine that Stephen believes the accusa-
tion, and has believed it all along.

> If he thought she could lie to him about such a fundamental issue as the parentage of her baby, then the idea of building any kind of lifelong relationship is a farce. She begins to pack her belongings.
>
> But she still needs the answer to one question: Why did he not even ask her about the child? Why did he assume the worst? He answers that he was afraid of what she would tell him—that he knew it would be the truth, but because he loved her and wanted her so much, it honestly did not matter to him whether her child was his as well.
>
> On the morning after their night together, when she gave up even her job in order to get away from him, he felt guilty about taking advantage of her pain. When he discovered her pregnancy, it seemed a chance to make up to her for the additional grief he had caused, as well as a chance to have her in his life—even if she could never love him. With the assurance of mutual love, they sort out the guilt that both have suffered and begin anew to create a family for their child.
>

categorize anything that asks "What if?" contrary to reality as we know it: science fiction, fantasy, horror, and magical realism.

In most cases, you'll need to open with a bit more backstory and setting than you would with other fictional genres like romance because these elements are so vital to the story. Specific examples include:

- **The year:** "It's 2080 and humans now live on Earth and Mars ..."
- **The setting:** J.R.R. Tolkien's Middle-earth in *The Hobbit* and *The Lord of the Rings*
- **The state of things:** The opening scroll in the original *Star Wars* movie could have been taken right from the synopsis:

  It is a period of civil war. Rebel spaceships, striking from a hidden base, have won their first victory against the evil Galactic Empire. During the battle, Rebel spies managed to steal secret plans ...

- **Backstory (how we got here):** J.K. Rowling's *Harry Potter and the Half-Blood Prince* had to include some backstory on the villain, which would probably have needed to find its way into the synopsis—had she been required to write one.

Can you imagine how a synopsis of a modern-day romance would read with the above-mentioned components?

> The year is 2007. Mary Jones is living in a blue house in the suburbs outside Waco, Texas. She used to be a hairdresser, then she worked at 7-Eleven for a few weeks before getting hired as a receptionist at the bank.

Year? Irrelevant. Setting? Irrelevant. Backstory? Irrelevant.

Not all synopses are created equal—and they shouldn't be. Craft yours to match your writing style, tone, voice, and genre.

Children's

First, a reminder that we're talking about children's (or young adult) *novels* here, not picture books. And because children's novels are generally shorter than adult novels, your synopsis will probably be much shorter (say, a couple pages as opposed to a whopping thirty-page tome for a four-hundred-page adult novel).

Because most children's or YA novels will be plot-driven, your synopsis will mirror the chronological order and action of the book's major events. You may want to break it into paragraphs as follows:

- **Beginning:** one to two paragraphs that introduce the main characters, their ages, the setting, and a circumstance or event.
- **Middle:** three or four paragraphs that describe the events and obstacles leading to the climax of the story.
- **Ending:** one or two paragraphs showing the climax and resolution, including the lesson learned.

As with adult novels, you'll want to touch on motivations, internal and external conflicts, growth of the character, and possibly a black moment (when all seems lost—right before the main character figures out an alternative solution).

There is one significant difference between writing a synopsis for a children's vs. adult novel: The voice in your synopsis will not necessary reflect the exact same voice in your book. A novel written for a ten-year-old reader will still have to be sold on a synopsis for an adult editor. Use your grown-up voice in the pitch while still conveying your ability to write for a young reader. Voice-driven novels are exceptions to this guideline: It would make sense that the pitch and synopsis for Megan McCafferty's YA/adult crossover *Sloppy Firsts* would sound like its narrator Jessica Darling. Likewise for Bruce Hale's middle-grade Chet Gecko series.

Cross-Genre

There's something edgy and fun about cross-genre fiction. Maybe it's the "something for everyone" factor, but writers have managed to make some major money off hybrid categories in TV, movies, and music, so why shouldn't cross-genre books make their authors rich?

Chances are, if you're writing cross-genre fiction, you already know it and can summarize it in layman's terms to nonwriters: "It's a paranormal romance, like the movie *Ghost* with Patrick Swayze and Demi Moore" or "It's a science fiction western, like *Wild Wild West* with Will Smith and Kevin Kline."

The tricky part comes in selling your idea in a synopsis, where it can often come across as hokey, campy, or outright bizarre. There are some easier sells: romantic comedies (think Helen Fielding's *Bridget Jones's Diary*) and black comedy (John Irving's *The World According to Garp*), but head out into new territory and you'll have to be just as inventive and likable in your synopsis as you are in your novel.

And unpublished authors take note: Cross-genre is a particularly tough sell with no prior books under your belt. That's not to say it can't be done, but you're asking a lot when you approach publishers with a neatly categorized genre. Now you want them to consider your fantasy-romantic-dramedy about a puppeteer who discovers a portal that literally transports people into the mind of a famous actor. Sound crazy? Although it's not a book, *Being John Malkovich* was nominated for three Oscars. See? Don't be so quick to doubt yourself! Cross-genre can work. But tread carefully.

# NOVEL QUERY FAQS

SHOULD I REWRITE MY SYNOPSIS IF MY AGENT SUGGESTS IT?

Unless it's a significant rewrite that doesn't represent your book accurately, I'd recommend making the change. Experienced agents often have a better grasp on what will get an editor's attention, especially if they've worked with the editor before. You always have the right to decline the agent's suggestions, but take into consideration the agent's experience (years in the business, books sold in your genre, the publishing houses to which he's sold books) before putting up a fight or moving on to another agent.

WHAT IF MORE THAN ONE PUBLISHER SHOWS INTEREST IN MY NOVEL?

You should be so lucky! In theory, you will make a decision when the first editor contacts you and offers to publish your book. If you sent simultaneous submissions, you'll need to make a decision rather quickly. Either take the first offer and contact the other publishers to withdraw your submission, or decline and see if anyone else bites. Never leave a publisher hanging. Sure, a bidding war would be great, but you don't want to blow your chances altogether by either not responding to the offer or saying, "Can you just hang on for a few months while I see what else comes in?" When in doubt, get yourself an agent (yes, after you have the book deal) and let him do some negotiating.

CHAPTER 5

AGENT QUERIES

New writers are often reluctant to use an agent because they hate the idea of giving up 15 percent of their profits. (Fifteen percent is the standard in the industry on domestic sales. For foreign sales, the standard is 20 percent. With few exceptions, agents that charge much more than this industry standard or ask writers to pay any up-front fees are considered shady and should be approached with caution ... and pepper spray.) I usually set these new writers straight with a math pop quiz: "Would you rather get 100 percent of four thousand dollars or 85 percent of seven thousand dollars?" After some head scratching and number crunching they'll inevitably and tentatively reply, "Um, seven thousand dollars?"

Good answer.

Reputable agents make 98 to 100 percent of their income from their clients' profits. You'll notice I didn't say "from their clients." That's because agents don't get paid by you, they get paid by what you *make*. This means that an agent will be eager to get you a bigger advance, negotiate higher royalty rates (when possible), and retain more rights to your work for future income.

You always have the option to represent yourself, but unless you're an expert in the legal intricacies of the publishing world, why would you? It's like trying to get an acting role in a Hollywood. Would you rather represent yourself and get a job as an extra making one hundred dollars for the day, or hire a well-known agent who takes 25 percent of whatever he gets you? You can bet he's going to use his connections to try to get you a good-paying gig, whether it's a toothpaste commercial or the sassy waitress in the new John C. Reilly comedy.

There are other advantages to hiring an agent. Your agent:

- **Knows the trends and changes in publishing.** This might mean that science fiction is hot and romance is dead (the genre, not the courtship concept) or that two publishing houses merged and are no longer accepting memoirs.

- **Not only gets your proposal seen by the larger publishing houses, but also gets you into the hands of the right editor.** Experienced agents often know the preferences of individual acquisitions editors.

- **Gets your manuscript to the front of the pile.** At publishing houses where unagented submissions are accepted, an acquisitions editor will almost always reach for an agented submission first, knowing that an expert in the industry has thought enough of the proposal to submit it.

- **Navigates the web of your contract's legalese.** Agents are intimately familiar with the standard, or "boilerplate," contract at each publishing house, so they can quickly assess your initial offer and decide what's in your best interest to negotiate and what is simply house procedure. For example, if a publisher typically has a book's indexing fees deducted from the author's first royalty check, the agent may push for higher royalties to offset the cost.

- **Advocates on your behalf.** This could include getting a bigger publicity push from the publisher's marketing department, making your book the alternate in the house's book club (if it has one), and insisting you have input on the book's cover design.

- **Makes sure you get paid on time and in the right amount.** Once you turn in your final manuscript, it's common for your agent to contact your editor to make sure any remaining advance money owed to you is in process. The publisher writers your advance check to your agent, who receives the money, takes her agreed-upon percentage, and sends the rest to you. This means your agent is personally invested in your being paid fairly, which is good news for you.

- **Sells subsidiary rights.** The more rights an agent retains for you, the more money-making opportunities you'll have after the book contract is finalized. This might include translation rights, movie rights, or audiobook rights. Unless you speak German or have experience producing (and funding) a Hollywood blockbuster, selling subsidiary rights means more money for you ... but no additional work.

- **Sometimes offers general career guidance.** Agents like to build long-term relationships. By taking you on as a client, they're hoping to represent you and your potential for future books—not just the one on the table at the time.

A very important note: If you're thinking about approaching publishers on your own only to try to get an agent if everyone rejects you, think again. Agents don't appreciate being a last resort. They're not miracle workers; if publishing houses rejected your proposal, chances are they'll reject the same proposal again—and not be happy that the acquisitions editors wasted their time reading it twice. Once your agent finds out you've exhausted all her options, she'll drop you as a client.

So why would anyone choose *not* to use an agent? It might be in your best interest to represent yourself if:

- You've worked in the publishing industry (or know someone who does) and feel informed.

- You know a lot about intellectual property and are comfortable negotiating rights.

- You've decided to hire a lawyer to review your contract instead of an agent so as only to pay a flat fee.

- Your writing focuses on a niche market (such as for a trade industry) so you're only pitching to small publishers.

- You've fired every agent (or they've quit). (READ: "You don't play well with others.")

COMPONENTS OF AN AGENT QUERY LETTER

The query you send to attract an agent will largely be the same one the agent sends to a publisher on your behalf. Obviously, the part at the end about requesting representation will be changed, but sometimes your agent may also suggest that you tweak the query's components a bit—especially if she is familiar with a particular acquisitions editor's likes and dislikes, or something that could be detrimental to your agent's efforts to get you published. Here are a few examples:

- The agent knows a particular publisher likes to work with authors who have published articles in national magazines (in which case, she may ask you to expound on your sentence about how you've worked as a freelance writer for several years).

- The agent knows one of the books you're comparing your book to wasn't a very big seller (and therefore may ask you to choose another comparative book).

- The agent knows a publishing house has stopped purchasing titles for the particular line you're referencing or that the publisher has just launched (or is about to launch) a new line that you *should* be referencing (e.g., "Harlequin has a new NASCAR line of romances. Since your lead character is a race car driver, we should pitch it to them for that line.").

- The agent knows a particular publishing house has very specific submission policies (e.g., only a one-paragraph pitch; no queries over two pages; writers must indicate if the book is completed).

In many cases, the agent will simply put your query on her own letterhead and open with a paragraph introducing you. (To see an example of this from the agent query used in **Example 5.1,** see the agent's letter to the publisher in **Example 5.2.**)

Of course, any of these changes will come from the agent after he agrees to represent you. So how do you get his attention initially? The same way you would with any query: Make it professional, interesting, and to the point.

EXAMPLE 5.1   GOOD YOUNG ADULT AGENT QUERY

January 1, 2007

Kate Schafer
kt literary, llc.
9249 S. Broadway, #200-543
Highlands Ranch, CO 80129

Dear Ms. Schafer,

One of my favorite young adult authors is Maureen Johnson. When I learned you represent her, I thought you might be interested in my 46,000-word YA novel, **UNBECOMING**. After getting caught cheating on her U.S. History final, seventeen-year-old Jacey Lowell has been sentenced to spend three days, six hours, and fifteen minutes in hell.

Cross-country bus. Hell. It's the same thing, as far as she's concerned.

When she boards the bus at Boston's South Station, Jacey has an overabundance of both luggage and attitude. She plans to spend the next three days flipping through foreign fashion magazines while ignoring the interstate as it rolls past her window.

But when Jacey misses her transfer in New York City, her boring bus ride becomes an adventure that will change her life. From spending the night in a squat on the Lower East Side to whitewater rafting with a group of gay men on the Green River in Utah, Jacey is exposed to life beyond Commonwealth Avenue.

Six days, six band T-shirts, and 3,400 miles later, she arrives in San Francisco with a cool new attitude … and a hot new guy.

Thank you for your consideration. I'd love to send you the manuscript and I look forward to hearing from you soon.

Trish Doller
(address, phone, e-mail)

[Note: This query got the author representation by the agent.
See Example 5.2 for the agent's letter to the publisher.]

EXAMPLE 5.2   SAMPLE OF AGENT LETTER TO PUBLISHER

February 1, 2007

Claudia Gabel
Delacorte Press
1745 Broadway, 15-3
New York, NY 10019

Dear Claudia,

As promised, I'm delighted to attach the manuscript for Trish Doller's debut YA novel, **UNBECOMING**. Trish has the same kind of voice as Maureen, and I think you'll love **UNBECOMING**, which is like *13 Little Blue Envelopes Across America.*

Rich, spoiled Jacey Abbott knows there'll be repercussions for her having been caught cheating on her history final, but having her summer trip to Europe canceled isn't the worst of it. No, her punishment's even more horrible than that—her dad's forcing her to take the BUS cross-country to meet her parents in San Francisco for her grandmother's birthday party. No BlackBerry, no credit cards, and a mere three hundred dollars to get from Boston to San Fran. And she has to prove she's made the trip by documenting the journey with photographs. At least her mom gets her a swanky new camera—even when she's traveling cheap, Jacey's used to traveling in style.

Bottom of the barrel? Hello, nice to see you. Jacey thinks her summer couldn't possibly get any worse, and she hasn't even made it out of the bus terminal yet. An obnoxious guy with a guitar case may prove to be the final straw—or he just may be the key to make whole trip worthwhile.

I'm so happy to share **UNBECOMING** as my first official submission from kt literary! I'm sending this to you and a shortlist of three other editors in hope that you'll be able to get back to me in two weeks. If you're unable to reach a decision by February 20, I'll expand my submission.

I look forward to hearing from you!

Cheers,

Kate Schafer
kt literary, llc.
9249 S. Broadway, #200-543
Highlands Ranch, CO 80129
http://ktliterary.com

[Note: The agent sold this book to Delacorte.
The title was changed to *My Way or the Highway*.]

The same basic rules of querying to a magazine editor apply when querying an agent:

1. Address your letter to the appropriate person. Many agencies have more than one agent and they may all represent different genres.

2. Open with a strong hook or, if you've met the person previously (such as at a writers conference), open with a reminder of your meeting.

3. Give a strong summary paragraph about your book.

4. Indicate why there's a market/need for your book (if it's nonfiction) or if it's completed (which is necessary if it's fiction).

5. Use the same voice/style/tone that you use in your book. If the book is funny, make sure your query is too.

6. List your credentials in a sentence or two near the end of the query.

7. Include an SASE if you're sending the query by mail.

8. Mention a platform if you've got one, and give specific numbers (blog or Web site hits, attendee numbers at conferences where you speak, etc.) when possible.

9. Follow the agency's submission guidelines. If they say to submit a query along with a proposal, do it. If they say "no e-mail queries," mail it.

10. Indicate if your query is a simultaneous submission to other agencies.

For samples of good and bad agent queries, see **Examples 5.3** through **5.8** (pgs. 152–158).

Take note: Not all agencies want just a query letter. Some will actually require a full book proposal on initial contact—or specific pieces of a proposal, such as an outline, table of contents, and sample chapters.

Your best approach is to create a full book proposal before contacting any agents. Then you can pick and choose the bits and pieces of the proposal based on the specific guidelines. For the most part, the same proposal will be used to shop your manuscript to publishers, so it's best to have it completed in advance anyway.

For two very different samples of good book proposals, see **Examples 5.9** (pgs. 159–165) and **5.10** (pgs. 166–170).

EXAMPLE 5.3   BAD AGENT QUERY FOR NONFICTION

January 2, 2007

Kate Austen
Austen Literary Agency
55 Park Place
Golden, CA 92014

Dear Ms. Austen,

As a pop-culture writer focusing on urban life, (A) I just had to pick up a copy of *Young, Black, Rich, and Famous: The Rise of the NBA, the Hip Hop Invasion, and the Transformation of American Culture* by Todd Boyd (B) when it came out this month. Although the book was very good, I was even more thrilled to learn that you represented Boyd. I've been searching for an agent and had the Austen Literary Agency at the top of my list!

Similar to Randy Kearse's *Street Talk: Da Official Guide to Hip-Hop & Urban Slanguage,* (C) my book will be a five-hundred-page dictionary of urban slang and colloquialisms for those living in the suburbs. More of a gag gift book (D) than an actual reference piece, **Blackspeak: A Translative Dictionary for Folks in the Burbs** will be a humorous guide that soccer moms (and dads) will want to give their friends. (E)

I'm enclosing an outline, table of contents, and resume. (F) You can e-mail your response to me at the address below. (G)

Thank you!

Al Most
(address/phone/email)

WHAT'S WRONG: AGENT'S COMMENTS

(A) This is good that he has a specific niche, though I would have liked to have known a bit more about his experience. Is he just calling himself a writer or has he written on the topic for magazines? (B) This is great that he mentions he bought (and read) a copy of a book by one of our clients. (We hate when people say they got it at the library!) (C) Another good reference he mentions a similar book. But I would have liked to know how his book will be DIFFERENT than what's already out there. You can't mention one side of things without the other. (D) He's starting to lose me with the whole "gag gift book." We want books that people will actually use/read. (E) Not sure I'm digging the whole "soccer moms" approach. (F) Our guidelines specifically state to send only a one-page query. (G) He didn't include an SASE—only his e-mail. This writer started off strong, especially mentioning one of our clients and taking the time to find out which of us at the agency represents pop culture. But he lost me when he didn't differentiate his book from what was out there or put the focus on it as a real book—as opposed to a gag gift.

EXAMPLE 5.4   BAD AGENT QUERY FOR FICTION

April 1, 2007

Chris Floundering
7000 Main St.
NY, NY 10001

Dear Chris, **A**

You've represented some fantastic books **B** and I'm hoping you'll be able to add my name to the list soon.

I've completed a 40,000-word novel **C** entitled, **We'll Cross That Bridge Later**, **D** about a young couple that struggles with the ups and downs of marrying too young. **E**

Synopsis paragraph: **F**

Rachel and Joey **G** were just eighteen when they got married. Rachel got pregnant on their honeymoon and that put a damper on their college plans. Rachel stayed at home with the baby and Joey got a job at a bank. **H** When the bank was robbed, Joey chased the robber on foot, managing to knock him out. **I** While he's waiting for the police to arrive, he hides the money in a nearby sewage drain. The police never find it and assume the robber tossed the bag while he ran. That night, Joey went back to get the bag. He returned home and as he and Rachel are making plans to flee the country, a woman knocks on their door. She tells them that she knows what Joey did and that if he doesn't figure out a way to (secretly) return the money to the bank on Monday, she'll tell the police. Joey and Rachel spend the night talking and decide that they need to silence the woman. They plan to track her down and offer her a bribe. If that doesn't work, they'll kill her. They begin canvassing the area for the woman, assuming she must live near the sewer. Can Joey and Rachel find Mrs. X before Monday? And if so, can they buy her silence or will their plans end in murder?

Thank you for your consideration. I'd be happy to send you the first chapter for your review. **J**

Sincerely,

Anita Help
(address/phone/e-mail)

WHAT'S WRONG: AGENT'S COMMENTS

A I don't know the author so it's a bit inappropriate for her to call me by my first name. I'm wondering if perhaps she didn't know if I was a male or female, and she didn't want to take the time to find out. **B** Oh really? I'm curious why she didn't mention any by name. **C**

This is way too short for a novel. **D** This title is horrible for a novel. Maybe a self-help book or something, but not fiction. Besides, the saying is, "We'll cross that bridge when we come to it." **E** I'm bored. This is too generic. **F** Spelling out (literally) that this is the "synopsis paragraph" is a bit like horrible business papers in which writers say, "In the next paragraph, I will talk about ..." **G** I'm immediately thinking of *Friends*. One of the characters names would have to change if the book ever got published because *Friends* fans are the same target market as romance novel readers. **H** Present tense always sounds better in a synopsis. (She changes tenses later.) **I** Finally, some action! But too little too late. **J** Why did she only offer one chapter if it's done?

EXAMPLE 5.5   GOOD AGENT QUERY FOR ROMANCE

January 4, 2007

Barbara Collins Rosenberg
The Rosenberg Group
2800 Harlanwood Drive
Fort Worth, TX 76109

Dear Ms. Collins Rosenberg,

I believe a writer in today's complex market needs to have someone in his or her corner. I am querying you for three reasons. You have been recommended to me by two completely different sources. Your agency's name has turned up in several respected RWA newsletters. And last, but certainly not least, you have offices in Texas. Fort Worth is a heck of a lot closer to Dallas than New York City.

EVERYTHING IN ITS TIME is a 96,000-word time-travel romance set in the Highlands of Scotland.

Katherine St. Claire has never forgotten the passionate night she shared with a stranger while staying at a castle hotel called Duncreag. He even haunts her dreams. Tired of loving a "Fantasy Man," as her brother Jeff refers to him, she decides to go back to Duncreag in search, literally, of the man of her dreams.

Iain Mackintosh wears the cairngorm earring of the only woman he will ever love. Eight long years ago she came to him in the night like a vision. News of his father's death brings Iain home to Duncreag where he finds himself questioning the circumstances surrounding his father's demise and wishing for the woman his cousin Ranald is convinced is a fairy.

Iain and Katherine arrive at Duncreag each longing to find the other. There is, however, a seemingly insurmountable obstacle. A 530-year barrier separates them. What follows is the story of a love so powerful it crosses the boundaries of time. Complicated by murder and abduction in the fifteenth century, their love will be tested even after they finally reunite. Only Jeff's twentieth-century discovery of events from the past can save them.

With Jeff's help, Iain manages to change history and save Katherine, but fate once more intervenes to separate the lovers. Iain is forced to allow Jeff to take Katherine back to the twentieth century, where she wakes up with no memory of him or the events that have transpired. A chance encounter with a history book brings everything full circle allowing the lovers to finally be together in the fifteenth century.

EVERYTHING IN ITS TIME is a first novel. The completed work contains twenty-seven chapters, a prologue, and an epilogue. It is a labor of love in tribute to the writers who have filled my life with magic, starting with Madeleine L'Engle and Mary Stewart and continuing on to authors like Diana Gabaldon and Leslie LaFoy.

In preparation for writing this book I thoroughly researched the romance novel industry, including reading several hundred romances of all genres over the last year. In addition, I did extensive research into fifteenth-century Scotland.

During a ten-year career in public relations I designed and edited three newsletters (one award winning), wrote television and radio commercials, wrote three award-winning PSAs, and wrote multimedia presentations for several large organizations. I have also written numerous brochures, press releases, and other business proposals. Many years ago, I won the National Council of Teachers of English award for excellence in writing.

In creating Duncreag and its neighboring holding Tur nan Clach, I have created characters that seem now like old friends. With the last sentence of this book completed, I find that I am eager to continue writing about the Mackintoshes of Duncreag. You see, Iain's cousin Marjory is being forced to marry a Cameron.

If you would like to read more about Katherine and Iain, I would be delighted to send a detailed synopsis, sample chapters, or the entire manuscript. I appreciate your time and interest in my work and I look forward to hearing from you. SASE enclosed.

Sincerely,

Dee Davis
(address/phone/e-mail)

[Note: This book sold to Jove.]

EXAMPLE 5.6   GOOD AGENT QUERY FOR LITERARY FICTION

January 3, 2007
Marcus O'Neal
The Ross Agency
1234 Church St.
New York, NY 10001

Dear Mr. O'Neal,

Joshilyn Jackson and Valerie Ann Leff recommended I introduce my novel **FULL ALIVE** to you. Set in 1952 rural Appalachia, **FULL ALIVE** is a novel of love and redemption in which a strong woman breaks tradition and makes unconventional choices. It is complete at 75,000 words.

Sometimes, a mother's arms are the most dangerous place for her son to be.

After Redmond Johnson lets good-hearted Caney Gentry die in a collapsed coal mine, he returns to their mountain hollow home to find Cane's widow Sarah. Holding tight to the secret that he could've saved Sarah's beloved husband, Redmond courts and marries the young mother. Shortly after, a Granny woman delivers a devastating prophecy: Sarah's son Jamie will leave the mountains before he's grown. Sarah makes an anguished decision to steel Jamie for his fate by withdrawing from him. In time, Redmond's volatile nature reveals itself, casting a shadow of abuse over the solitary family. But when ten-year-old Jamie befriends Jack, a man of the world with secrets of his own, everything changes as the stranger becomes an unlikely guardian angel in the unfolding of the prophecy. Sarah experiences her own inner awakening while she watches. After Jamie leaves, she accepts the unconventional gifts that give her a second chance at life. **FULL ALIVE** is about the power of the choices made in determining a life lived.

I moved to the western North Carolina mountains ten years ago after a twenty-year love affair with the region. I am a member of the NC Writers Network, and one of the producers of The Honeybee Project, a multimedia education initiative whose goals include enlivening children's interest in nature. I am currently developing a marketing plan to help promote **FULL ALIVE**. Attached is advance praise from Cassie Robinson, the Coordinator of Regional Studies at Mars Hill College, NC, and authors Ron Rash (*Saints at the River, The World Made Straight*), Wayne Caldwell (*Cataloochee*), and Valerie Ann Leff (*Better Homes and Husbands*).

Thank you for your consideration. The first twenty-five pages and an SASE for your reply are enclosed. I look forward to hearing from you soon.

Sincerely,

Heloise Jones
(address/phone/e-mail)

[Note: This query garnered the author two immediate offers of agent representation.]

EXAMPLE 5.7   GOOD AGENT QUERY FOR HOW-TO

January 8, 2007
Ms. Jan Miller, President
Dupree/Miller and Associates Inc.
100 Highland Park Village, Suite 350
Dallas, TX 75205

Dear Ms. Miller,

The days of hand-washed, line-dried diapers are gone, thank goodness. So that should signal an era of more relaxed, less anxious parents, right? WRONG! According to the American Academy of Pediatrics, helping the twenty million parents with eleven million children under the age of four through the potty training process can be one of the toughest challenges for parents.

In the pages of **POTTY TRAIN YOUR CHILD IN JUST ONE DAY: PROVEN SECRETS OF THE POTTY PRO**, you will find a fun, time-tested method for helping parents to potty training victory. In the fast-paced, multitasking society in which we live, parents need a training tool that will teach them how to potty train their child in ONE day. And, this book will argue, that means a well-planned fun and exciting potty party.

Why is this ritual so important? It's simple: Children ordinarily have absolutely no incentive to become potty trained—none. Even if the entire culture in which they're raised seems focused upon—at times, obsessed by—their graduation from Pampers University, the toddlers themselves remain blissfully unaware of all this. Which is where the potty party comes in. Here, we're talking a child's language, a dialect in which they're highly conversant: parties, fun, yummy treats, balloons, and lots of attention on little me. Now you're talking toddlerspeak!

I have launched my own speaking tour promoting my potty training products throughout the Great Lakes region. I also conduct a wildly popular boot camp for new parents and I am currently in negotiations with Babies"R"Us to be their regional resident speaker through their in-house seminar series.

I will obtain endorsements from the two consultants for this book: *New York Times* best-selling psychologist Sylvia Rimm, Ph.D., and Philip Caravella, M.D., F.A.A.F.P of the renowned Cleveland Clinic (who has also provided the foreword).

You've heard of the *One-Minute Manager*, haven't you? Consider this an all-purpose guide to becoming the One-Day Potty Trainer, presented in a fun, hip, easy-to-follow format. Potty training and party planning, two books in one; it can be yours, it can be done.

A forty-page proposal is available at your request.
Most sincerely yours,

Teri Crane
(address/phone/e-mail)

[Note: This query landed the author agent representation
and a book deal with Fireside, an imprint of Simon & Schuster.]

EXAMPLE 5.8   GOOD AGENT QUERY FOR YA PARANORMAL

February 27, 2007

Kristin Nelson
Nelson Literary Agency
1732 Wazee Street, Suite 207
Denver, CO 80202

Dear Ms. Nelson,

I am seeking representation for my completed 62,000-word young adult novel, **IN MEMORY OF**.

Sixteen-year-old Cass McKenna would take the company of the dead over the living any day. Unlike her high school classmates, the dead don't lie or judge, and they're way less scary than Danielle, the best-bud-turned-backstabber who kicked Cass to the bottom of the social ladder in seventh grade. Since then, Cass has styled herself as an avenger. Using the secrets her ghostly friends stumble across, she exposes her fellow students' deceits and knocks the poseurs down a peg.

When Tim Reed, the student council VP, asks Cass to chat with his recently deceased mom, her instinct is to laugh in his face. But Tim's part of Danielle's crowd. He can give Cass dirt the dead don't know. Intent on revenge, Cass offers to trade her spirit-detecting skills for his information. She isn't counting on chasing a ghost who would rather hide than speak to her, facing the explosive intervention of an angry student, or discovering that Tim's actually an okay guy. Then Tim sinks into a suicidal depression, and Cass has to choose: run back to the safety of the dead, or risk everything to stop Tim from becoming a ghost himself.

Told in Cass's distinctive voice, at turns sarcastic and sensitive, **IN MEMORY OF** will appeal to fans of Scott Westerfeld and Annette Curtis Klause.

My short fiction has appeared in *Brutarian Quarterly* and *On Spec*. I maintain the Toronto Speculative Fiction Writers Group, and I've worked with children and teens as a recreational programmer and behavioral therapist for several years.

Thank you for your time.

Sincerely,

Megan Crewe
(address/phone/e-mail)

EXAMPLE 5.9   GOOD LONG PROPOSAL

[Separate cover sheet]

A Proposal for

The Writer's Guide to Keeping Your Day Job

By Wendy Burt-Thomas

Wendy Burt-Thomas

address

phone

e-mail

[Proposal begins on new page]

Introduction

Overview

Everybody wants to be a writer, and there are lots of books on the market that encourage writers to quit their day jobs:

- *Secrets of a Freelance Writer: How to Make $85,000 a Year*
- *Achieving Financial Independence as a Freelance Writer*
- *The Well-Fed Writer: Financial Self-Sufficiency as a Freelance Writer in Six Months or Less*

But where does that leave most aspiring writers who must struggle to write while holding down a full-time job? **THE WRITER'S GUIDE TO KEEPING YOUR DAY JOB** is a 125-page guide and workbook for the beginning or struggling freelancer who can't afford to give up the security of a full-time job. Chapters average ten pages each and cover:

- finding time to write

- creative exercises

- brainstorming sessions

- examples of what works and doesn't

- short writing exercises for when writers have only minutes to spare

- the five-minute character

- query letters with samples

- personal experiences

- simple ways for beginners to break into the business

- how and when to tell the boss when moonlighting

- writing a book proposal

- getting an agent

Beginning and intermediate writers will learn step-by-step tips to help them begin and build their careers as writers without the pressure to quit their day jobs in hopes of striking it rich as an overnight success.

Promotion

To promote the book, the author will:

- Send press releases and make follow-up calls to all major writing magazines and Web sites including *Writer's Digest* magazine, FundsforWriters, AbsoluteWrite, and *Poets & Writers* magazine.

- Contact one hundred local, regional, and national radio shows to appear as a guest. Promotion for the author's previous two books included radio appearances on iVillage.com and six-hour stint as a co-host on Denver's KOSI 101FM.

- Contact national general consumer television shows such as *The Oprah Winfrey Show*, *Good Morning America*, *Today*, and *Live With Regis and Kelly* to appear as a guest. Promotion for her previous two books included appearances on Pure Oxygen on the Oxygen network.

- Contact one hundred metropolitan newspapers to raise interest in reviews. Her previous books were written about in newspapers in Denver, Seattle, Detroit, Albany, and Lincoln.

- Contact one hundred publications throughout Colorado. She has written for fifteen publications in the state and can get publicity from most of them. Many covered her previous books.

- Contact writing-related radio programs including *Authors' Secrets Radio* with Vijaya Schartz; *Booknotes* on C-SPAN; the *Diane Rehm Show* on National Public Radio; *Writing on the Air*, an Austin-based radio show; and the *Writer's Roundtable* on World Talk Radio.

- Print 250 postcards and mail them to friends, family, former writing students of six years of workshops, writing/business contacts, and writing conference directors.

- Contact bookstores to set up signings as she did with her first two books. At her very first signing, which took place at the Tattered Cover in Denver, she sold seventy-five books.

- Contact well-known writers conferences in the Southwest about speaking. Shawguides.com lists more than 1,500 conferences and workshops. The author led a workshop on "Breaking into Freelance Writing" for eight years and taught at the Pikes Peak Writers Conference, the country's sixth largest conference.

- Continue to line up speaking engagements with regional writing and business groups, including Front Range Fiction Writers, Pikes Peak Romance Writers, Colorado Springs Fiction Writers Group, Pikes Peak Writers, American Business Women's Association, and National Business Women's Association.

- Promote the book through two Web sites: www.wendyburt-thomas.com and www.burtcreations.com.

- Continue to sell books, as she does with her first two books, to friends, family, and writers in her two-hundred-plus member creative women's group.

- Continue to accept the publicity offered by friends' two large writing-related newsletters and one large business newsletter.

- Continue to promote her books through her two regular columns; one for a national dating Web site with more than three million members and a Q&A column in which she answers questions about writing to the newsletter's readers.

- Promote the book through meetings and newsletters for PEN Women, the Better Business Bureau, and Just CAWS (Creative Alliance of Women's Support).
- Continue to mention her book in her bylines for local and national magazines, newspapers, and Web sites. Her five-hundred-plus published pieces have included work in *Family Circle*, *Christian Parenting Today*, Bally Total Fitness's *FIT.STYLE*, *Complete Woman*, *Woman's Own*, *Home Cooking*, Cub Foods' magazine, and Kay Jewelers' international magazine.
- Attempt to get published again in writing magazines where she has already been published: *Writer's Digest*, *The Writer*, *ByLine*, *Writers Exchange*, *The Ultimate Writer*, *New England Writer's Exchange*, *The Writer Gazette*, *Jus' Write*, WritersWeekly.com, *Writers' Journal*, *Canadian Writer's Journal*, and CoolStuff4Writers.com.
- Send review copies to online booksellers' top reviewers who are willing to review the book. Her previous books were written about favorably by several major reviewers including RebeccasReads.com, Carrie Hampton, and Linda Linguvic.
- Contact media in states where she has personal connections: Maine, Vermont, New York, and Colorado.
- Attempt to get promotional quotes for the book flap from three friends who are authors and have taken the author's class.
- Contact national writers organizations that might
    — ask her to speak at a conference
    — plug the book in their newsletters and on their Web sites
    — buy a large quantity of books for its members

    These organizations include: Associated Business Writers of America, Association for Business Communication, the International Association of Business Communicators, and the National Association of Women Writers.
- Take her father up on his offer to sell books across New England for many months out of the year at book fairs, craft fairs, book shows, and speaking engagements. Steve Burt is the author of twelve books and sold 2,800 copies of the author's first two books in just over two years.
- Contact two writing program teachers who took her class to ask them to sell her book or incorporate it as part of their curriculum.

The author will provide the promotional copies the house can't, and will coordinate her efforts with yours.

About the Author

Formerly the editor of Colorado Springs' largest-circulated business newspaper, Wendy Burt-Thomas knows about the commitment it takes to be a successful freelancer. In addition to her job, she managed to teach writing, sell freelance articles, write monthly columns, run a two-hundred-plus member women's creative group, speak to writers' groups and conferences, and promote her first book, *Oh, Solo Mia! The Hip Chick's Guide to Fun for One* (McGraw-Hill, 2001). Her second book for McGraw-Hill, *Work It, Girl! 101 Tips for the Hip Working Chick* was published in 2003.

At thirty-seven, Burt-Thomas has published more than one thousand articles, short stories, and essays in national, regional, and local magazines and newspapers, and has been teaching "Breaking Into Freelance Writing" for eight years. Her work has appeared in such publications as *Writer's Digest, The Writer, ByLine, Family Circle, Complete Woman, Woman's Own, American Fitness, FIT.STYLE*, and *Christian Parenting Today*.

Wendy's writing club memberships include PEN Women, Front Range Fiction Writers, and the National Writers Union, and she is the founder of Just CAWS, a two-hundred-member creative women's group.

Burt-Thomas has won contests, including first place for fiction in PEN Women's "Soul-Making Literary Contest." Her books have been excerpted/quoted in *Cosmopolitan, Woman's Own, Complete Woman*, and other publications.

In 2001, at the age of thirty, Burt-Thomas was named one of the "25 Most Dynamic Business Women" of Colorado Springs—a city with 400,000 people. Now a full-time writer and editor, Burt-Thomas still teaches "Breaking Into Freelance Writing."

For years, her students have been asking her, "How do you balance a full-time job and a freelance career?" This book will tell them how.

The Outline

Foreword: About the Book   1 page

The foreword includes an overview of the book, why the author wrote it, and a preview of how she managed to maintain a freelance writing career while holding down a day job.

Chapter One: Moonlight Serenade: Telling Your Boss About Your Writing (Included)

Keeping a day job means readers have to tell their bosses they're moonlighting. Or does it? Readers learn what they should and shouldn't tell bosses and when to tell them. Other advice includes:

• Making twice the money by writing about the readers' employer

• Getting paid to publicize the company readers work for

• Getting paid by the company's publication

• Building a portfolio of clips

The chapter closes by discussing other factors for freelancers to consider such as when they have a responsibility to tell clients or editors at publications about other assignments.

Chapter Two: Easy Street: Simple Ways to Break Into the Business (Included)

Breaking into freelance writing can be tough for a beginning writer with no published pieces. Chapter two will offer simple ideas on how to build your clips, including writing for nonprofits, using your nonwriting experience, and writing for free to build clips.

Chapter Three: Making the Masthead: Getting Regular Assignments

Obtaining regular assignments is a vital part of building credentials and making a steady income. This chapter shows writers how to increase their chances of getting regular assignments and selling column ideas to magazines, newspapers, and Web sites.

Chapter Four: Knowing Rights From Wrongs: Selling Your Work

This chapter covers selling one-time, First North American, and all rights, and teaches writers how to maintain more of their rights so they can resell their work. It also discusses contracts, negotiating electronic rights, how to obtain additional money for photos, artwork, and sidebars, and what to do when conflicting markets accept the same piece.

Chapter Five: Editors and Predators: Attracting the Good Ones

Contacting editors at magazines, newspapers, Web sites, and small press publications, and how to write a query letter, cover letter, and e-query. It also includes guidelines for submitting articles, reviews, personal essays, and short stories.

Chapter Six: Book Smarts: Writing a Book Proposal

Explains how to write a book proposal and discusses the overview and outline, the importance of a marketing section, and finding competitive books.

Chapter Seven: To Whom It May Concern: Finding an Agent

What writers need to know about synopses, agent etiquette, manuscript formats, and simultaneous submissions.

Chapter Eight: Finding your Hallmark: Writing and Selling Greeting Cards

Tapping into the greeting card market is the subject of the chapter. It describes brainstorming, formatting, and where to send ideas.

Chapter Nine: Thinking Straight: Organizing Your Writing

The importance of organizing writing, including practical tips on how and why to file paperwork, store folders, label properly, and name computer files. Tips include how to follow-up on queries and submissions, and organize multiple projects.

Chapter Ten: Going it Alone: Setting Goals (Included)

Writing can be a lonely business, so readers learn how to set daily, weekly, and long-term goals for projects as well as how to get support from outside sources. From accountability groups to critique groups, the chapter shows how to stay motivated while juggling the demands of a full-time job and writing.

Chapter Eleven: Now or Never: Fighting Procrastination

How and why writers procrastinate as well as tips for overcoming procrastination by changing one's patterns, goals, and motivations. Tips from other writers on what works and why. Creative exercises and brainstorming tidbits for even the smallest bits of free time including "writing" in traffic.

Chapter Twelve: Where Do I Go From Here? References and Resources

Search engines can help writers find what they need, but what if they don't know what they're looking for? From key phrases like "call for submissions" to writing Web sites, online publications and writing e-zines, the chapter tells where and how to find the good stuff without wading through the junk.

[Note: Sample chapters were included, as indicated in outline]

EXAMPLE 5.10   GOOD BOOK PROPOSAL (SIMPLE)

[Pitch sheet, with contact information omitted for privacy]

BORN ON A ROTTEN DAY

In love with an obtuse Taurus, drunk Pisces, or hot-headed Aries? Fed up with whining relatives and backstabbing co-workers? Discover how to use your own inner brat to outwit bullies, outmaneuver manipulators, and win those endless games that lovers play.

Forget traditional astrology and take a trip to the maladjusted side of the universe. **BORN ON A ROTTEN DAY** debunks the myths, reveals the flaws, and examines the dubious virtues of each sign. Find out who's the compulsive cheater, the hypochondriac, emotional blackmailer.

BORN ON A ROTTEN DAY takes a cheerfully jaundiced jab at each sun-sign personality. It exaggerates the bad, exorcises the good, and puts a new spin on the age-old question—what's your sign?

About the Author

Hazel Dixon-Cooper is a professional astrologer and teacher of astrology. She is a member of the American Federation of Astrologers and writes a horoscope column for a weekly entertainment magazine.

She is also a freelance journalist, most recently writing three columns for McClatchy newspapers.

She is currently writing a second humorous astrology book, *Love on a Rotten Day*.

[Condensed proposal]

BORN ON A ROTTEN DAY

Illuminating the Dark Side of the Zodiac

Overview

Traditional astrology books dispense advice on health, money, and the pursuit of true love. **BORN ON A ROTTEN DAY** is the first book to focus on the unenlightened qualities of each sign. It explores the dark side of the sun sign personality types and describes what to expect if you love, live, or work with one of these disagreeable characters. It reveals how to outwit bullies, outmaneuver manipulators, and thwart emotional blackmailers.

BORN ON A ROTTEN DAY takes a cheerfully jaundiced jab at each sign. Anecdotes and quotes involving famous characters from both fiction and life illustrate various churlish behaviors.

Joan Crawford and Bette Davis are classic examples of why the Aries female is known as Queen Bitch of the Universe. The Ayatollah Khomeini, Saddam Hussein, William Randolph Hearst—all the best dictators are born under the sign of Taurus. Think double-trouble when thinking about the Gemini twins. The Norman Bates character in Psycho was no doubt an Oedipus-obsessed Cancer. But Mother had to be a Virgo. Congenitally nitpicky Virgo can drive a saint to kill. Leos will stand on their heads, or someone else's back, to get attention. Libra lover boys and girls are vain, indecisive, and easy targets for insincere flattery.

Scorpios will self-destruct to prove a point. Sagittarians make the best serial killers. That constant smile covers a volcanic hostility. Capricorns, even the ones crawling out of the gutter, are stodgy, social-climbing snobs. Aquarians are so preoccupied with themselves they frequently forget where, and with whom, they live. Pisces goes with the flow, right into the sewer of humanity.

BORN ON A ROTTEN DAY invites readers to take a saucy trip to the maladjusted side of the universe. Readers will be shown their own petulant inner child and how to use its power to goad the powerful, torment the chronically anal, and win those endless games that lovers play.

At an approximate length of 55,000 words, the book will consist of thirteen chapters and an introduction.

BORN ON A ROTTEN DAY reveals all the flaws and dubious virtues of each sign. The barbs are sharp. The tone is biting. But the premise is that, in humanity's fevered search for peace, love, and the meaning of life, the universal common denominator is humor.

About the Author

Hazel Dixon-Cooper is a professional astrologer and teacher of astrology. She is a member of the American Federation of Astrologers and writes a horoscope column for a weekly magazine. She also writes three columns for *The Fresno Bee*, the largest daily newspaper in the San Joaquin Valley (circulation 450,000).

She is currently working on a second book, *Love on a Rotten Day*.

Market Analysis

Target Readers

Primary target readers for **BORN ON A ROTTEN DAY** are women, aged eighteen and above, who are the principal buyers of all self-help and relationship books, and New Age materials, including astrology books and horoscope magazines. This audience is familiar with the names of the zodiac signs and also with some of the basic character traits of each sign. They often read the daily horoscope in the newspaper and frequently peruse astrological Web sites. This audience will appreciate the fact that the author is a professional astrologer and that the book is astrologically accurate. They will enjoy the unique perspective and the humorous tone.

Secondary audiences are men who appreciate astrology and frequently buy astrological and other New Age materials, and the skeptical, who will find the book entertaining and fun to read. The latter group will discover that **BORN ON A ROTTEN DAY** is the perfect put-down gift for their New Age friends.

Professional or amateur astrologers and astrology students will enjoy the premise and see it as a lively change from typical astrology books. The book will also make an excellent all-occasion gift.

BORN ON A ROTTEN DAY was developed from the author's lifelong appreciation of human character and twenty-five years' study of astrology.

Competition

More than 16 percent of books published today fall into the category of New Age/Spirituality, and the popularity of astrology continues to soar throughout the world. Amazon. com lists 3,274 books with astrology titles alone. However, less than 2 percent are written from a humorous perspective. Humor is an enduring nonfiction genre, and the time is right to include an astrology book.

Sun Signs by Linda Goodman (Taplinger Publishing Co.,1968; Reprinted by Bantam Books, 1971) is still popular after more than twenty years. Goodman's conversational style is easy to follow and reader-friendly. She offers advice on love, friendship, children, and work, with an overview of each sign. Her book emphasizes the good qualities of each sign and softens the negative ones.

BORN ON A ROTTEN DAY is deliberately presented as an exposé of common astrology personality types. It assumes everyone is a crank, crackpot, or emotional vampire and instructs the reader in the fine art of handling these obnoxious characters.

The Only Astrology Book You'll Ever Need, by Joanna Martine Woolfolk (Stein & Day, 1982) is a best-selling how-to guide presented from the traditional viewpoint. Written for the amateur or student astrologer, it leads the reader through the process of casting and interpreting a simple horoscope chart. Woolfolk provides a brief look at the mythology behind astrology and gives a short history lesson of astrology throughout the ages. Although she presents a wealth of information, the negative qualities of each sign are presented as a list of dangers, without further explanation or application.

BORN ON A ROTTEN DAY discloses the bad behavioral traits of each sign. Readers will easily recognize their own irascible sides as well as those of family, friends, coworkers, and other acquaintances.

The Secret Language of Birthdays and *The Secret Language of Relationships* by Gary Goldschneider and Joost Elffers (Penguin Studio, 1997) are two oversize, coffee-table volumes that use the day of the month as a further indicator of the sun sign personality. The former focuses on the individual and the latter on relationship compatibility. Goldschneider and Elffers have divided the zodiac into forty-eight personology periods, with subtitles such as The Week of the Child or The Week of the Empath. They give an overview of each sign that includes some dark-side qualities, however, the primary focus is on the positive, as well as the various layers of compatibility.

BORN ON A ROTTEN DAY's primary focus is entertainment. It suggests there are no compatible relationships, only the Sturm und Drang of maneuvering for control.

Promotion

Hazel Dixon-Cooper will actively promote **BORN ON A ROTTEN DAY** through New Age and general bookstores, and will travel to promote the book. As an astrology teacher and practicing professional, she will secure book reviews and interviews through contacts in the local news and media, and is constructing a Web site and will promote the book through links to other astrology and New Age sites, as well as additional sites that are of interest to women.

As a member of the American Federation of Astrologers, the author can also arrange to promote **BORN ON A ROTTEN DAY** at various astrological conferences, including the AFA's annual convention, which attracts more than fifteen thousand participants. The author will also seek endorsements from world-renowned astrologers, such as Jonathan Cainer.

The author will arrange speaking engagements for astrology and writers groups, as the book will fit into each category comfortably. For an astrological audience, she will use her book as an example that is both accurate and entertaining.

LANDING AGENT REPRESENTATION

There are lots of ways to go about finding an agent.

You can ask for recommendations from fellow writers or writing instructors who are familiar with your genre. Be forewarned: Not everyone is eager to share their agent, or to offer a direct referral—especially if they feel your work is not ready for publication. Asking for recommendations is one thing; asking for a referral (or the right to mention your friend's name) may put her on the spot. I get a lot of requests from fellow writers to share the name and contact information of my agent. Some even ask if I'll put in a good word for them. I usually explain that referrals haven't worked out in the past, and recommend they simply do some research on their own to find a good fit.

It's not unheard of for writers to land a book deal with a publisher before hiring an agent. In many cases, it's still beneficial for the author to acquire representation. Such was the case with this book; I landed the deal without an agent and then asked the editorial director at Writer's Digest Books if she could recommend some agents with whom she enjoyed working. She seemed delighted that I was open to her suggestions, and the agent I chose knew the standard Writer's Digest Books contract so well that we were able to expedite the process.

Another approach is to search the dedications or acknowledgments pages of books similar to your own. Many authors thank their agents in their books, and a simple Google search or a search in an agents directory (see list on page 174) will easily turn up contact information. This is a quick and easy way to track down agents who represent your genre, although there are a few caveats. For one, agents sometimes stop representing certain genres. Also, some agents don't represent unpublished authors, so don't assume that Stephen King's agent is on the prowl for undiscovered horror writers. This just means it's still your responsibility to research agents you find this way and familiarize yourself with their areas of representation and submission guidelines.

For most new writers, the quest for an agent begins with a search through a directory of agents. There are several great resources that list the important details of credible agents, including:

- *Guide to Literary Agents* (updated annually): www.guidetoliterary-agents.com
- *Jeff Herman's Guide to Book Publishers, Editors, & Literary Agents* (updated annually): www.jeffherman.com/guide
- The Association of Authors' Representatives: www.aar-online.org
- *Literary Market Place*: www.literarymarketplace.com

Although books are not always as up to date as Web sites, it's often easier to use a book when doing the following steps because you can use the indexes and make notes on the pages next to the agencies' listings.

To start, you'll need to do a search by genre. Make a list of all the agents that represent your book's genre or topic. Rule out any that aren't taking new clients.

Next, look at the important statistics. These include percentage of books from first-time authors, number of queries and manuscripts received each year, rejection rate, number of clients represented, and number of books sold each year. You may also be able to find the percentage of client representation by category (e.g., 40 percent nonfiction, 55 percent fiction, 5 percent textbooks). Some directories also allow for detailed comments from the agent, such as:

- Most common mistakes authors make
- Description of a dream client (or client from hell)
- Best way to initiate contact ("camping out in my front yard")
- Areas most interested in agenting

- Tips to increase chances of landing the agent
- Titles the agent has represented
- A description of the agent's business/management style

Now rule out agents that don't take simultaneous submissions. If you choose not to do this step, you'll have to wait to hear back from each one before pursuing another.

Finally, visit the agency's Web site to review its submission guidelines. If no guidelines are posted on the Web site, contact the agency to request them. You may also want to review a list of titles that the agent has represented (and sold) in the past and mention one or two in your query letter.

Once you've got your list narrowed down, begin submitting your (perfected!) query letter.

Approach With Caution

If you find an agent from another means (e.g., an ad posted on the Web, solicitation through the mail), you'll need to confirm that the agency is legitimate. There are a lot of scam artists out there posing as agents when in fact they're merely preying on the dreams of unknowing authors. While you should always cross-reference the agent with a reputable source (such as one of the aforementioned books or Web sites), there are a few red flags that should send you running for the hills.

Up-front fees

Agents only make money when they sell your book. If they charge a reading fee (or "handling" fee), scratch them off your list and don't look back. However, some reputable agents will take their photocopy and postage reimbursement (used to mail your manuscripts to publishers) out of your advance check. (Your advance check goes through your agent, who takes his cut before mailing you the remainder.)

An offer to edit your book

Although a legitimate agent may make some editorial suggestions, reputable agents aren't in the business of book doctoring. If she offers to do so (or refer you to one particular person or company), she's probably making money off the deal. This is a conflict of interest and a sign that the agent isn't making her living off selling books, but rather, editing services.

Lack of communication

This is a broad category but in general it refers to three things: an agent who won't answer your questions promptly, who won't supply you with a direct phone number to his office, or who won't supply you with responses from publishers.

Yes, agents are busy, but they make their money off their clients and therefore should be able to respond to your questions—no matter how big or small—in a timely manner.

And any agent that directs you to a generic voice message that is never answered by a human may be a sign that you're dealing with a front, like a vanity press.

If you've requested copies of publishers' rejection letters and your agent can't (or won't) supply them, cut ties and run. It probably means that your manuscript was never submitted.

No published clients

If your agent can't supply you with the titles (and authors) of books she's gotten published by commercial book publishers (read: not self-published/vanity presses), she's either brand spanking new, not reputable, or not very good at her job. In any of the three cases, you're better off searching for representation elsewhere.

While there are a few legit agents who claim to specialize in unpublished writers, in most cases, these claims are made by con artists who know that new (and often, less knowledgeable) writers are easier to fool.

Legitimate agents are also willing to give you the names of a few clients they've represented so you can call and ask questions about the authors' experiences with the agent.

Trolling for clients

Good agents don't have to post solicitations for new writers on the Web (especially sites geared to amateur writers) or in classified ads in the back of magazines. Also, be wary of agents who make the initial contact with you

---

(instead of the other way around), especially if they "guarantee" they can get your book published. Real agents can barely keep up with the submissions they receive! (There are notable exceptions—writers who've been contacted by big-name agents after having short fiction or articles published in reputable literary or commercial magazines or after winning a prestigious prize. If this is your experience, my advice is to research the agent who contacts you before you even respond to his query.)

There are some great Web sites that help keep track of scam artists (or just plain horrible agents). Although you can certainly do a search for a particular agent on your own, you may want to scan a few of these lists first and keep a running blacklist in your notes.

- Writer Beware (www.sfwa.org/beware): Perhaps the most famous of all warning sites for writers, hosted by the Science Fiction and Fantasy Writers of America

- Agent Research & Evaluation (www.agentresearch.com): A consulting company that offers a free agent verification search

- Preditors & Editors (www.invirtuo.cc/prededitors or anotherealm. com/prededitors): Offers an alphabetical search with notations on illegitimate or irresponsible agents and publishers

- Absolute Write Water Cooler (www.absolutewrite.com/forums/): Features a forum called "Bewares and Background Check" under the Conference Room section.

Choosing Wisely

If you think choosing which editors to submit to was difficult, wait until it's time to choose among those agents offering representation. (Yes, you may get more than one offer. And yes, you're starting to garner some power. Don't let it go to your head. Yesterday you were eating ramen noodles for dinner.)

You can put your penny away. There are more precise ways to choose representation than flipping a coin. Probably the best route is to ask the (competing) agents a list of questions. Of course, some of these may have already been answered as you muddled through the trenches of agency guidelines and Web sites. (You did do that, didn't you?) But the remaining questions may offer not only some factual information for your big decision, but also some personal insight into with whom you'll click, develop a long-term relationship, and (hopefully) make money.

Before contacting agents for representation

Search their Web sites for:

1. What genres do they represent?
2. Do they charge any reading or handling fees?
3. Are they a member of the AAR?
4. What percentage do they charge? (Usually 15 percent for domestic sales and 20 percent for foreign)
5. Do they handle other rights? (Audio, film, foreign translation, etc.)
6. What percentage of their clients are first-time authors?
7. Are there other agents at the agency or is it a one-person operation?

After you've received an offer of representation

You should ask:

1. Can you give me the author, title, and contact information for a few previous clients (preferably in my genre) so I can ask them questions about their experience with your agency?
2. How many authors do you represent?
   Of those, how many are published?
3. Who will typically answer the phone when I call?
   You? An assistant? Voice mail?
4. Do you work with a publicist?
5. Will I receive copies of publishers' rejection letters?
6. Do you provide an agent representation agreement?
7. What if things don't work out? Can I look for another agent?
8. How involved are you in critiquing work?
9. How involved are you in your clients' career paths?
10. Have you ever fired a client? If so, why?
11. Have you ever sold audio, film, or foreign rights?

Questions to ask your (prospective) agent's clients

1. In general, would you recommend this agent? Why or why not?
2. On a scale of one to ten, how hard did he work for you?
3. Did the agent keep you updated regularly?
4. Was most of your correspondence with the agent by phone or e-mail?
5. How promptly did she return your calls?
6. How valued did you feel as a client?
7. How long did it take him to sell your book(s)?
8. Did you keep the agent for your next book? (If applicable)
9. Were you satisfied with the advance, royalties, and rights she negotiated for you?
10. Did he offer editorial suggestions, and if so, to what degree?

Questions to ask the agent you choose to represent you

1. Will you be submitting my query/manuscript to several publishers at once (simultaneous submission) or one at a time?
2. How many publishers will you approach? (The new writer's dream response: "As many as it takes, but this manuscript is so wonderful that I expect it to get picked up pretty quickly. Have you picked out your mansion yet?")
3. Which publishing houses are you most eager to approach?
4. What are your hours?
5. Who is my contact when you're not available?
6. How often should I check in? Or how often will you update me?
7. What will you be submitting to publishers—the entire manuscript, a proposal, a synopsis and sample chapters?
8. What kind of advance can I expect to get as a first-time author?
9. What's your biggest pet peeve with clients?
10. What should I be doing while you're shopping my manuscript?

Remember, you are under no obligation to accept any representation. If you don't like the responses of any of the agents who offer to represent you, you can always go back to the drawing board and look for more agents, or approach publishers on your own.

BECOMING THE MODEL CLIENT

Ask agents what they like in a client and you'll probably be surprised at how similar the responses are. For the most part, they'll all mention something along the lines of "professional," "hard-working," and "easy to work with." (Those adjectives alone will help new writers understand what agents *aren't*: babysitters, drill sergeants, or sadomasochists.)

Delve a bit deeper and the commonalities still remain. Sure, agents will have their own preferences when it comes to favorite genres, levels of author experience (sorry newbies), and even financial potential ("Now how am I supposed to sell this critique of Yugoslavian feminist literature from the 1800s to Hollywood?!"), but for the most part, you can count on these ten standard qualifiers when it comes to agents describing their dream clients.

Have a Platform

Here's a news flash that most creative types don't want to hear: Successful writers aren't necessarily successful for their writing; they're successful for their marketing. Ouch!

Yes, there are lots of great (even award-winning) writers out there, but there are just as many average writers out there who have a means of promoting themselves and their work. While the ideal would be an author who has both (talent to write *and* market themselves), many agents would rather have the latter if they had to choose. Why? Because book sales depend as much on the writer's promotional efforts (or more so) as they do those of the publishing house. (An agent has virtually nothing to do with marketing a book to the reading public. After the book comes out, the agent's job is to keep track of your royalties and try to sell other rights—like film, TV, audio, or foreign translation—to earn you extra money.)

Many new writers are disheartened to learn that publishing houses (yes, even bigger ones) don't always send their authors on huge cross-country book tours. Many publishing houses do little to promote your book at all, leaving you to find your own avenues (speaking gigs, teaching workshops, book signings, author readings, blogs, mass mailings, published excerpts in magazines, radio/TV interviews) to sell books. To an agent, who only makes money when *you* make money, finding an author with an established platform is a sign of potential income above and beyond the advance. See **Example 5.11** (pgs. 179–180) for an agent query from an author with a good platform.

Understand the Business and Its Processes

No agent expects an author to be as knowledgeable about the industry as *she* is, but it's certainly nice to represent a writer who knows the basics of how publishing works. A client who understands the importance of a strong query (and synopsis, outline, or book proposal), the steps that go into shopping a manuscript, and the effort and knowledge it takes to get from point A to point B is a godsend in a time when everyone with a computer has dreams of being the next Tom Clancy or Danielle Steel.

Be Willing to Rewrite

If you're one of those writers who falls in love easily (with your words), you either need to self-publish or get over it. Manuscripts almost never go to print exactly as they came in from the author and many undergo several revisions. The same goes for titles (which are often changed at the last minute due to recently released books with similar names) and even query letters. If an experienced agent suggests changes to your query letter (or synopsis, outline, or book proposal), you don't have to agree—or make the changes. But know that he's only trying to increase your chances of getting published—not flaunt his power or expertise. Agents only make money when you make money, so you can rule out the power trip theory ... and make the tweaks.

Respect Your Agent's Opinions

This isn't just about revising your work; it's about heeding your agent's advice when she says a publisher isn't right for you, it's worth waiting to hear from a publisher that doesn't take simultaneous submissions, or she can negotiate more money. (Don't worry, publishers don't change their minds about accepting an author just because her agent tries to squeeze a bit more money out of them.)

EXAMPLE 5.11   GOOD QUERY FROM AUTHOR WITH PLATFORM

February 27, 2007

Kristin Nelson
Nelson Literary Agency
1732 Wazee Street, Suite 207
Denver, CO 80202

Dear Ms. Nelson,

Think that annoying spam clogging your computer is just so much cyber-junk? Top-notch TV reporter Charlotte McNally suspects some of it may be much more than that—in fact, she's certain it carries secret big-money messages to a powerful inner circle of executives who possess the key to its code.

Turns out—as Charlotte discovers—the last outsider who deciphered the spam's hidden clues now resides in the local morgue. Was his car accident really a car accident? Charlotte's spidey-sense for news may have put her on the trail of the biggest story of her life—or the one that may end it.

PRIME TIME introduces Charlotte McNally, a hip and attractive fifty-something journalist who's facing some life-changing challenges. Charlie's smart, successful, and devoted to Italian clothing designers—but she's worried her news director is about to replace her with a younger model. Even though she's won a row of Emmys for her investigative reporting, she's convinced that unless she digs up another blockbuster in time for the next ratings book, she may be fired from the job she loves.

Charlie's got too many pairs of shoes, too many graying hairs, and even a hot flash or two—but she puts her life on the line for a story, and her heart on the line for a guy. **PRIME TIME** —approximately 95,000 words—is a mystery in a lady lit voice. It's an action-filled page-turner, with humor, romance and a stock market scheme so timely and innovative you'll wonder why someone hasn't tried it. A twist of an ending will have readers going back to the beginning to check for all the clues they missed.

It's also a look from inside at the world of television news: its ambition, cynicism, tyrannical managers, clothing allowances, ratings wars, power struggles, and even a few devoted journalists.

On a personal note, my twenty-second year of reporting at WHDH-TV (NBC/Boston) has been a terrific one so far. I won two more Emmys for my investigative and consumer stories (that makes twenty-three), and three more Edward R. Murrow Awards, including the one for best writing.

After all my years in journalism and affiliation with investigative reporters and editors, I have lots of pals in local TV and newspapers across the country, as well as at all the networks. So I figure, add those publicity and blurb resources to the millions of TV viewers who already recognize my name and we could have a ready-made marketing platform.

For experienced and savvy women who are weary of reading about chick lit chicks swilling Cosmos (not that there's anything wrong with that), **PRIME TIME** is a satisfying selection for beach, book club, or curling up with a cup of tea. And they'll never look at spam the same way again.

What happens next to Charlie, her career, and her future with a dishy professor? I'm currently working on the next in the series, **FACE TIME**, where Charlie contemplates cosmetic surgery to stave off on-the-air aging and uncovers a series of murders in a luxury hospital.

You don't say on your Web site whether your interest in chick-lit mysteries extends to chic but older chicks—I hope it does. May I send you the completed manuscript? Thanks so much for your time and consideration. I look forward to hearing from you.

Best,

Hank (Harriet Ann) Phillippi Ryan
(address/phone/e-mail)

[Note: This query landed the agent and sold to Harlequin.
The title remained unchanged.]

And all of this is not to say that you shouldn't question your agent if you have legitimate cause for concern. It simply means that agents like to feel appreciated and valued for their opinions and their expertise, whether it's about your work, your publishing options, or the future of your career. (Besides, you don't want an agent with *no* opinion about what you do as long as you make her money. That's what spouses are for.)

Have a Book Deal With a Publisher

Yes, I know, it sounds crazy. And while it's easy to see why agents would love this, there *is* still work involved once a deal is made (negotiating money and contract rights, selling other rights outside the publishing house). Besides, just because you sold one book yourself doesn't mean you can sell future books. It also doesn't mean you can approach some of the big publishing houses. Even with one book under your belt, some publishers will still only accept agented submissions.

In some cases, authors can generate advance interest in other media rights as well. If you happen to have run the idea by your cousin, who turns children's books into Saturday morning cartoons, or your brother-in-law at a production company said he might be interested in turning your book into a movie, mention it. You don't have to have anything set in stone. Just indicate that there's an interest and explain more later. (But this interest must be from a legitimate, connected source. Saying your high school Spanish teacher thinks the book would sell well in Colombia does not count.) See **Example 5.12** (pg. 182–183) for an agent query that uses this tactic.

Have Incredible Talent (Without the Ego)

Every agent dreams of discovering the next great writer, especially if she doesn't act too big for her britches. Authors with both incredible talent and humility are as likely to happen as your Great Aunt Louise leaving you millions in her will "on the condition you keep being you." Authors with incredible talent and egos are as likely as your Great Aunt Louise leaving you millions in her will if your promise to take care of her thirty-nine cats until they die of natural causes. The first one is vastly preferred, but you'll put up with the second one because it's a package deal that could pay for your kid's college tuition.

Have Patience

Your book took a year to write and now you're eager to make some money, right? The bad news is, the majority of book deals don't happen overnight. The worse news is, there's not much you can do about it. Agents are as eager to sell their clients' manuscripts (OK, maybe not *as* eager) as their clients are to have them sold. And unless your agent is in the hospital (or rather, thanks to the slush pile, *mental* hospital), chances are he is doing as much as possible to get you a publisher. Checking in once in a while is allowed—even encouraged. E-mailing a daily equivalent of "are we there yet?" is not.

Strive for More Than One Book

No one likes a one-hit wonder. (In the music world, the label itself is enough to make a grown man cry.) Agents rarely rule out a prospective client based on the fact that she's not pitching a series, but that doesn't mean they're not hopeful you have other projects in the works. Agents like long-term relationships, especially if the author has the qualities mentioned above (professional,

EXAMPLE 5.12   GOOD QUERY OF AUTHOR WITH MOVIE INTEREST

February 27, 2007

Kristin Nelson and Sara Megibow
Nelson Literary Agency
1732 Wazee Street, Suite 207
Denver, CO 80202

Dear Ms. Nelson and Ms. Megibow,

I am a big fan of Ms. Nelson's blog and the dedication and positive attitude obvious in every post. I would like you to consider **THE DEMON'S LEXICON**, my YA urban fantasy set in modern-day England. The manuscript is complete at 75,000 words.

What would be the first word to come to mind about the runaway romance between a beautiful, headstrong woman and a darkly fascinating magician?

For Nick, it's "embarrassing," since said beautiful, headstrong woman was his mum. Sixteen-year-old Nick has been brought up on the run from the darkly fascinating magician after things really didn't work out between him and Nick's mother. He resents his mother for the predicament they're in, and he was mostly raised by his older brother, Alan.

Nick has also been brought up knowing that there are certain people who have limited magical abilities. Some of them, the magicians, increase these magical abilities by summoning demons who give them more power—in return for the magicians giving them people to possess. The other magically gifted people have considerably less power and rely on magical trinkets and information, exchanged every month at a "goblin market." As the only people who know about the magicians and their victims, they do try to control things, but it's an endeavor that is not going well.

Nick, who can summon demons and is pretty handy with a sword, is mostly concerned with just getting by, but his life is greatly complicated by the advent of his brother's latest crush. Not only is she a little too attractive for Nick's peace of mind, but she has a boy in tow who bears the marks of demon possession. Added to that the fact that Nick has started to suspect that Alan, the only person in his life whom he trusts, has been lying to him about a few very serious things, and not only Nick, but everybody else, are in for some surprises.

I have a popular online blog, some contacts in the writing and publishing world, and movie interest in this project from Dino De Laurentiis Productions. I want to move ahead on this with an agent, and I also want an agent for the long term, for negotiation and guidance—in fact, everything it says on the tin—that is to say, your Web site.

Thank you for your time, and I look forward to hearing back from you.

Yours,

Sarah Rees Brennan
(address/phone/e-mail)

[Note: This query landed the agent and sold to Margaret K. McElderry Books
(Simon & Schuster). The title remained unchanged.]

easy to work with, hard-working). Prolific writers who can produce multiple quality manuscripts are gems by any standards.

Be Careful With Referrals

If you're a good writer, you probably know good writing (and conversely, crappy writing) when you see it. Once you land an agent, you can expect that everyone you know who has ever written so much as a line of poetry will ask you to refer them to your agent. Don't do it. Or at the very least, choose wisely, Grasshopper.

If you've read a friend's, co-worker's, or family member's manuscript and you think it has real potential to be made into a book, go ahead and give them the name of your agent and permission to use your name. But consider the consequences if any of the following occur:

- Word gets out to all the other wannabe writers in your circle to whom you were *not* willing to give a referral.
- Your agent declines to represent your friend.
- Your agent agrees to represent your friend and then your friend doesn't accept or accepts and then never follows through (e.g., misses deadlines to complete the book or proposal).
- Your agent agrees to represent your friend and lands him a publisher before landing you one (or doesn't get you one at all).
- Your agent agrees to represent your friend and he becomes a household name and gets a $603 million advance plus 90 percent royalties.

Okay, so the last one is probably the least likely of the five to occur, but you do need to think about what will happen if your friend ends up being more successful than you. What happens when the apprentice becomes the master?

If you're not the jealous type, go ahead and make the referral. Your agent will appreciate it and so will your friend. Besides, you can always write a tell-all book about how you knew him and helped him get his first big break. And maybe *that* will be the book that makes you money.

A CLIENT ONLY A MOTHER COULD LOVE

Want to avoid being that ignored (or blacklisted) writer at the top agencies? Here are some sure-fire ways to tick off (or just bore) literary agents.

Sending Unfocused Queries
An unfocused query is made of one page (or worse, multiple pages) of rambling with no specific point. These scattered thoughts often leave the agent feeling confused (about your topic, genre, or experience) and will quickly send you to the recycle bin. If you can't get your point across in a query, an agent is never going to ask to read more.

Not Following Through on Deadlines
This is one of the biggest sins in the publishing industry. If an agent agrees to represent you and you continually drag your feet on getting him a complete proposal (or manuscript), why would he ever expect you could meet your deadline to finish writing the book?

Including Irrelevant Information in Your Query
We're back to the "my friends all love this idea" concept. Leave out anything that doesn't pertain to the topic or genre of your book, your writing experience, or your experience directly relevant to the topic (e.g., twenty years as a nurse qualifies you to write a book on nursing). No one cares if it took you five years to write your novel or if you ate only vanilla pudding while doing so.

Lying/Exaggerating

Were you really the president's mistress for three years? Did you really scale Mt. Everest by yourself? Is your novel really finished or are you just too lazy to complete it before landing representation? Agents are like bloodhounds when it comes to sniffing out the truth. Don't start off on the wrong foot. It's a smaller industry than you think, and word travels fast.

Nagging

Since we've focused on the importance of brevity and tight writing throughout this book, let's stay on the topic. When you need to talk to your agent (or a prospective agent), follow his protocol and, when in doubt, learn to write short, sweet e-mails. "Just wanted you to know that I received your agent agreement and sent it out via UPS today" is a great example of staying in touch without coming across as a nag. Calling and e-mailing daily to ask for updates on your agent's search for a publisher is neither necessary nor appreciated. Dropping him a note about a prize you won or another journal or magazine publication you earned could be an important step toward getting published. Calling him to announce that you've just finished chapter two makes you a nag *and* insecure.

Pushing for Too Much Control

There's good news when it comes to your book's layout, illustrations, and cover design: Sometimes you have a say. The bad news is, that doesn't mean you have the final word. Good agents may try to negotiate to allow for more of your input, but even the great ones can't set the rules at the big publishing houses. Don't insist on creative control over everything. You may even lose some of your favorite parts in the book if the publishing house's editor deems it necessary. (Despite initial tantrums, most writers admit once the book is finished that the cuts were the right decision.)

Unless you feel very strongly about the proposed changes, don't push back too hard. The more books you get published, the more control you'll have.

Expecting an Unrealistic Advance and Royalties

Chances are that as a first-time author, you're not going to get rich. In fact, you may not even be able to buy yourself a new car (maybe a Hyundai).

New authors often make the mistake of assuming that the few-and-far-between stories they hear about huge advances apply to most authors. (Or, if they've got big egos, apply to them.) The reality of book publishing is that you probably won't make enough money to quit your day job until several (published) books down the road—if *ever*. In fact, for most first-time authors, the advance (if there is one) isn't even enough to live off of while you finish the book.

In addition, many first-time authors never see any royalties. That's because the advance is just that: an advance against royalties. So if your advance is based on what you'd earn in royalties from the first print run (say ten thousand books), you don't earn any royalties until book number 10,001 sells. For many first-time authors, that never happens. On the bright side, you don't have to pay back your advance if your first print run doesn't sell out.

AGENT QUERY FAQS

WILL AN AGENT GIVE ME FEEDBACK ON MY MANUSCRIPT?

This depends on the agent. Most agents don't have time to read (let alone critique) the entirety of every manuscript that comes through their doors. Much like a magazine editor, if a query doesn't spark an agent's interest in the first few paragraphs, it's generally returned to the writer with a standard (form) rejection letter.

Some agents do take the time to include a sentence or two about why your piece was rejected. Things like "We don't represent science fiction" or "We are inundated with romance novels right now" or "The manuscript is too long for a picture book" may not necessarily indicate that your writing isn't up to par, just that you need to revise it or seek out another agent. (Note: Many responses like the above can be avoided by reviewing each agency's writer's guidelines *before* you submit.)

If you're lucky, you'll stumble upon an agent who sees the potential in your work and is willing to give you general feedback in order to allow you to revise the manuscript (query, book proposal, or novel). While it's always your decision to take or leave the advice, it's important to remember that a good agent is more likely to know and understand the current publishing industry better than you do. If she recommends that you add more competition to your book proposal, do it. If she believes your synopsis needs to open in the middle of the action instead of with lengthy backstory, revise it.

If the feedback comes from the very first agent you target, you may want to try a few others before making the revisions. But if you've tried several agents and no one has bitten, revising your work might be just what you need to get representation.

CAN I FIRE MY AGENT?

Yes, you can fire your agent, and there are times you should.

An agent who isn't staying in regular contact with you or updating you on responses from publishers may not be serving you well. You have a right to know to which publishers your manuscript is being submitted and what type of responses you're receiving.

Also, an agent who takes forever to get back to you with answers to your questions (especially once you're his client) may be overwhelmed with too many clients.

Don't necessarily jump to fire an agent just because he hasn't immediately landed you a publishing deal, however. Some deals take time and some manuscripts (even those with merit) will *never* find a publisher, no matter what agent represents you.

IS IT EASIER TO GET AN AGENT THAN A PUBLISHER?

Not necessarily. Although it's true that publishers plan to publish everything they buy while agents expect that they can't sell every project they represent, the competition is still stiff when it comes to getting an agent. (This is especially true in tough economic times when fewer books are being bought—both by publishers and readers—and with first-time novelists.)

The typical agent only agrees to represent about 2 percent of the manuscripts (or ideas, in the case of nonfiction) that are submitted to him. If you're wondering why agents don't accept a higher percentage of pieces, the answer is twofold:

• Agents don't have time to represent hundreds of clients at once.

• Agents have to keep up their reputations among publishers. If they continually shop low-quality pieces, publishers will no longer consider them to be respectable agents.

Remember, reputable agents make all (or darn near close to all) of their money by selling books. Just as an Oscar-winning actor wouldn't want to take every single role he was offered (Hear that, Cuba Gooding, Jr. in *Boat Trip*?), agents know that a few deals gone bad (authors missing deadlines or never completing manuscripts at all) or shopping too many subpar manuscripts ("it's like *Catwoman* meets *Moby-Dick*!") can end their career. You don't necessarily need to consider yourself *lucky* if you get an agent, just *talented.*

CHAPTER 6

FOLLOWING UP

So you've sent your query, had a celebratory cocktail, and got right to work on your next query letter. (You're not putting all your eggs in one basket, are you?) Soon, one of several things will happen:

1. You'll get an acceptance, assignment, or request for a proposal.
2. You'll get a "possible" (e.g., "We like your idea and are holding it for possible use ...").
3. You'll get a rejection.
4. You'll get impatient.

While numbers one and two are good, number three isn't a lost cause. As you'll read in this chapter, you can learn a lot from your rejection letters, increasing your chances of hitting the mark with your *next* query.

There are even some tips in this chapter for number four. (No, they don't requiring busting anyone's kneecaps!) Though, truth be told, you'll need to start building your patience as you build your writing career.

MAGAZINE ARTICLE QUERIES

Waiting around for a magazine editor to respond to your query can be as agonizing as watching televised bowling. This is especially true with magazines that don't accept simultaneous submissions. Rejections are hard enough without waiting around for six months before learning your article "just isn't a good fit" with the publication. The publishing industry is probably the only one in which "no news is good news" doesn't apply—thanks the likes of eight-foot slush piles.

If you're not the patient type, take note: You've got options.

1. Send queries *only* to magazines that accept simultaneous submissions.
2. Send follow-up correspondence to ask about the status of your query.
3. Break the rules (not recommended!).

There's an advantage and disadvantage to all of the above.

If you choose the first option, you're probably taking the safest route possible. You're following the rules like a good little writer and planning to wait things out as your responses trickle in. This is the least likely choice of the three to elicit any problems.

The second choice is also relatively safe, though there's a reason that magazines post their response times in their writer's guidelines. Following up to ask about the status of your query too early ("I haven't heard from you since I mailed my query last week ...") could send you straight to the rejection pile (not exactly the type of prompt response you were hoping for). On the other hand, some editors will make the extra effort to pull out your query if your follow-up letter indicates that you sent a timely (or fascinating) pitch.

The third choice isn't one I recommend, though I'll admit I did it myself quite a bit when I was a new (and eager, unrealistic) writer. I sent my queries to *all* the magazines that seemed an appropriate fit (and few that were completely inappropriate)—even those that said "no simultaneous submissions." I never indicated so much in my query and for the most part, it was a nonissue because the acceptances came from noncompetitive publications. I did have one instance where I pitched two (very small, but competitive) markets and both planned to run the article at the same time. This did not go over well and I forfeited payment from one of the publications. (One of the magazines has since gone out of business, so thankfully I can stop worrying that the editor has highlighted my name on her "never again" list of writers.)

If you're dead-set on getting your article into a magazine that doesn't accept simultaneous submissions, there is a safe compromise. Send your query and then follow-up *exactly* at the cited response deadline. That is, if a magazine says, "We respond to queries in six months," put your follow-up letter in the mail two days before the deadline with a gentle reminder that you've waited the obligatory half a year. For a sample follow-up letter to a query, see **Example 6.1**.

QUERIES TO AGENTS

There's probably not as much of a risk in following up with an agent a bit too soon—especially if she doesn't accept simultaneous submissions. Since

EXAMPLE 6.1   SAMPLE FOLLOW-UP LETTER TO ARTICLE QUERY

March 20, 2008

Jeremy White, Editor-in-Chief
Pizza Today
908 S. 8th St., Ste. 200
Louisville, KY 40203

Dear Mr. White,

Thank you for choosing to publish my article, "Say Cheese! Turning Your Pizzeria's Press Release Into Free Publicity" in your recent issue. I appreciated the contributor's copies that you sent.

I am writing to follow up on my January 21 submission for an article entitled, **"The Juicy Details: Should You Be Offering Fruit Juice to Your Customers?"** The 1,000-word piece would cover topics like the future of juice trends, making a profit, marketing juice to your customers, and choosing juices. I have several pizzeria owners and a juice distributor that I could interview.

I am eager to get started on this piece but wanted to wait the two months (as per the standard response time indicated in your writer's guidelines) before pitching the idea to other magazines.

Thank you in advance for your consideration. I look forward to hearing from you.

Best regards,

Wendy Burt-Thomas
(address/phone/e-mail)

---

agents make their money from their clients, they'll likely be hesitant to pass up a book with great potential just because you followed up too early. Good writing is good writing and a quick follow-up e-mail or postcard (similar to the follow-up letter to the magazine editor in **Example 6.1**) is respectful and professional. Besides, there are a lot more agents than publishers out there and agents know that a good writer will likely eventually land representation—and make *that* agent money.

QUERIES TO BOOK PUBLISHERS

You've probably got a bit more at risk if you're waiting to hear back from a publisher. There are only so many publishing houses in the world that accept work from new, unagented authors in your genre. The last thing you want to do is start annoying an acquisitions editor with immediate "have you read it yet?" e-mails. (Don't even think about calling.) Wait for the length of time listed in the publisher's guidelines and then follow-up up with a short, to-the-point postcard. (Publishers are often inundated with e-mails.) It should be professional, informational, and perhaps a bit complimentary.

INTERPRETING REJECTION LETTERS
(AND THE CODED PHRASES WITHIN THEM)

As much as you'd probably like to burn your rejection letters or mold them into little voodoo dolls of the respective editors, *don't*. There's a lot to be learned from the responses (even those that arrive with nothing more than a standard checkbox of reasons the pieces weren't accepted).

Think of your rejections as responses from first dates: Some will be very general ("Sorry, I'm just not that into you."), some will offer minimal feedback ("You talked nonstop about your ex. I don't think you're ready for a new relationship."), and some will offer detailed information to help you improve for your next attempt ("You were charming, attractive, and we had a lot in common, but I just don't date smokers.").

EXAMPLE 6.2   FOLLOW-UP POSTCARD TO BOOK PUBLISHER

March 21, 2008

Nick Beilenson, Editorial Director
Peter Pauper Press, Inc.
202 Mamaroneck Ave.
White Plains, NY 10601-5376

Dear Mr. Beilenson,

Just a quick note to see if you've had a chance to review my January 21 query for **THE THREE-GENERATION MEMORY BOOK FOR WOMEN**, a do-it-yourself book of questions for grandmothers, daughters, and granddaughters.

As you are my top choice for a publisher, I wanted to wait the appropriate two months before querying other publishing houses.

Although I sent an SASE with my query, please feel free to e-mail me as well.

Thank you,

Wendy Burt-Thomas
(address/phone/e-mail)

While it may be hard to swallow, the feedback provided in the last two examples is your best hope of improving your work (query, proposal, or manuscript) in order to eventually get published (or fall in love). Be grateful for it. Most editors are so busy sorting through their slush piles (in addition to all their other work) that they don't have time to offer advice. If they do, it could be because they truly believe your work has potential or because your approach is so far off the mark that they're trying to help you correct your mistakes (and avoid potential embarrassment) before you approach one of their colleagues. Either way, they wouldn't respond if they weren't sincerely trying to help you.

So what are some of the specific types of responses you might get and what can you glean from them?

First, the responses that could have been avoided:

- "No simultaneous submissions."
- "No previously published/reprints." (In the case of magazine articles)
- "Not our genre."

- "Too long." (For magazine articles)
- "Too short." (For book manuscripts)
- "No unagented submissions." (For book publishers)
- "Not right for our audience." (I once sent a query for a parenting article to a magazine for senior citizens because I didn't read the guidelines—or the magazine—first. Not only did I waste my time and postage, but I burned a bridge to ever write for the publication.)
- "No business profiles." (Or personal stories, anecdotes, fiction, etc.)
- "No freelance material accepted." (i.e., everything is staff-written)
- "No e-mail queries."
- "No queries without clips."
- "Query only." (i.e., don't send a proposal, manuscript, or synopsis)
- "That issue is already laid out. Try again next year." (e.g., "You're too late to pitch a Christmas-themed piece but this idea has potential so try us again in six months or so.")
- "No anthropomorphic characters."
- "We just ran something on this topic." (i.e., "Didn't you skim our last couple issues?")
- "We only cover *local* businesses." (Or artists or people)
- "We only publish books from experts in their field." (i.e., "You're not quite qualified to tackle this topic for us.")

Now, the responses that you may or may not have been able to predict:

- "Not our style/voice/tone."

    Translation: This could simply mean that the writing or idea was good, but the magazine or publishing house doesn't print pieces like yours.

    Your next move: Try another magazine/publishing house.

- "We no longer accept this genre."

    Translation: The publishing house has found that it can be more profitable in other genres. That doesn't mean your genre isn't profitable; it's just not for them.

The Writer's Digest Guide to Query Letters

Your next move: Try another publisher who recently printed a book in your genre.

- "We are not accepting new clients at this time."

    Translation: The literary agency could be overwhelmed with clients, in the process of restructuring, or about to fold.

    Your next move: Try another agency.

- "We're already planning to cover this topic in the near future."

    Translation for a magazine article: The editor has already assigned this topic to a writer.

    Your next move: Hurry up and pitch it to another magazine.

    Translation for a publishing house: Another book on the same or a similar topic is in the works. *Your next move:* Pitch it to another publisher fast and see if you can find anything on the Web about the upcoming book. If it looks too similar to yours, see if you can find a way to tweak yours a bit to make it different.

- "This topic has been done to death."

    Translation for a magazine: There's obviously an interest on this topic in general, but find a way to slant it in order to create a new angle.

    Your next move: Pitch the magazine something else (the editor didn't say there was a problem with your writing) or find a way to approach the topic from a new angle. You can also pitch the idea to another magazine after skimming some back issues to make sure they didn't cover the topic recently too.

    Translation for a publishing house: The editor may not be saying that her publishing house in particular has covered this topic in numerous books, but rather that several publishing houses have printed books on the topic recently and the market is saturated.
    Your next move: Find a fresh angle for your book to avoid getting this response from all the other publishers.

And finally, the responses that may blindside you:

- "It doesn't feel as though you've zeroed in on a niche."

  Translation: You were all over the map. The editor or agent couldn't understand the query/synopsis/proposal, or the topic is too broad to fit into one book.

  Your next move: Get a second or third set of eyes to give you feedback on tightening the idea. Hire a book editor if you're serious about seeing your manuscript get published, and don't fall in love with your words because it could need some major rewriting.

- "I really like your protagonist but just can't get on board to represent you."

  Translation: You're great at developing characters but other areas (like plot, motivation, dialogue, or conflict) are still lacking or weak.

  Your next move: Ask a professional editor who works in your genre to give you feedback on your strongest and weakest areas. You may also want to consider taking a class (or attending workshops at a writers conference) specific to your genre.

- "Numerous grammatical errors."

  Translation: You either didn't proofread and spell-check your piece or you don't know grammar. Both are bad but the former is just lazy.

  Your next move: Paying someone to proof your work will only help with the initial step. If you're going to write more articles, finish your book, write another book, or do your own press releases, you'll need to take a few English classes and invest in a copy of Strunk & White's *The Elements of Style*.

- "The book didn't quite live up to my expectations."

  Translation: "The first few sample chapters you sent were great; that's why I requested more. But the book lost its appeal the more I read."

  Your next move: Revisit your book and see where it went off track. Did it change focus? Did the action slow down? Did the main characters lose their charm or do something that no longer made them believable? Rewrite portions of your book if necessary. Don't be afraid to cut words. Just because you hit the word count for a novel doesn't mean it's done.

- "We only publish authors with platforms."

  Translation: "We're a small publishing house with no budget to promote new authors. It's up to you to promote yourself and your book, and since you didn't mention anything about having a platform in your query, we'll have to pass."

  Your next move: Create a platform for yourself now—and mention it in your query to the next publishing house. It could be something as simple as a blog on the subject, teaching a half-day seminar on the topic, or developing or buying an e-mail list of potential customers.

- "I would recommend that you read some of the work of great authors in your genre."

  Translation: Your writing was mediocre or did not adhere to the conventions of the genre in which you are writing, and you need to learn about basic narrative elements like plot, structure, motivation, character development, etc.

  Your next move: Read several classic and contemporary works in your genre and take a writing class before heading back to revise your book. Then, join a critique group or attend a writers conference where you can get feedback from an industry professional. Don't submit your manuscript to any other publishers until someone knowledgeable about your genre has "approved" your piece. And no matter how many Agatha Christie books she has read, your mom does not count. The person who critiques your work should not have given birth to you, dined at your home, or owed you a favor.

- "This isn't quite right for us, but have you tried contacting [*insert name of agent or acquisitions editor*]? This might be a good match for them."

Translation: "This is a good, solid piece of writing. We can't publish it, but it's good enough that I'm willing to put myself out on a limb to give you a referral to another publishing house. I want them to call and thank me when they make money off your book."

Your next move: Call the acquisitions editor at the second publishing house and tell her who referred you. Ask if you can e-mail your query/synopsis/proposal/manuscript immediately. Write the first editor a nice thank-you note and keep him updated in the process.

- "You may want to consider self-publishing."

Translation: Unfortunately, this may mean, "There is nothing that can be done to salvage this book. You need to take ten writing classes, hire an editor, join a writers' group, attend every writers conference in your area over the next three years, and then start from scratch." But it may also mean that your topic or audience is so niche that it's not commercially viable. The editor may be able to tell that this story is one that means a lot to you (like the history of your hometown or a memoir of your boarding school days), but she also knows enough about the industry to see that the book is too "small" to appeal to larger audiences.

Your next move: In case of the first scenario, ask your mom to tell you how great you are. In the second, start researching local printers if you're determined to see your story in print.

RESPONDING TO AN ACCEPTANCE OR REJECTION

While most rejection letters shouldn't elicit a response from you, there are a few exceptions. These include:

- An agent or acquisitions editor referring you to another agent or editor (in which case, a thank-you note would be nice)

- An agent or acquisitions editor referring you to another agency or publishing house (in which case you could respond by asking if there is a specific person that he recommends you contact)

- An agent or acquisitions editor rejecting your piece but suggesting you make changes and then resubmit (in which case you should respond saying if you're planning to make the changes or not—either way thanking her for the feedback)

- A magazine editor rejecting your article query but indicating he'd be open to other ideas (in which case you could respond by asking if he has a particular topic or section of the magazine for which he is in need of articles)

Even acceptance letters require responses. The three primary reasons being:

1. Acknowledgment and gratitude for the acceptance
2. Rejection of the acceptance (such as in the case of a simultaneous submission to magazines or literary agents)
3. Questions regarding the acceptance

In the third case, you will want to contact the agent who has agreed to represent you to get your agent's opinion of the acceptance terms and to discuss negotiation strategies. If you don't already have an agent, it's a lot easier to get one with an acceptance in hand.

For a magazine editor, be sure to inquire as to when he thinks your article will be printed if he hasn't already specified an issue. (An editor that replies, "We're not sure exactly. We're just hanging onto it for now" might cause you to rethink things if another editor offers to publish the piece immediately.) You may also be able to negotiate rights. If the editor agrees to one-time rights, you'll be free to shop the piece elsewhere in the meantime.

In the case of an acquisitions editor, you may need to clarify your next step. If you sent the query saying, "a full proposal including two sample chapters is available upon request" and the publisher wrote back to say, "yes, please send an outline and three sample chapters," you'll need to either send what you've got or request an extension to get the third chapter written. Either way, don't blow your chances by dragging things out. If a publisher shows an interest in your query, send the requested materials out ASAP while the book is fresh in his mind.

 **FOLLOW-UP FAQS**

HOW OFTEN SHOULD I UPDATE MY EDITOR ON MY PROGRESS?

When in doubt, go for short and frequent updates. If you've got a three-month deadline for a magazine article, a once-a-month update should be plenty. Just shoot the editor a quick e-mail saying where you are in the process ("I've got a rough draft done"), any roadblocks you've run into ("Doctor Reed is in the Bahamas on vacation for two weeks so I can't interview her right now"), and how you're addressing them ("I have a back-up pediatrician lined up on the off chance that Doctor Reed doesn't contact me within a week of her return"). Reassure her that you're still on track for your deadline and you'll contact her again if any snags turn up that you can't handle on your own.

Much the same should be done when working with your book editor. Monthly e-mail status updates to your editor would likely bode well for a six-month deadline to turn in your nonfiction book (or edits to a novel). Many contracts are designed to have the first half of your book submitted several months before your second half to make sure your writing is on course with the publishing house's expectations. In such cases, a good check-in point would be halfway between deadlines for both halves of the book. Questions, however, can and should be submitted as you go. Don't worry about bugging your editor. She'll appreciate that you're not making assumptions, and she may nip something in the bud before you turn in a 70,000-word book that completely went off course because you were too shy to ask for guidance.

WHAT'S A REASONABLE NUMBER OF AGENTS OR EDITORS TO TRY BEFORE GIVING UP?

Most writers have probably heard the stories about famous authors like Stephen King getting hundreds of rejection letters (read King's fabulous book, *On Writing*, which details these accounts) before hitting the "big time." Personally, I'd probably sit down to re-evaluate my decision to be a writer if I hit that many walls. But on the other hand, I often hear of first-time authors who give up after only pitching to a handful of agents.

Since the question is subjective, I'll recommend that you read your rejections and look for a pattern. If everyone is telling you that your work is great but they just can't offer representation, keep trying. If, on the other hand, you're getting the same comments over and over again (or worse—a standard rejection form), it may be time to hire a professional editor to get some feedback. Yes, it'll cost you money, but it will be worth it in the long run if you learn where your writing is weak and rectify the issues to create a stronger manuscript/query/proposal.

CHAPTER 7

OTHER FORMS OF CORRESPONDENCE

Not all your correspondence will include intensely researched ideas and cunningly crafted pitches. Sometimes you'll just need to head back to the basics, drafting a simple follow-up note or handwriting a thank-you card.

It's true: Being a writer isn't just about the creative process. Some days, you're an editor. Other days, you're a salesperson. Once in a while, you're a heavy. ("Dear editor, where's my money/contributor's copy/tear sheet?") And more often than not, you're a secretary. (Sorry, *administrative assistant.*)

Yes, the admin in you often works overtime, coming in before the writer, editor, salesperson, and heavy and staying long after everyone has gone to bed. She's underpaid and overworked, but be you'll be glad she does her job well as the need continues for the following forms of correspondence.

COVER LETTERS

Chapter three touched on cover letters for book proposals. There is another instance in which you'll use a cover letter rather than a query: when submitting a completed manuscript to a magazine editor.

The two most frequent occasions that call for cover letters to magazine editors are as follows:

1. When a magazine's writer's guidelines specifically state "no query necessary; send manuscript"
2. When your query has led to the editor's request for your manuscript

In each case, the cover letter will be slightly different. In the first case, you'll still be trying to "sell" your article to the editor. And while a query-style cover letter isn't necessary, you still have to get the editor interested enough to read your manuscript. This means summarizing the topic of your article; mentioning your sources, interviews, and hands-on experience; suggesting a specific section of the magazine (if applicable) where your article might fit; referencing word count (to show it fits the magazine's writer's guidelines); and citing your credentials. (For a good sample cover letter for an unsolicited article, see **Example 7.1** [pg. 204].)

In the second instance, you should have already provided most of this information in the initial query letter, allowing for a more simplified letter with a "thank you for requesting my manuscript" near the end. (For a sample cover letter for a previously solicited article, see **Example 7.2** [pg. 205].)

In both cases, you'll be including an SASE if sent by postal mail.

THANK-YOU NOTES

Thank-you notes are not only a courtesy; they can also help you stand out from the slew of other writers vying for an editor or agent's attention. While it's not necessary to send one for every single response ("Thanks for the lovely rejection!"), there are a few standard instances that call for etiquette.

- Upon first assignment from the magazine editor (thank-you card should be mailed after you turn in your assignment)
- Upon first acceptance of a solicited or unsolicited submitted article
- Upon an agent's offer for author representation
- Upon an agent landing your book a publisher
- Upon an agent selling foreign, translation, or film/TV/audio rights
- Any referral from an agent, magazine editor, or acquisitions editor
- Upon completion of book edits (This thank-you note should go to your book's editor at the publishing house. Although few first-time authors like the process of rewrites, the editor's job is to make your book better. Show him you appreciate the effort!)

EXAMPLE 7.1   GOOD COVER LETTER FOR UNSOLICITED ARTICLE

March 26, 2008

Patricia Moade, Editor
Old House, New House
Roddingham Publishers
982 Main St.
White River Junction, VT 05001

Dear Ms. Moade,

I'm writing to submit my article, **"Superstitions, Folklore, and Old Wives' Tales in the Home."** From common to bizarre, the 981-word piece (plus sidebar) entertains readers with information on the histories of blessing a new house, warding off evil when building a new home, and cleaning properly to "avoid bad luck."

I believe the piece might be a good fit for your "Generations of Wisdom" section.

My credentials include more than five hundred published pieces with articles in *Church Construction Magazine, Complete Woman, American Fitness,* and *Woman's Own,* as well as a Healthy Home column in *Nexus.*

Thank you for your time. I look forward to hearing from you.

Best Regards,

Wendy Burt-Thomas
(address/phone/e-mail)

Encl: SASE and manuscript

With the convenience of the Internet, a thank-you e-mail is nice, but it doesn't show nearly as much effort. Take the time to snail mail an actual card or postcard.

One of my favorite ideas is to buy a set of funny postcards or note cards that represent your specialty (if you have one). If you write a lot of parenting articles or books, buy some of those cute Anne Geddes cards with babies in flowerpots or dressed like animals. If you're an equestrian writer, spend the money for some classy horse-themed cards. If you don't have a specialty—I write about everything under the sun—buy a twelve-pack of scenic photo or watercolor note cards that highlight your region's beauty.

EXAMPLE 7.2   GOOD COVER LETTER FOR SOLICITED ARTICLE

May 5, 2005

Erin Eagan, Managing Editor
Bally Total Fitness Magazine
RB Publishing Inc.
2901 International Lane
Madison, WI 53704

Dear Ms. Eagan,

Thank you for requesting to review my article, **"The Skinny on Fats."**

I have attached the 1,017-word piece for your review. As mentioned in my query, the piece covers bad fats, good fats, and a sidebar of twenty ideas for reducing bad fat intake and increase good fat intake. Because my mother has been a registered dietitian for more than twenty years, I asked her to review the piece for accuracy. (I'm happy to report that she gave it two thumbs up!)

Thank you again for your interest. I look forward to hearing from you.

Best regards,

Wendy Burt-Thomas
(address/phone/e-mail)

TURNING DOWN AN ASSIGNMENT

I know it may seem hard to believe at this point in your career if you're a beginner, but there are times in which you'll want or need to turn down an assignment. You may be too busy with other work or just find the assignment to be, well ... *boring.* I should point out, however, that you likely will never have to turn down an assignment because you already sold the idea to a competitive magazine. Ideas aren't copyrighted—only articles—so you should simply find a way to write the articles on the same topic in two different ways.

If and when the time comes to turn down an assignment, there are three important pieces of information to share with an editor:

1. You appreciate the offer

2. You're open to future assignments
3. Your availability and schedule

What you don't need to include is why you can't accept the assignment—unless you feel it's incredibly relevant (or impressive!) to the editor. Examples of the latter might include:

- Major life event (just got married, had a baby, death in the family)
- Travel (at which time you won't have time or access to a computer)
- Major project (book due)

While telling an editor you're too busy with other work does make you sound "in demand," it could also imply that you can't handle multiple assignments. Instead, keep the note simple and to the point. If you're interested in the assignment but can't make the deadline, ask if the topic is time-sensitive and indicate when you could have the piece turned in. For example:

> Dear Mr. Van Camp,
>
> Thank you for the offer to write an article on the rising number of shark attacks off the coast of Florida. Unfortunately, I'd be unable to accept the assignment at this time to meet your March 15 deadline. If, however, the piece is not time-sensitive, I could accept the assignment and turn it in by April 15. Either way, I certainly hope you'll continue to contact me for future assignments. If you have other assignments, my schedule should be free again after April 2. I'll await your response regarding the shark-attack assignment.
>
> Thanks again,
>
> Wendy Burt-Thomas

PULLING AN ARTICLE SUBMISSION

Just when you were thinking that simultaneous submissions were the greatest thing since sliced bread, along comes a glitch. What if you submit your completed article to multiple (competitive) markets and several editors write back to say they'd like to publish it? (Granted, as a new writer, you should *be* so lucky—but it does happen.)

The minute the first editor responds, you should contact the other magazines. Don't offer any explanation; just send a simple note asking that they pull your submission. Something like this will do:

> Dear Ms. Tratter,
>
> I would like to request that you withdraw my submission "Marathon Kids: Running With the Country's Best Teens" for consideration. Please confirm you received this request by e-mailing me at [*insert e-mail address*]. Thank you for your time.
>
> Best regards,
>
> Wendy Burt-Thomas

As long as you haven't signed a contract with the other magazines yet, you're under no obligation to allow them to publish the article you submitted for review.

A word of caution: It's difficult to turn down a second magazine that pays more money. Don't get greedy. Yes, there may be time to change your mind about the first magazine's acceptance before signing the contract, but you'll likely be burning a bridge for any future work for the publication. (This is why it's generally much safer to pitch ideas rather than *completed* manuscripts. You can always rework the same idea for multiple publications and produce completely different articles on the same topic.)

Once you give an informal agreement (by phone or e-mail), keep your word. You can always explain to the second magazine's editor what happened and agree to rewrite the piece to make it completely different. Hopefully—if you've indicated the piece was a simultaneous submission—the editor will realize she was just a bit too slow to beat her magazine's competition to the punch ... and she'll give you an assignment.

REQUESTING INFORMATION FROM A SOURCE

While you might assume that everyone likes free (good) publicity, you'd be wrong. Well technically, you'd be right. The difference is that not everyone likes to do the work to get free publicity.

I've contacted businesspeople to be listed as expert sources in my articles only to have them ignore me, take forever to get back to me, or tell me they were too busy to talk to me (even if my deadline was in a month and I only needed five minutes).

On the other hand, I've contacted others who have gone above and beyond to send me information, free samples, and even their home phone numbers just to get a two-sentence blurb in a 2,000-word story.

In general, you'll find that most people are somewhere in between. Nonprofits, PR agencies, and marketing divisions tend to be the best at helping writers and journalists, probably because it's their job to get the word out about their companies and they recognize a free ride when they see one. Small-business owners also want the free publicity (due to their limited advertising budgets), but they're often hard to connect with because they're running every aspect of their businesses. In my experience, the worst sources are CEOs, who often don't prioritize their schedules for journalists unless they know the article will make them look good in *Time*, *Newsweek*, or *Entrepreneur*. Plus, they always want to (dis)approve everything before you send it to your editor (which means you'll be rewriting until retirement—yours or theirs).

Here are five "tricks" to help you get the information you need quickly and without hassle:

1. When possible, choose to request information from a nonprofit. Your second choice could be a local business (locals tend to trust local writers more—maybe because they can hunt you down) or a larger company that has a dedicated PR division or agency. (These people are hired specifically to promote the company.)

2. E-mail first to introduce yourself, then follow up with a phone call a few days later (to give your expert time to read your e-mail). This will save you some hassle when you call and are greeted with, "Who are you? What do you want again? What is this for?" In the subject line of your e-mail, write "MEDIA REQUEST."

3. Visit the nonprofit's or business's Web site before making contact. If you see the information you're looking for, you'll simply have to ask

for permission to use it. This makes your expert's job much easier and will save you both time.

4. In your initial e-mail to experts, (A) be clear about your deadline and always give them a fake deadline that is much, much earlier than your real deadline; (B) state that they will not be able to proof the piece before you send it to your editor and explain that you just have too many sources to let everyone proof and provide feedback; and (C) tell them you will be happy to send them a tear sheet when the article comes out, but don't promise a copy of the magazine as you may only get one contributor's copy, which you'll want to keep for yourself.

5. Be clear about how much (or how little) time you'll need for a phone interview. People are more likely to commit if you tell them you'll only need ten minutes of their time. It also helps if you can e-mail the questions to them in advance and give them the opportunity to answer by e-mail if they prefer. For small-business owners who are very busy, I sometimes ask if it would be more convenient to talk at night, after their businesses have closed. Most are thrilled to have options and feel much more relaxed when they don't have customers to take care of.

One, perhaps unexpected, twist: Nonprofits tend to be so helpful they'll mail or e-mail you ten times more information than you need, making it incredibly time-consuming to sift through to get the few tidbits of data you need. Be specific about your time crunch and the exact specifications of the type of info you require or be prepared to read through 612 pages on the importance of proper hand washing while vacationing in Cambodia. Here's a short, specific example of a media request to the PR department at McDonald's

Dear Ms. Hathaway,

I am writing an article on healthy fast food for *Men's Health* and am hoping you can provide me with a high-res (300 dpi) photo of your Premium Grilled Chicken Classic Sandwich. (I was able to get all the nutritional information about this healthy choice off your Web site.)

Also, if you have any new healthy choice options for adults (under 500 calories, 10 grams of fat or less) that are not yet posted on your Web site, please send me a description, nutritional information, and a high-res photo so I might consider it for use in the article.

Thank you for your assistance. Please don't hesitate to contact me with any questions.

Sincerely,

Wendy Burt-Thomas
(address/phone/e-mail)

COMPLAINING TO AN EDITOR

It's rare, but you may run across the occasional need to complain to an editor. I've seen this most frequently among fellow writers whose articles were butchered by an overly eager editorial intern. One friend of mine went so far as to request that her name be removed from an article before going to print because she felt the piece no longer had any of her original writing in it (and she didn't like the new version). Yes, you have that option, but I only recommend using it if you feel the final piece is worse than your original version.

There are several other reasons you may want to complain to an editor: late payments (see below), missing contributor's copies, omitted (important) parts to your article, or grammatical mistakes that were made by the copy editor. In the last case, you can indicate such on your tear sheets when submitting them to other editors.

The "sandwich" method is always a good choice: Wedge the complaint between two nice comments. In addition, the comment should be factual—not personal—and if applicable, recommend a remedy (such as reimbursement, a printed correction, or a personalized note explaining that the mistake was made on THEIR end, not yours). Of course, humor usually helps to soften the blow and to demonstrate that you aren't taking the offense too seriously.

Here's a simple example of a complaint letter to an editor:

Dear Mr. Dallas,

Thank you for choosing to run my article, "The Busy Mom's Workout." I enjoyed working on the piece and thought that the photos you chose to accompany it were beautiful.

By now, I'm sure you've noticed the mistake in the subtitle. Luckily, your readers are likely smart enough to figure out that our intention was not to encourage them to get "the FATTEST postpartum abs ever," but rather, "the FLATTEST postpartum abs ever." (We certainly don't need help figuring out how to shovel in the Ben & Jerry's!)

I checked my original manuscript and felt a sigh of relief that the mistake was not on my end. (Hope I'm not getting anyone in trouble!) With that said, I'm wondering if it would be possible to get a corrected version of the PDF so I might use the article as a feature in my portfolio.

Again, thank you for the great opportunity. I enjoy not only writing for your magazine, but also reading it, and hope you will consider me for future assignments.

Sincerely,

Wendy Burt-Thomas
(address/phone/e-mail)

FOLLOWING UP ON A "MAYBE"

Whoever said that freelancing was black or white? There's a third option between acceptance and rejection—I call it the "possible."

A "possible" refers to a response from an editor who says, "We're interested in your article and will be holding it for possible use in the future." Generally this is accompanied by something like, "Please let us know if the work is published in any other publications in the meantime."

A possible is actually better than it sounds (when followed by the second phrase) because it allows you to continue shopping your piece to other magazines while you're waiting. I usually respond to a possible with a short thank-you e-mail and a promise to check in down the road. Then, if I don't hear anything after several months, I send a nice follow-up reminder:

Dear Ms. Zellum,

Thank you for your April 3 e-mail regarding your interest in my article, "Honey, I Shrunk the Kids: Helping Overweight Children Lose Weight as a Family." I'm just checking in to see if you have slated a publication date for the article yet. Thank you again for your consideration. I appreciate your interest and your time.

Sincerely,

Wendy Burt-Thomas

Notice that there is no threat of taking the piece elsewhere. (There's no need, as they gave you the option to continue shopping it.) There's also no pressure, just a simply inquiry that also acts as a reminder to an otherwise busy editor who may have filed your piece away in a long-forgotten folder.

FOLLOWING UP ON PAYMENT

I've had a few occasions in which I've had to contact a publication regarding late payment issues. Sometimes, such as at small publications, the editor is also in charge of paying the writers. But in most cases, the editor and accountant are completely separate people (and divisions) and a complaint to an editor is only justified after several attempts to work directly with the accountant.

Always address editors as if you're simply "enlisting their assistance" rather than placing blame, even if you know they're responsible for the late payments. An editor who is embarrassed about a late payment (for which she is to blame) may be less likely to give you more assignments.

Your best bet is a short, to-the-point e-mail. Although a phone call is also an option, be sure to stay focused, polite, and remain calm. If you're calling about a late payment, be sure to cite the specifics (amount promised, dates invoiced, contract payment terms—such as thirty days) and fax or e-mail a copy of the signed contract if necessary. Always end your note or call with "thank you for your assistance on what I assume to simply be an oversight." (Unless the accountant slammed the phone down in your ear after yelling, "We will never pay you! *Ha ha ha*!" while twirling the ends of his moustache and tying another writer to railroad tracks.)

Give the publication the benefit of the doubt (oversight rather than intentional fraud) and you'll increase your chances of getting paid in a timely manner. Your grandmother was right: You catch more flies with honey than vinegar. If the honey doesn't work, get a third party—like Angela Hoy of Writers Weekly (www.writersweekly.com)—involved. She's an amazing advocate for writers and probably the most reputable source on things like self-publishing, avoiding scams and con artists, and spreading the word about editorial fraud.

SOME PARTING WORDS

So, do you feel ready to submit? I hope so.

As a freelance writer who has received hundreds of rejections, I'll admit it's overwhelming to try to absorb so many rules. That's why I prefer the term "guidelines." After all, you'll always hear stories about writers who broke all the rules, opting to do things their own way, only to land a six-figure publishing deal or a two-dollar-a-word assignment for a huge national magazine. But on the other side of the coin, there are probably a lot more writers who followed protocol and channeled their need to be rebellious into great out-of-the-box writing instead.

As a writer, your job is to find the balance between cookie-cutter submissions and extreme attempts to get an editor's attention. It's like kindergartners competing to be teacher's pet. Susie is politely raising her hand to answer every single question. Johnny is jumping on his desk screaming the answer at the top of his lungs. Both get points for participation because the teacher knows she can't play favorites. But she's secretly awaiting another genius, like the last teacher's pet, who crafted a four-story, modeled-to-scale, sixteenth-century Scottish castle out of nothing more than dust bunnies and recycled plastic spoons. Now *that* kid made her look good.

Let the work shine.

APPENDIX

RESOURCES

GLOSSARY OF TERMS

ADVANCE: Payment to the author before a book's publication. Because the payment is based on expected sales, it is deducted from royalties.

BYLINE: The author's name on a published piece. A longer version, a *bio,* includes a sentence or paragraph about the author. Bios typically run at the end of the author's work or with a photo on the contributors' page.

CLIPS/TEAR SHEET: Often used interchangeably, these terms represent the writer's published pieces from a magazine, newspaper, or Web site.

CONTRIBUTOR'S COPIES: Free copies of the magazine or newspaper in which the writer's work appears.

COVER LETTER: A short (generally less than one page) letter accompanying a completed article, book manuscript, or book proposal.

GENRE: A classification of literature by common components, styles, or themes, such as science fiction, romance, mystery, or narrative nonfiction.

IRC: An abbreviation for *international reply coupon.* Used when sending materials to other countries, this is required in order for an editor, agent, or publisher to respond to a query, proposal, or manuscript sent by mail. Non–U.S. countries cannot use U.S. postage to return materials.

LEAD TIME: The time between an editor receiving a manuscript and its publication in the magazine or newspaper.

MASTHEAD: The staff, circulation, and operations information about a magazine, newspaper, or online publication, usually published in the first few pages of the magazine (near the table of contents) or in a newspaper's opinions and editorial section.

MULTIPLE SUBMISSIONS: Sending more than one query or manuscript to an editor, agent, or publisher at the same time.

ON SPEC: Short for *on speculation*. The term refers to an editor's agreement to review a proposed piece of work (usually, an article) with no promise to purchase or publish the completed manuscript.

OUTLINE: A rough written sketch of a book's contents using headings and one or two sentences per section to describe each chapter's subject matter.

PITCH: A catchy summary of your book or article used to pique the interest of an editor, agent, or publisher. In some cases—such as at writers conferences—pitches are done verbally. Your pitch is also used as the main paragraph of your query.

PLATFORM: A writer's reputation and visibility as an author and/or expert. This could include blogs, columns, media appearances as an expert, Web sites, e-zines, and more.

QUERY: A letter (typically one to two pages) to a magazine editor, agent, or publishing house acquisitions editor crafted to generate interest in an article or book you have written or plan to write.

RESPONSE TIME: The time between an editor receiving a manuscript and responding to the writer with a rejection, acceptance, or hold.

ROYALTIES: Payment to the author based on a percentage of the retail price of each book sold.

SASE: An abbreviation for *self-addressed, stamped envelope*. This is required in order for an editor, agent, or publisher to respond to a query, proposal, or manuscript sent by mail.

SIMULTANEOUS SUBMISSION: A manuscript or query sent to more than one editor, agent, or publisher at the same time.

SLUSH PILE: The stack of unread manuscripts (articles, stories, queries, proposals, or books) waiting to be read by an editor, agent, or publisher.

SUBSIDIARY RIGHTS: Ancillary book rights sold to movie studios, book clubs, foreign publishers, magazines, etc.

SYNOPSIS: A detailed summary of the complete plot arc of a book. When presented as part of a book proposal, the summary is typically only a few pages. Presented alone, it can be as long as thirty pages, depending on the length of the work it's synopsizing and the restrictions dictated by the publisher's or agent's submission guidelines.

TRADE JOURNAL: A specialized publication geared to a targeted occupation (e.g. doctors) or industry (e.g. Human Resources).

UNSOLICITED: A manuscript (article, story, proposal, or book manuscript) that an editor, agent, or publisher did not specifically request. Sending an unsolicited manuscript is the equivalent to "cold calling" in the sales world.

FOR FURTHER STUDY

It's easy to become overwhelmed by the vast number of resources for writers. Here are a few of the most respected, most useful, and most frequently updated.

Trade Magazines

ByLine – www.bylinemag.com

Editor & Publisher – www.editorandpublisher.com

Poets & Writers – www.pw.org

Publishers Weekly – www.publishersweekly.com

Small Publishers Association of North America – www.spannet.org

Writer's Digest – www.writersdigest.com

Writers' Journal – www.writersjournal.com

The Writer's Chronicle – www.awpwriter.org/magazine/

Books and Reference Guides

The Associated Press Stylebook and Briefing on Media Law by Norm Goldstein (Basic Books, 2007)

The Chicago Manual of Style, 15th ed. (University of Chicago Press, 2003)

Children's Writer's & Illustrator's Market by Alice Pope (Writer's Digest Books, annual)

Guerrilla Marketing for Writers by Jay Conrad Levinson, Rick Frishman, and Michael Larsen (Writer's Digest Books, 2000)

Guide to Literary Agents by Chuck Sambuchino (Writer's Digest Books, annual)

How to Write Attention-Grabbing Query & Cover Letters by John Wood (Writer's Digest Books, 2000)

How to Write Irresistible Query Letters by Lisa Collier Cool (Writer's Digest Books, 2002)

Jump Start Your Book Sales by Marilyn and Tom Ross (Writer's Digest Books, 1999)

Novel & Short Story Writer's Market by the Staff of *Writer's Market* (Writer's Digest Books, annual)

Writer's Market by Robert Brewer (Writer's Digest Books, annual)

Writer's Market Companion, 2nd ed. by Joe Feiertag and Mary Cupito (Writer's Digest Books, 2004)

Web sites

Agent Query – www.agentquery.com

The Association of Authors' Representatives, Inc. – www.aar-online.org

Guide to Query Letters – www.GuideToQueryLetters.com

Writer's Digest – www.writersdigest.com

Writer's Market – www.writersmarket.com

E-Zines

Absolute Write – www.absolutewrite.com

FundsforWriters – www.fundsforwriters.com

WOW! Women on Writing – www.wow-womenonwriting.com

Writers on the Rise – www.writersontherise.com

WritersWeekly – www.writersweekly.com

Fiction Addiction – www.fictionaddiction.net

The Purple Crayon (children's writing) – www.underdown.org

Organizations and Genre Groups

Crime-Writers – www.groups.yahoo.com/group/crime-writers

Horror Writers Association – www.horror.org

Mystery Writers of America – www.mysterywriters.org

National Writers Union – www.nwu.org

Romance Divas – www.romancedivas.com

Romance Writers of America – www.rwanational.org

Science Fiction and Fantasy Writers of America, Inc. – www.sfwa.org

Sisters in Crime – www.sistersincrime.org

Society of Children's Book Writers & Illustrators – www.scbwi.org

Western Writers of America, Inc. – www.westernwriters.org

Online Writing Courses

Gotham Writers' Workshop – www.writingclasses.com

WorldWideLearn – www.worldwidelearn.com

Writers Online Workshops – www.writersonlineworkshops.com

Writers.com/Writers on the Net – www.writers.com

Favorite Writing Blogs

Ask Wendy – http://askwendy.wordpress.com – Based on the popular "Ask Wendy" column from the author, this blog offers visitors a chance to get their writing-related questions answered by a full-time freelance writer and author.

C. Hope Clark – www.hopeclark.blogspot.com – The blog for the founder of FundsforWriters.com, this site is full of interesting contests, funds, a word of the day, and tales from a day in the life of a writer.

Writer Mama – http://thewritermama.wordpress.com/ – One of the best ways to stay connected to other writing moms and the news, blogs, and tips that help them succeed.

Erik Sherman's WriterBiz – www.eriksherman.com/WriterBiz – A great blog that focuses on the business side of writing: marketing, sales, contracts, copyright issues, and more.

Freelance Folder – http://freelancefolder.com – This multi-authored blog covers all things writing thanks to the hundreds of contributions from "writers helping writers."

Jane Friedman's "There Are No Rules" – http://blog.writersdigest.com/norules/ – Written by the publisher and editorial director of the F+W Writing Community (*Writer's Digest* magazine, Writer's Digest Books, Writers Online Workshops, et al.), this blog offers an inside look at the ever-changing publishing industry.

The Well-Fed Writer Blog – www.wellfedwriter.com/blog – Peter Bowerman, author of the award-winning Well-Fed Writer series, is more than generous on this blog, sharing income-boosting resources for commercial writers.

Discussion Forums for Writers

Writer's Market – www.Community.WritersMarket.com – Much like a "Facebook for writers," this community Web portal was created by Writer's

Digest to offer networking, discussion, and information to writers around the globe. A great way for new writers to "meet" published authors.

LibraryThing – www.librarything.com/groups/writerreaders – This forum is dedicated to "those who create as well as consume," offering a place for readers to share thoughts and books from a writer's perspective. Visitors can scroll through recent topics or search by most commonly shared books.

Media Bistro – www.MediaBistro.com/bbs – The bulletin board for MediaBistro.com, this site covers freelancing, media issues, sources for stories, news, contests, anthology submissions, and more. There's even a section for "Beginner Issues."

WritersNet – www.Writers.net/forum – With more than ten years under its belt, this forum offers writers a chance to share their knowledge—and questions—about the craft and business of writing.

FreelanceWriting – www.freelancewriting.com/forums – Offering a wide variety of discussion topics, this site encourages writers to share their success tips, talk about markets, list favorite freelance Web sites, and more.

National Novel Writing Month – www.nanowrimo.org/forum – Despite its name, this Web site's forum is active year-round. Discussions include plot, character development, writing prompts, helpful sites, and resources. There are also "genre lounges" and groups divided by the writer's age.

ABCtales – www.abctales.com/forum – For those seeking feedback on work, this forum offers a chance to hear what others really think of it. Other areas encourage writers to share tips on getting published, competitions, and book recommendations.

INDEX

S

Sales pitch, query (equivalence), 2

Sample copy, receiving (process), 47

Savvy Author's Guide to Book Publicity, The (Warren), 80

Scholars, usage, 92

Second serial rights, 66

Self-addressed stamped envelope (SASE), 5, 10
inclusion, 11

Self-published material, submission, 100, 102

Self-publishing, consideration, 198

Self-representation, advantages, 147

Serial rights. *See* First serial rights; Second serial rights

7 Habits of Hibhly Effective Teens, The (book/workbook pairings), 96

Sidebars/sidelights, inclusion, 24

Simultaneous queries, submission number, 69

Simultaneous submissions, acceptance, 47

Slush pile, 10

Snail mail query, 11

Solicited article, cover letter (example), 205f

Source, information request, 207–210
tricks, 208–209

Special issues, contribution, 48

Speculative genre, novel query (considerations), 139, 141–142

Stewart, Martha (impact), 95

Story representation, examples, 102, 104

Submissions, tracking, 7–8

Supporting details, 35, 73

Synopsis. *See* Nonfiction book proposals; Novel synopsis example. *See* Bad

novel synopsis; Romance focus, 78

T

Table of contents. *See* Nonfiction book proposals

Tattlers, usage, 92

Tedder, Lorna, 81

Textbooks
query, example, 113f

Textbooks, nonfiction book considerations, 107–110

Thank-yous
notes, 203–204
usage, 35

Thriller/suspense, novel query (considerations), 139

Tobias, Ronald B., 107

Turnarounds, reasonableness, 26

20 Master Plots (And How to Build Them) (Tobias), 107

U

Unsolicited article, cover letter (example), 204f

W

Warren, Lissa, 80

Web-Savvy Writer: Book Promotion with a High-Tech Twist (Rutledge), 80

Web site, usage, 40

Wooden Horse Publishing, resource, 50

Word counts
estimation process, 69
guarantees, impossibility, 27
preference, 41

Worldwide Freelance Writer, resource, 49–50

World Wide Web, usage, 5

Writer Mama (Katz), 58–59

Writers (authors)
advance/royalties, expectations, 185–186
agent search, 173–174
bragging, 56
control, impact, 185

credentials, 123, 125
deadlines, following, 184
expenses, publication payment, 49
experience, lying (avoidance), 74
guidelines, understanding, 39–49
identification, 64
location, 65
lying/exaggeration, impact, 185
multiple book projects, availability, 181, 183
patience, 181
platform query, 179f–180f
promotional plan, 81
qualifications, 35, 74
query
information, inclusion, 184
movie interest, example, 182f–183f
referrals, caution, 183–184
rewriting, willingness, 178
talent, ego (absence), 181
threats, problems, 55–56
unfocused queries, avoidance, 184

Writer's Digest Guide to Query Letters, The, 74

Writer's Market
listing, example, 39–40
resource, 50
table of contents, usage, 36–37
usage, 7, 82

Writers Weekly, resource, 49

Writing
content, 64–65
details, absence, 54–55
enjoyment, 31–33

Y

Young adult
agent query, example, 149f
paranormal, agent query (example), 158f

"Your Book Promotion Countdown Checklist" (Tedder), 81

Your Road Map for Success (book/workbook pairings), 96

ACKNOWLEDGMENTS

Much thanks to my wonderful editor, Lauren Mosko, my agent, Rita Rosenkranz, and to Christina Katz and Sage Cohen for your continual nudges and support.

Thank you to Jane Friedman for having faith that I was the right person to write this book, and to all the authors and agents who provided great queries in hopes of helping other writers.

Special thanks to my parents, who have always supported my writing efforts, and to my husband, Aaron, though he still thinks I play online solitaire all day.

ABOUT THE AUTHOR

Wendy Burt-Thomas is a full-time freelance writer, editor, copywriter, and PR consultant. Her more than 1,000 published articles, essays, and stories have appeared in such varied publications as *Family Circle*, *American Fitness*, *ePregnancy*, NYTimes.com, MSNBC.com, *Woman's World*, and *Home Cooking*. Wendy's columns—on business, marketing, parenting, writing, and healthy living—have appeared in countless newspapers and magazines.

Wendy's previous two books, *Oh, Solo Mia! The Hip Chick's Guide to Fun for One* and *Work It, Girl! 101 Tips for the Hip Working Chick* were written with co-author Erin Kindberg and published by McGraw-Hill.

Her workshop "Breaking Into Freelance Writing" has led her to a variety of speaking engagements on the topics of writing, PR, marketing, and copywriting. She taught a version of her seminar at the Pikes Peak Writer's Conference and to numerous business and networking groups around the region.

On any given day, Wendy is editing magazines, drafting ad copy, working on a column, writing greeting card copy, or doing PR consulting. She lives in Colorado Springs with her husband Aaron, daughter Gracie, son Ben, and two black labs.

www.WendyBurt-Thomas.com

MORE GREAT RESOURCES FROM WRITER'S DIGEST BOOKS

The Craft & Business of Writing
Essential Tools for Writing Success

For more than eighty years, the Writer's Market series has provided the timeless advice and detailed instruction writers have come to depend on to achieve their goals. In *The Craft & Business of Writing*, writers, agents, and editors offer their insights into every genre and facet of the publishing industry, so whether you write fiction, nonfiction, children's books, or poetry—or a little of everything—this all-in-one reference includes everything you need to start and maintain your writing career.

ISBN-13: 978-1-58297-487-3, spiral-bound hardcover, 400 pages, #Z0717

The Writer's Digest Weekly Planner

This essential week-by-week tool helps writers chart their entire writing lives for a year, providing space for creative notes, goals, deadlines, submissions, and to-do lists. In addition, it offers invaluable tips for submitting and selling your work, collaborating with an editor, and navigating the business side of publishing and also provides sample query letters.

ISBN-13: 978-1-58297-553-5, spiral-bound hardcover, 256 pages, #Z2302

Get Known Before the Book Deal

Use Your Personal Strengths to Grow an Author Platform

Becoming visible is more crucial to landing a book deal than ever; simply churning out a book isn't enough. In this book, author Christina Katz (*Writer Mama*) empowers writers to take charge of their writing careers and partner with agents, editors, and publishers. Introverts and extroverts alike will find effective and diverse strategies for growing their platform in ways that complement their own style and pace of working. From developing a readership to increasing the odds of a book deal to having a greater impact on book sales, this book is every aspiring writer's guide to success in the world of publishing.

ISBN-13: 978-1-58297-554-2, paperback, 272 pages, #Z2389

The Daily Writer

366 Meditations to Cultivate a Productive and Meaningful Writing Life

This devotional for all writers emphasizes the importance of deep thinking in the context of writing and cultivating a meaningful writing life. Professor and author Fred White provides action-oriented entries that prompt you to integrate practice into your daily life and dedicate thought to your writing pursuits. From getting in a creative frame of mind to maintaining good writing habits to breaking through writer's block, this guide will help you develop the discipline, focus, and dedication needed to become successful.

ISBN-13: 978-1-58297-529-0, paperback, 384 pages, #Z1982